S0-BJJ-104

Armed and Dangerous

ARMED AND DANGEROUS

The Rise of the Survivalist Right

James Coates

The Noonday Press

Farrar, Straus and Giroux
New York

Copyright © 1987 by James Coates
All rights reserved
Printed in the United States of America
Published in Canada by Collins Publishers, Toronto
Designed by Constance Ftera
Second printing, 1988

Library of Congress Cataloging-in-Publication Data
Coates, James.
Armed and dangerous.
Includes index.
1. Radicalism—United States—History—20th century.
2. Prejudice—United States—History—20th century.
3. United States—Social conditions—1980–
4. United States—Politics and government—1981–
5. Survivalism—United States—History—20th century.
6. Right and left (Political science)   I. Title.
E839.5.C59   1987   973.9   87.9278

In memory of Mary Garden Brennan Coates

Contents

Since a holocaust is a wholly prospective rather than a present calamity, the act of thinking about it is voluntary, and the choice of not thinking about it is always available.
—*Jonathan Schell*, The Fate of the Earth

Armed and Dangerous

I stick it to the audience and they just love it.
—Alan Berg

Introduction:
The Denver Connection

Alan Berg was a pushy Jew. A master of the fine art of arguing, Berg was a hard-living, fast-talking, fifty-year-old radio personality, a manic chain smoker with a love for life and a once blond beard quickly going gray. His expensive cashmere sports jackets, hand-sewn shirts and even the custom leather upholstery in his DeLorean and Bricklin sports cars bore the scars of his carelessly wielded Pall Mall cigarettes.

Berg's friends in Denver news media circles loved him for his iconoclastic and spirited wit. They appreciated him for his eagerness to take a fatherly interest in each of their personal problems, and they enjoyed him for his love of a good time. But, above all, they admired him for his fierce Jewishness, for his combativeness whenever the ugly ghost of anti-Semitism surfaced, as it does far more often in the American West than most realize. But those same media friends had to agree that, indisputably, Alan Berg was pushy—pushy about his opinions, pushy about his roots and particularly pushy with those who would scorn him for those roots.

Being a pushy Jew got Alan Berg killed. He was shot down like a dog on the street by a latter-day Nazi who boasted afterward to his friends about how fast Berg's body hit the pavement.

3

It was the quest for the how and the why of Berg's slaughter that led investigators to start piecing together the mosaic of interlocked hate groups that is the focus of this book. Some of these groups are well-known players on the fringes of the far right that suddenly find themselves reenergized. Others strive to keep their very existence secret. Working together in many instances, these groups have created a network with roots in the western states but with shoots spreading all too quickly throughout the rest of the country.

The situation, in fact, is much worse than even Berg feared when he used his radio show to "flush out" those right-wing hate groups he knew were out there. Alan Berg went to his grave not knowing just how right he had been while warning about the resurgence of murderous radicals in the hills, mountains and plains surrounding his adopted home of Denver.

Berg liked to brag on his top-rated program on Denver's 50,000-watt KOA radio that he had migrated from the criminal courts on the Near West Side of Chicago to the Mile-High City in 1969 to "dry out" from alcoholism brought on by the pressures of being an honest man employed as a mob lawyer. He would joke about how the Sicilians in the Mafia hired Jews to be their lawyers and accountants but didn't trust them to be gunsels. With obvious delight, he called his ballpoint pen a "Jewish machine gun." Berg would recall how in Chicago's criminal courts he was just one more syndicate mouthpiece representing such clients as hit man "Ice Pick" Alderisio and Pat Cerone, nephew of crime boss Jackie "the Lackey" Cerone, who had gotten his start as Al Capone's errand boy. Fifteen years after Berg had arrived in Denver and become a major molder of opinion in the Rocky Mountain and plains states reached by his broadcasts, he was mowed down on a Denver street in precisely the same manner that so many cheap Chicago hoodlums have died.

It should have been obvious from the first that the move West was risky. If Berg was just one more outfit lawyer in Chicago, to the establishment in Denver he was just one more in a seemingly endless procession of smart-aleck flatlanders who had immigrated to the high country eager to share the scenic wonders of the Rocky

Mountains and to immerse themselves in the Colorado lifestyle of Aspen hot tubs and folk music, left-wing politics and ardent environmentalism. But as Berg's tragic tale illustrates, these outsiders had dangerous and hidden enemies waiting for them from the first day they arrived.

When Berg moved into his first Denver apartment in 1969, his fellow outlanders were just seizing political and cultural power in Colorado and the rest of the West. They ran for the state legislatures and won seats, edited the local newspapers, dominated the TV and radio stations, and even rose to become major players in the region's centers of commerce and industry. Theirs was a revolution from without powered by the sheer numbers of newcomers brought by the national shift from the Northeastern and Midwestern Frostbelt to the Sunbelt and founded on a credo of opposition to Nixon and the Vietnam War and support for environmentalism.

Many of these newcomers quickly rose to national prominence, and that fame helped the revolution grow. Among the more noteworthy were folk singer John Denver with his albums *Rocky Mountain High* and *Country Roads*; Aspen-based Hunter S. Thompson, the "gonzo journalist" author of such best-sellers as *Fear and Loathing in Las Vegas*; Sam Brown, the anti-war movement's master strategist, who stunned the nation by setting up the massive "New Mobilization" march against Washington in 1971; and feisty congresswoman Patricia Schroeder, who rose to prominence as one of the most effective of the Pentagon gadflies.

As the foreigners' revolution flourished, resentment at their clamorous intrusion grew among the natives of the Rocky Mountain states who had lived on the lofty spine of the continent in beautiful surroundings for more than a century, suspended in splendid isolation from the complexities of life on both coasts. The natives complained bitterly of the "Californication" of the West. To the straitlaced old-timers, the newcomers like Berg were characterized by their low-grade Mexican marijuana and their top-quality cocaine, likely as not brought from Peru by some overprivileged hippie mountaineer bum in granny glasses. The old-timers took substantial, if belated, pains to keep the influx in its place. A brisk business was done in bumper stickers patterned after the green mountain peaks on the official Colorado license plate but with the word "Native" printed where the numbers should be. The newcomers copied the sticker with tags like "Alien" or "Semi-native" or "Who Cares?"

The old guard went out of their way to taunt the liberals. They installed rifle racks in the rear windows of their pickup trucks, and over their rear tires bolted mud flaps blazing with the Confederate flag. They cinched their waists with belt buckles bearing the National Rifle Association logo and donned T-shirts with slogans like "The only way the government will take my gun will be to pry it from my cold, dead, clenched fingers." And these were just the workaday natives. The hard-liners were yet to be heard from.

Most decidedly, Berg, the acid-tongued Chicagoan, was just another Californicating liberal from the East, a man like Illinois-raised governor-to-be Richard Lamm or Gary Hart, the transplanted Kansan who parlayed a year as press secretary for George McGovern's 1972 presidential campaign into a career as the United States senator from Colorado. These men—Lamm, Hart and Berg—employed similar styles to rise to prominence in a state long dominated by conservative ranchers, oilmen and traditional Republican Chamber of Commerce business types. If they were called Californicators, these glib intruders tweaked the establishment by calling the old guard, men and women alike, "Cowboys."

It was the Cowboys versus the Californicators, and the Cowboys never had a chance. The paranoids were right. There indeed was a conspiracy, albeit a very open one, by outside forces to seize power in the West.

Lamm made his political mark by attacking Cowboy Governor John Love's plan to bring the 1976 Winter Olympic Games to Colorado's stunningly scenic ski country. Warning that the Olympic facilities that would have to be built—bobsled runs and ski jumps, athlete housing and parking lots—would sully the environment, Lamm not only defeated the game plan but won the governorship in 1974. That same year, Hart campaigned against Cowboy plans to build a beltway extension of the interstate highway system around Denver and won one of the state's two seats in the United States Senate.

Berg too opposed the Olympics and championed fewer highways and more extensive environmental planning. But he also spent much of his time as the leading radio talk show host in Denver berating his Cowboy audience about another blemish on the soul of the American West, deep-seated racism and anti-Semitism.

"Are there any Nazis out there?" Berg would taunt his audiences. "I'm a Jew and I'd like to talk to them."

And the Nazis telephoned, in such numbers as to both dismay Berg and egg him on to future baiting sessions. So too did the Klansmen call, as did the John Birchers and the fundamentalist Mormon Freemen, the tax protesters from Posse Comitatus, the adherents of the White American Bastion and the militant farmers from *The Primrose and Cattlemen's Gazette*. They called eager to talk about a litany of conspiracy—of the "Trilateralist Rockefellers," the Kissingers and the "Jew Rothschild bankers"—about plans by a cabal of international financiers to sap the moral strength of Americans by conning them into putting fluoride in their drinking water and by getting God-fearing people to eat shellfish. They spoke with agitation about their conviction that these bankers had spirited all the gold from the vaults at Fort Knox and that the Jews had infiltrated a cadre of Baptist Zionists into the Soviet Politburo itself. Neo-Nazis called to say there had never been a Holocaust, while Klansmen phoned to warn about the "mongrelization" of the white race caused by civil rights legislation. Extremists of the religious right called with rantings about the arrival of Armageddon, claiming that signs everywhere pointed to the presence of the Beast in our midst. A cleansing nuclear war was just around the corner, they forecast, and "your mongrel, your Jew and your Negro" soon would be eradicated by God.

And Berg, always the master of the put-down, made the fatal mistake of teasing them. He led them on and then hanged up on most—"You're a jerk," he would say, or "That, my friend, is right out of Looney Tunes," while most of his faithful audience of Cal-ifornicators listened with approval. Berg's popularity became enor-mous. He told an interviewer, "I stick it to the audience and they just love it." Ultimately, however, the audience stuck it to the talk radio czar.

On the balmy summer night of June 18, 1984, Berg was mowed down by slugs from an illegal automatic pistol known as an Ingram MAC 10 as he stepped out of his favorite car, a Volkswagen Beetle, in front of his Denver town house. With the headlines blazing, Berg's murder triggered a massive spurt of investigations by FBI agents, private detectives, reporters and others who, when they ul-timately found the killers, also uncovered a previously unnoticed network of dangerous hate groups that had evolved right along with the flower children and liberal politicians in the beauty spots of America. These most decidedly were not the well-known cocka-mamie right wing of yore, the Wallaceites or even the bigots of groups like the John Birch Society or the Knights of the Ku Klux Klan. This was the real thing. The investigators learned that the real conflict in the West hadn't been the Cowboys versus the Cal-ifornicators at all. The real conflict had been everybody else versus the Survivalists.

Until Berg's death the phenomenon of Survivalism largely ap-peared to be the province of widely scattered individuals who spent far too much of their hard-earned money buying freeze-dried food and military equipment to store under their beds until that long-dreaded day when the Russians finally come. Men's magazines have long been peppered with ads for hunting knives painted in cam-ouflage colors with hollowed handles where one can store waterproof matches, a bit of fishing line and a few hooks in preparation for the day survival depends upon living by one's wits off the land. Indeed, learning self-confidence in the wilderness is considered a noble goal, a character-building pursuit for healthy young prep school Epis-copalians in walking shorts and boots from L. L. Bean.

Could somebody who went one step further and stockpiled a couple of deer rifles be all that different?

Yes. Different and very dangerous. In the sense that the Berg investigation isolated it, the philosophy and practice of Survivalism is a previously unnoted and uniquely American phenomenon. The Survivalists who killed Berg, in fact, became what they were for the same reasons that Berg became what he was. Both the Survival Right and the Californicators were adapting in their own way to the terrors of post-Hiroshima life on a fragile and unfriendly planet. One group became "tree huggers" and the other group started stock-piling chain saws. In ways that people rarely discuss in polite society, both the Californicators and the Survivalists were simply trying to cope with modern-day nuclear anxiety.

All Americans, of course, must deal with that unrelenting curse of late-twentieth-century life—the prospect of standing by impotently as leaders in Washington and Moscow haplessly or by design plunge the world into a thermonuclear holocaust. Coping with this underlying terror of current life takes many forms. Some find solace in religion. Others work in political movements. Many find relief in alcohol, Valium or other chemical solutions to anxiety. Most just choose not to dwell on the nasty subject.

The Survival Right, on the other hand, has developed a very different strategy for coping with the specter of Armageddon. Instead of worrying about how to prevent the coming holocaust, these Survivalists have devoted their energy to planning how to prosper by it. They reason that a nuclear war would cleanse the world of their enemies, leaving them alone to emerge from the irradiated rubble, new Adams and Eves ready to start the human saga over, this time with a single pure white race. The Survival Right really did learn how to stop worrying and to love the bomb.

The common thread linking these ardently violent people together is a belief that the U.S. government has been taken over by a conspiracy of Jewish bankers and nebulous other dark forces who plan to bleed the country dry, then bring a nuclear attack down upon the withered shell. This final attack is what the Bible calls Armageddon and, the Survivalists hold, once the attack has cleansed the earth, their new order of white people will start history over again.

Neither the scope nor the virulent aspects of the Survival movement had been grasped until investigators tied it to the sensational Berg murder. Once the link was made—by matching bullets from an Idaho Survivalist's gun to those taken from Berg—the investigators discovered that the Survival Right was rampant. The trail led everywhere, from spectacular commando raids against armored cars in California and Washington to polygamous communes along the Missouri–Arkansas border in the Ozarks.

These investigations ultimately led to a series of spectacular trials and numerous grand jury indictments, including the lodging of sedition charges in 1987 against many of the Survival Right's most prominent figures, a legal tactic used very rarely in recent U.S. history and a development that underscored just how seriously the federal government regards the movement. The evidence offered in various courtrooms showed the common thread that stitches the Survivalists together. Whether strutting about Idaho in jackboots bought at J. C. Penney's or stalking deer in Montana wearing hand-made moccasins, each group is convinced that the world is on the verge of some form of catastrophic renewal, after which the stage will be set for them to eliminate the Jews, blacks, Hispanics, Catholics and others who are their targets.

Investigators learned early on that having somebody to hate is a crucial element in the Survivalist credo, and its adherents have borrowed from a vast global tradition of intolerance. From the eighteenth century they have adopted the conspiracy theory that an elite group called the Illuminati works behind the scenes to move humanity toward evil. From the anti-Masonic movements of the nineteenth century they have taken up the view that Masons are simply latter-day manifestations of the Illuminati. From the resurgence of the Ku Klux Klan in the early twentieth century comes their rampant hatred of blacks. Most emphatically of all, the Survivalists have taken to their bosoms the rich tradition of anti-Semitism from throughout Western history with a virulence rarely displayed by the world's fringe-group haters.

Tying the Survival Right to the Berg assassination and to scores of other dramatic crimes throughout the United States underscored that the single most significant characteristic of the Survivalists is their willingness to act, indeed to lay down their lives for their bigotry. Above all, it is this activism that separates the Survivalists from other hate groups in America from pre-Revolutionary days to the present.

Talk long has been cheap on both the left and the right of the American political spectrum. Certainly there has been rhetoric aplenty from the right, as white-robed Klansmen burn their crosses in front of TV cameras and self-proclaimed Nazis milk the maximum amount of notoriety out of such gimmicks as demanding permission to stage a march down the main street of Chicago's largely Jewish suburb of Skokie. Followers of the enigmatic extremist Lyndon LaRouche harangue busy crowds at the nation's airports about his National Democratic Policy Committee's belief that international bankers and the drug-dealing British royal family are part of the same Zionist plot. Members of tax protest groups hold seminars in rented Holiday Inn rooms to urge farmers to burn their crop loan papers and strike out against their Zionist oppressors.

By contrast, the Survival Right doesn't just talk hatred. Machine guns blazing, ranting their rhetoric of anti-Semitism, anti-Catholicism, race war and paranoia, they are translating that hatred into a nascent political movement that, while still in the seed stage, threatens to erupt with far more vigor than anyone would have forecast before five members of a hit squad from a neo-Nazi Survivalist group that called itself Bruder Schweigen (the Silent Brotherhood) opened the debate in Berg's dark driveway with a MAC 10.

Since then Survivalist groups throughout the country have been linked to sophisticated counterfeiting schemes, terrorist bombings, masterful loan fraud operations, daring armored car robberies, theft rings, a raft of murders, and thousands of federal firearms and explosives violations. Several of their number have won status as martyrs by dying in shoot-outs with state, local and federal police.

But every bit as disturbing as the violence itself is a preponderance of evidence that the Survivalists' murderous exploits (and their courage, no matter how horribly misdirected a form of bravery it is) do not go unnoticed by the men and women who live around them in the rural pockets of the United States—people who, on the whole, were already more than intolerant and suspicious enough long before the new breed of haters surfaced.

That same audience of Cowboys who served so well as foils for the Lamms, Harts and Bergs now is listening to the cant of hatred from the Survival Right along with the rest of the political background noise in their lives. The Survivalists are being heard right along with the cable television evangelists whose words and pictures are beamed to outstretched parabolic satellite dishes in farmyards and backyards across the land. One minute, the Cowboys are listening to figures like Republican power broker Pat Robertson calling down the fire and brimstone of Armageddon on abortionists if not on Democrats in general. The next minute, the message from Survival Right groups like the White Aryan Resistance comes in on cable public-access channels followed by that of visionaries such as Reagan's former Interior Secretary, James Watt, who wanted to clear-cut the timber and mine the national parks because of a religious conviction that his will be the last generation to see them before the Four Horsemen ride, just as it says in the Book of Revelation.

Neo-Nazis stockpiling Uzi machine guns in underground bunkers aren't the only ones waiting for the Apocalypse. Many fundamentalist Christians such as best-selling paperback writer Hal Lindsey preach that this is the "Terminal Generation" for "the Late Great Planet Earth," and that the Second Coming is at hand. President Reagan told *People* magazine in 1983, "There have been many times in the past when we thought the end of the world was coming, but never anything like this . . . We're heading very fast for Armageddon right now." Not surprisingly then, for some in the heartland, the Survival Right doesn't sound all that out of sync anymore. And its conspiracy message has a certain political appeal, just as its cosmology has a familiar ring. In more ways than most Americans would like to think, the Survivalist rampage is acting out the anger and frustration felt by growing segments of the embattled farm economy.

Smack-dab in the middle of the American continent is a group of people who really are being driven into poverty by a system under which outside bankers foreclose on their government loans, force them to sell their hard-earned property at public auction, then drive them off their land jobless, penniless and unwanted by their equally beleaguered neighbors. And the far right has moved quickly to exploit the situation—from flagrant neo-Nazi types openly mouthing ethnic slurs to the clipboard-grasping disciples of Lyndon LaRouche, whose followers in the mid-1980s received as much as 30 and 40 percent of the vote in some congressional districts and won the 1986 Democratic nomination in Illinois for lieutenant governor.

A common tactic on the far right has been to declare that the Survivalists who have died in gun battles with police agencies are martyrs, victims of a Zionist-controlled establishment of the press, the banks and the government—precisely the cabal that anti-Semites of Hitler's era evoked and then damned to rounds of applause in the beer halls of Munich and Berlin.

Notably, in the mid-1980s the well-financed, anti-Semitic American Populist Party deftly incorporated the farm crisis into its long-standing rap about international bankers, Zionist infiltration of the Federal Reserve System and race mixing. The party, which was able to place its candidates on the ballots in fourteen states in the 1984 presidential election, is heavily financed by what is arguably the most solidly entrenched far-right group in America today, the Liberty Lobby, a Washington-based operation whose nationally circulated tabloid, *Spotlight*, has been the leading organ of the extreme right for several decades.

The Anti-Defamation League of B'nai B'rith views the Populist Party's campaign to exploit the farm crisis as the most sophisticated political move by the anti-Semitic right in recent memory. In study after study, the ADL's analysts warn that the Populists are particularly dangerous because they cloak the movement's underlying gospel of hatred with a mantle of respectable-sounding rhetoric. Instead of openly caviling against Jews, blacks and other targets, Populist literature employs code words linked to powerful themes that also can be heard in the American political mainstream, such as questioning the wisdom of spending billions on foreign aid (especially the aid to Israel) when America's own farmers are going bankrupt in record numbers because they can't repay federal loans.

The ADL has cited the following example of the Populists cleaning up their rhetoric but keeping their message intact. Jim Yarbrough, the Populist Party's vice-chairman, was quoted in *Spotlight* as saying:

> The Populist Party and the overwhelming majority of the American people are more concerned about the small farmers, whom America's first populist, Thomas Jefferson, called "the chosen people of God," than we are concerned with bankrolling a free-spending, inflation-ridden, politically unstable Middle East aggressor state that is not, and never has been, an ally to the United States.

What Yarbrough left unsaid is that the Survival Right bases much of its ideology on a mixture of pseudo-science and theology called Identity Christianity, which maintains that God's chosen people are the descendants of the whites who founded the United States and that all nonwhites and Jews are descendants of Satan who labor to destroy the white race by undermining the American economy with inflation and entangling the nation in dangerous foreign alliances. Identity preachers accuse Jews of hiding behind the label of "God's chosen people" and argue that the real chosen people, the Jews of the Bible, actually left the Holy Land in the last millennium before Christ to settle Western Europe and Great Britain. The people known as Jews to the world today are actually the progeny of an Indo-European tribe founded by Adam's evil son, Cain, called Khazars, according to Identity Christianity. The bizarre credo also holds that one tribe of the true Jews, a tribe called Mannaseh, crossed the ocean and became the founding fathers—Thomas Jefferson,

George Washington, John Adams and the rest. Further, they preach, the Declaration of Independence and the U.S. Constitution were given to this "Lost Tribe of Israel" by God, only to have generations of conspirators posing as Jews, but who actually are the satanic Khazars, surreptitiously amend the Constitution to give blacks and women the vote, to establish a federal income tax and to permit Federal Reserve banking, all as part of a plot to ruin the country and bring about the final battle of Armageddon. Yarbrough's brief quote in *Spotlight*, then, spoke volumes to the initiates of the Survival Right, while seeming to most readers just a fairly ordinary bit of rhetoric against foreign aid.

Spotlight continues today to be the most significant voice of the entire far right, with a paid circulation of roughly 150,000 readers each week, according to its reports filed with the U.S. Postal Service. To be sure, this publication has been around far longer than the Survivalist movement it now touts, and for many years has carried laudatory pieces about old-line Klansmen like J. B. Stoner or radical visionaries like the John Birch Society's patriarch and leading writer, Robert Welch. But today it is the haters with machine guns instead of those with fountain pens who are holding sway, and the pages of *Spotlight* reflect the change. In addition to its staple of articles about the need to stockpile gold, silver and freeze-dried food as investments for a very uncertain future, the tabloid carries numerous ads for Identity literature and the sort of paramilitary gear that no good Survivalist should be without.

So the concerns raised by the Survival Right are twofold. First, armed to the teeth and demonstrably erratic, they already are a dangerously active domestic network of terrorists who continue to pose the threat of political assassination, racial violence and virtually any type of armed mayhem one can conjure. Second, the Survivalists, with their alarming willingness to act, are pumping a vitality into the far right that it never before enjoyed. Instead of weak-chinned wimps in rented Nazi uniforms whining about getting a permit to parade in Skokie, the Survivalists offer Robert Jay Matthews, the Bruder Schweigen founder, who held off two hundred heavily armed FBI attackers for two days until the lawmen set afire the house on Whidbey Island, within sight of Seattle, from which he fought alone with no quarter asked or given. They evoke the memory of charismatic Posse Comitatus leader Gordon Kahl holding a small army of federal and local lawmen at bay in Arkansas until he too died in a holocaust of his own exploding ammunition after authorities set his barricaded farmhouse afire. They speak glowingly of Jim Jenkins and his son Steve, who reacted to their local banker's efforts to foreclose on their modest Minnesota farm by shooting the banker and his chief loan officer to death with their Army-issue automatic rifles.

If economic conditions continue to worsen in the American agricultural heartland, and if the sophisticates of the entrenched right, whether the Liberty Lobby Populists or the surprisingly powerful LaRouche group, manage to strike the proper political chords, the day may come when we realize that the Survivalists really were the vanguard of new Aryan warriors that they claimed to be. Or maybe the Survival Right's dream of political power will continue to be denied them by a decent and informed American electorate, leaving them a frustrated corps of armed zealots with only acts of terror to express their canon of hatred and conspiracy.

Either way, it behooves all to learn who and where these dangerous people are, what they are saying and, above all, how they came to be this way. We'll start with the landscape of the Survival Right—its history, its geography and the troubled and troubling people who are its denizens.

Most of the prophecies that had to be fulfilled before Armageddon can come have come to pass. Everything is falling into place. Ezekiel said that fire and brimstone will be rained upon the enemies. That must mean that they'll be destroyed by nuclear weapons.
—Governor Ronald Reagan, August 1971

1: Where They Come From

During Ronald Reagan's first presidential campaign in 1980, which was to take the United States on the biggest swing toward the right in its history, the candidate's speechwriters sought to emphasize that he no longer was merely a hired actor railing the cant of the ultra-conservative businessmen who had spent millions during the 1950s and 1960s making Reagan their TV spokesman. Instead, the 1980 campaign sought to present Reagan as the leader of a well-entrenched and totally respectable conservative American political movement. The vehicle for this transformation came to be known among the national press corps as The Speech.

Each time he delivered the Speech on the long campaign trail, the Great Communicator superbly used the skills he had learned in Hollywood and honed in the Sacramento governor's office to assure ordinary Americans that despite the fact that his stance was the most extreme right-wing posture ever assumed by a successful presidential candidate, it nevertheless was a reflection of the changed psyche of mainstream U.S.A. The Speech comforted millions of skeptics, who walked away with the feeling that this particular candidate was neither the dangerous warmongering extremist nor the lowbrow movie actor that his opponents claimed.

The syntax of The Speech was slightly different at each delivery; but always the message was the same.

"These people who share our dream," the candidate would ask his audience, "where do they come from?"

Of course he had a ready answer: "They come from the fields, the farms, the small towns and the big cities. They come from all over America and they share a dream. They dream of a shining city on the hill. So do I."

The shining city was Washington, D.C. And as the ballots cast that year demonstrated, the people who shared Reagan's conservative dream were everywhere.

The same question can be asked about the Survival Right. Where do they come from? They come from the high pine forests of Montana and the coastal plains of Texas. They come from the hills and hollows of North Carolina and the rugged Ozark Mountains along the Missouri–Arkansas border. They labor in downstate Illinois and press the good fight in Wisconsin's dairy land. They clamor for what they deem to be righteousness on the Nebraska–Kansas–Missouri border and in the bayous of Louisiana.

And they too fear an uncertain future even as they dream of a shining city on a hill. But for them it will be a city without blacks. A city free of Jews. A city of like-minded white Christian right-wingers, a bastion of bigotry.

Even Reagan's most rabid critics can't accuse him of harboring the hatreds that so infect the Survival Right, but many scholars speculate that just as the American mainstream moved rightward in the Reagan years, so did the far right move even farther to the right. John Birchers shifted rightward to join the Klan while Klansmen moved to their right to become neo-Nazis even as a Democratic majority was moving toward Reagan.

It should be noted as well that in years when the national trend leaned leftward, such as the 1970s, the violence on the political fringes came more from the ultra-left than from the right wing. A decade ago it was the Weather Underground, Students for a Democratic Society and other zealots on the far left who were robbing armored cars, killing guards and using the proceeds to send donations to like-minded fellow radicals. Today the crimes are the same, but the perpetrators come from the opposite end of the political spectrum.

Between 1971 and 1981, when Reagan moved into the White House, the Weather Underground alone claimed responsibility for twenty-five bombings, including those of the U.S. Capitol in 1971 and the Pentagon in 1972. In 1981, a half dozen Weather Underground radicals were charged with the commando-style attack against a Brink's truck in Nyack, New York, in which $1.6 million was taken and two policemen and a guard were shot to death. That crime, which took place just as Reagan replaced Democrat Jimmy Carter, marked the most lucrative single outing for the left-wing radicals in their history. It also was the last major crime attributed to the extremists from the far left.

Another parallel surfaces when one examines who is living in communes today. Twenty years ago hundreds, if not thousands, of leftish idealists were living in remote compounds hoping to escape the hassles of congested urban life and seeking rural security from the prospect of the Bomb. Today most of those communes are gone, while increasing numbers in the Survival Right are becoming compound dwellers, stockpiling large stores of weapons, food and medicine in preparation for what many of them have taken to calling "the end time," the final period of "Tribulation" foretold in the Book of Revelation.

And in common with the left-wingers before them, today's right-wing zealots have like-minded fellow radicals to support them all across the American landscape. That became obvious as investigators began to trace the network of hatred that joined forces in the enterprise that ended in the murder of Alan Berg.

The MAC 10 used in the assassination was acquired by a Survivalist commando instructor who lived in a right-wing religious commune on the Arkansas–Missouri border called the Covenant, the Sword and the Arm of the Lord. He converted the weapon into full automatic mode in the church's sophisticated gun shop and gave it to a unit of Survival Right commandos who were training at camps in Troy, Montana, and Metaline Falls, Washington, to prepare for planned armored car raids in California and Washington State.

After Berg was shot down in Denver, the gun was seized by FBI agents in Sandpoint, Idaho. At yet another Idaho compound, this one called the Aryan Nations, the group had planned a counterfeiting operation that they executed with the help of allies in Philadelphia. Funds acquired by the sundry crimes allegedly went to Survivalist sects in Washington, D.C., Michigan, California, Texas and Idaho. In Texas they apparently used money donated from an armored car heist to make a movie extolling the Ku Klux Klan that was aired on cable television. The other funds sent to right-wing leaders scattered about the country went to buy literature and otherwise proselytize their common credo of conspiracy, hatred and Armageddon.

Particularly indicative of the scope of the Survival Right is the fact that, after the five members of the "Aryan death squad" that slaughtered Berg fled the law, they ultimately were captured only after fellow Survivalists had attempted to hide them in Texas, New Mexico, Georgia, the Carolinas, Virginia and Arkansas.

This group of well-connected assassins, members of the self-styled storm troopers who called themselves Bruder Schweigen, will be dealt with at some length later. Here their movements serve best to illustrate their connection to a fervent and impressive Survivalist underground that shares the same vicious dreams.

Those dreams have been dreamt for a long time in the United States of America. The Survival Right is merely the latest to do the dreaming. At first the targeted opponents were the dark-suited Jesuits and the vilified Freemasons who were said to be "Illuminati," keepers of ancient wisdom given by Satan to his pawns on earth to work toward hastening the onslaught of Armageddon.

The ravages visited upon the national psyche by the Civil War and Reconstruction transformed blacks into the enemy. Unwilling to view the sons and daughters of slaves as brilliantly evil, the haters simply focused their sexual tensions against this new target, warning of race mixing, which would dilute the hardy white race.

Jews were added to the list after the waves of immigration from Eastern Europe passed through Ellis Island at the turn of the twentieth century. Of course, a rich body of hate lore had been already prepared by Old World anti-Semites, which made it easy for American haters to cite chapter and verse about how these mercenary "sons and daughters of Satan" were out to ruin the country.

During the 1920s, for instance, Henry Ford used substantial amounts of the money he made selling automobiles to advertise an anti-Semitic document forged in Europe called *The Protocols of the Elders of Zion*. Concocted by Russian Czarists at the dawn of the Bolshevik Revolution, the document purports to be a master plan by an ultrasecret council of Jewish elders to seize world power by manipulating finance through a cabal of bankers, puppet non-Jewish politicians and "our press." A 1920 series about the *Protocols* in Ford's newspaper, the Dearborn *Independent*, entitled "The International Jew: The World's Foremost Problem," was distributed not only in Michigan but by every Ford dealer in America.

Ford had adopted the conspiracy theory about Jewish elders after years of feverish personal efforts to prevent his own version of Armageddon, World War I. He had sailed a "peace ship" through German submarine patrols in 1915, hoping to convince Europe's warring parties to cease hostilities. He ran for the Senate in 1918 and was narrowly defeated after campaigning in favor of President Wilson's efforts to create a League of Nations. Then he concluded that the Jewish bankers whom he perceived to be the cause of his own financial troubles were out to plunge the world into ruinous wars, and began urging his fellow Americans to study the *Protocols*. Finally, in the face of a massive libel suit, Ford issued a public apology in 1927 and acknowledged that the *Protocols* were a forgery.

But his many biographers note that he went to his grave convinced a final collapse was imminent.

For the purpose of understanding the Survival Right's historical roots and gaining a glimmer of its potential as a political force as well as a seedbed of terrorism, one needs to go back to the anti-Catholic tradition that the country's English colonists brought to the New World along with beads and blankets to trade with the Indians. Then the target was the Papists instead of the Jews and the conspiracy was directed by the "Pope of Rome" instead of the "Elders of Zion."

The English colonists who first settled the Americas were molded by the profound forces of the Protestant Reformation. These colonists were the grandchildren of men and women who had been alive when Henry VIII bolted the Church of Rome and established the Anglican tradition by attacking "Popery" and claiming that an evil cabal of Jesuits was secretly in control of world economic activity.

Throughout colonial times Catholics were a tiny minority in the Americas, with openly practicing congregations only in Rhode Island and Maryland until after the Revolution. And their fellow colonists wanted to keep it that way. In 1704 the Maryland legislature enacted an "Act to Prevent the Growth of Popery," which imposed a heavy fine for attending Catholic religious services. In 1750 Harvard College offered lectures "for detecting and convicting and exposing of the idolatry of the Romish church, their tyranny, usurpations, damnable heresies, fatal errors, abominable superstitions and other crying wickedness in her high places." After the American Revolution, New Jersey incorporated in its state constitution a clause stipulating that Catholics might not hold state offices. Similar measures were included in the constitutions of North Carolina and Georgia in 1776. The 1777 Vermont constitution required all holders of state offices to swear they were Protestants.

Generally called the nativist movement by social historians, the American anti-Catholics were holding rallies as early as 1814 to talk about how the Pope was planning to take over the New World by infiltrating Catholics in such numbers that they would rise up on orders from Rome, shoulder the guns they stored under the altars of their churches and visit havoc on their Protestant neighbors. Posters were tacked on the sides of barns showing a bitch nursing a teeming litter of pups representing immigrants from Europe with the caption: "Catholics in search of their dog-ma."

By the late 1820s, nativist mobs were harassing convents and beating up nuns and priests all along the eastern seaboard. In 1834 Samuel F. B. Morse, inventor of the telegraph, wrote a series of twelve anti-Catholic letters to the New York *Observer* entitled "A Foreign Conspiracy against the Liberties of the United States," which warned that the Pope was about to send hordes of his hench-men into America under the guise of immigrants to establish a Romish kingdom in the Mississippi Valley. Once established, the Papists would rise up and take over the entire nation and turn it over to Rome. Morse explained to the *Observer's* readers:

> The conspirators against our liberties, who have been admitted from abroad through the liberality of our institutions, are now organized in every part of the country; they are all subordinates, standing in regular steps of slave and master from the most abject dolt that obeys the commands of his priest, up to the great master-slave [Austrian Count] Metternich, who commands and obeys his illustrious master, the Emperor [of Austria] . . . Every unlettered Catholic emigrant, therefore, that comes into the country, is adding to a mass of ignorance which it will be difficult to reach by any liberal instruction; and however honest (and I have no doubt most of them are so), yet, from the nature of things, they are but obedient instruments in the hands of their more knowing leaders out to accomplish the designs of their foreign masters.

The same year that Morse launched this attack, a mob of "No Popery" activists stormed the Ursuline Sisters' Mount Benedict, the largest convent in Boston, and burned it to the ground after chasing the nuns and priests until they found refuge in the Irish shanties of Charlestown. Such attacks against Catholic churches became com-monplace over the next two decades. A dozen churches were burned in 1853–55 alone, according to one survey of newspapers by scholar Ray Allen Billington. Far more churches were vandalized, their crosses stolen, their altars violated and windows broken. Churches in Sidney, Ohio, and Dorchester, Massachusetts, were bombed. A New York mob laid siege to the Cathedral of St. Peter and St. Paul. When the Pope sent a block of Leonardo da Vinci's marble as a Vatican contribution to the Washington Monument, a nativist mob stole it from a shed and tossed it into the nearby Potomac River.

Nativist preachers took to their pulpits to warn that the events unfolding in America as a result of Catholic emigration from Europe were foretold in the New Testament Book of Revelation, which ends in the final battle on a field called Armageddon when the forces of God and goodness do battle with Satan and his evil seed in the person of "the Beast."

Over twenty-two symbol-laden chapters, St. John tells of the last seven years of humanity when a tremendous "Tribulation" is visited on humankind as God fulfills all his stern Old Testament warnings with a series of plagues, natural calamities and wars until the Second Coming of Christ. Wrote John in Revelation 13:18:

> Let him that hath understanding count the number of the beast: for it is the number of a man; and his number is six hundred threescore and six.

The nativist sermonizers produced labored computations to associate the papacy with the number 666. One popular formula dwelled upon the Latin name assumed by the Pope, "Vicar General of God upon Earth" or "Vicarius Generalis Dei in Terris," to reach 666. Yet another found that by turning the printed words "Pius the Ninth (9th)," the Pope of the time, upside down one could produce the dreaded 666. More than a century later, doomsayers on the American Fundamentalist Right were noting with far more easily comprehensible zeal that the words Ronald, Wilson and Reagan each contained six letters.

From the nativists who burned the Ursuline convent in 1834 up to the neo-Nazis who slaughtered Alan Berg, American hate movements have been inspired by and driven by those last few pages of the New Testament in which John describes the revelations that came to him toward the end of his days while living as a hermit on the Aegean island of Patmos shortly after the Crucifixion. Here the Four Horsemen ride across a sky rendered blood red while sinners gnash their teeth in hopeless despair. Here 200 million infidels from the East die at the hands of avenging angels while, at the same time, God marks 144,000 of his chosen people on the forehead so that they can escape the "Tribulations" and carry the message of salvation to the rest of humanity's beleaguered survivors.

Just as it was a century ago in the heyday of American anti-Catholicism, the Book of Revelation is absolutely crucial to the chemistry that pits much of today's Survival Right against the rest of the world. In scores of fundamentalist, anti-Semitic congregations of the modern-day religious movement called Identity Christianity, a new generation of haters uses this biblical prophetic book to explain a Jewish conspiracy and to justify their hatred. These Scriptures likewise drive large segments of what may be the nation's largest single segment of the Survivalist Right, the loosely structured Posse Comitatus tax protest, underground.

Later in this book we will deal at some length with how the Survival Right is driven by Revelation's prophesies of slaughter for millions of Jews and forecasts of the final, world-ending battle between the forces of good and evil. Here it suffices to explain that these are the holy writings that foretell the nuclear nightmare of the Survivalists and that the biblical interpretations sounded by Identity Christians, such as the Idaho-based Aryan Nations' Reverend Richard Butler, are virtually the same as those proffered by the anti-Catholic forces after the battle was joined in 1840 over the King James Version of the Bible. But in the 1840s the cancer had not yet progressed to the stage of advocating genocide. The nativists would have settled for a few laws keeping the Irish with their whiskey and the Germans with their beer at home.

In that quest, the nineteenth-century anti-Papist crusaders had seized upon the unwillingness of the American Catholic clergy to accept the Protestant King James Version of Scripture as evidence that the Pope of Rome had forbidden his immigrant followers to read the unadulterated word of God out of fear that once exposed to the holy writ they would bolt the Romish Church and become loyal Americans. Protestant Bible Societies were formed in most states to press legislatures to incorporate the King James Version into the school curricula and force Catholic children to read it. Protestants accused the Catholics of not allowing the true Bible in their homes. The Catholic Douay Version of Scripture was edited to permit such lurid abuses as the sex orgies and child stealing that the fundamentalist nativists charged went on behind the doors of convents and monasteries. Some priests made the staggering public relations error of responding by publicly burning King James volumes. The bonfires proved that Holy Scripture was more than the satanic Pope of Rome could bear, argued the nativists. The Papists were burning Bibles because the Holy Book of Revelation shows that the Pope is the Antichrist, the demon who bears the mark of the Beast—666.

Then, in 1844, the Irish potato blight struck, America opened its doors to the world's starving masses, and the nativists became a force to reckon with in U.S. politics. They became the American Party, known popularly as the Know-Nothings because that was what members of the secretive "native Protestant" group were instructed to tell anyone who asked them what they knew about the party.

The founding force behind the Know-Nothings was E. Z. C. Judson, the flamboyant writer of more than four hundred dime novels under the pseudonym Ned Buntline whose florid fictions transformed an obscure Indian scout named William Cody into the American archetype Buffalo Bill. Buntline's Know-Nothings too were archetypes, archetypes for all the hate groups to follow. Their platform was simple and uncompromising: No Catholic whether foreign-born or native to the United States could hold any form of public office. No foreign-born Protestant could hold office. No person could apply for naturalization until he or she had lived inside the United States for at least twenty-one years, instead of the five years that the law prescribed.

The waves of emigration that followed the potato blights in Europe produced an ample supply of newcomers for the Know-Nothings to hate. In 1845 the United States accepted 100,000 immigrants. In 1853, 300,000 were admitted. In addition to establishing religious intolerance as a basis for an American political movement, the social dynamics of the period pitted secretive, "populist" rural Americans directly against their urban counterparts, a dichotomy that can still be seen today in the Survivalist phenomenon with its compounds in rural pockets. The immigrants whom the nativists hated did not live among the Know-Nothings; they gravitated instead to the cities, where they became major forces in the urban Democratic machines.

Just as the neo-Nazis of Idaho have to drive all the way to Denver to find a Jew to hate, the rural Know-Nothings often had to take a trip to town to find an Irish Catholic. In fact, a key element in the chemistry of scapegoat hatred is that the targeted minorities tend either to be very small ones or else to have very few members living in close proximity to the people doing the hating. It is very difficult to live around large numbers of Jews or blacks or whatever and maintain the fictions that fuel the hatred. In 1856, the year of peak political influence by the nativists, the U.S. government estimated that only 7 percent of its residents were immigrants, with most of them, particularly the Irish, clustered in a few major cities such as New York, Boston and New Orleans.

Nevertheless, a widely quoted passage by the American historian Ray Allen Billington explained the Know-Nothings' rather stunning political successes during the 1850s in terms of urban citizens' reaction to the newcomers about them:

> The average American had only to look about him to find tangible evidence of the propagandists' worst fears. He could see quiet city streets transformed into unsightly slums by the foreigners' touch. He could see corrupt political machines thriving upon foreign votes and deadlocked political parties struggling for the

support of untrained aliens. He could see the traditional policy of American isolation threatened by immigrant blocs seeking to embroil the United States in the affairs of their homelands. He could see intemperance, illiteracy, pauperism, and crime all increase with the coming of the foreigner. He could see alien labor, content with a lower standard of living, taking over more and more of the work which American hands had formerly performed. Here were arguments which required no propagandist embroidery. *

Ultimately the Know-Nothings sent seventy-five members to Washington to serve in Congress and controlled several state legislatures, including that of Massachusetts, where anti-Irish hatred allowed the nativists to control the entire state government. In 1856 the American Party's candidate for the presidency, Millard Fillmore, won 21 percent of the vote, a showing that no domestic hate group has ever approached since. Fillmore had served as President between 1850 and 1853 as a Whig and attempted to regain power in 1856 via the anti-Catholic route. It was a turbulent era in American politics as conflicting views over economic issues and slavery had forced the breakdown of the traditional Democrat versus Whig political system. The time was ripe for the Know-Nothings, and they seized it. In addition to the 21 percent turnout for Fillmore, the party won congressional races in New York, Massachusetts, Rhode Island, New Hampshire, Connecticut, Pennsylvania, Delaware, Maryland and California.

By 1860 the Know-Nothings were once again just another bitter minority. Most of the people who had voted for Fillmore on the American Party ticket had moved into the ranks of the Republican Party—founded in 1854.

The Civil War followed. The South lost and, because it lost, the saga of America's haters resumed in 1867 in room 10 of the Maxwell House Hotel in Nashville, Tennessee. In that room, shortly before Independence Day, 1867, Confederate general Nathan Bedford For-

---

* From *The Protestant Crusade: A Study of the Origins of American Nativism* (New York: Macmillan, 1938).

rest, second only to Robert E. Lee as a hero of the South, presided over the inauguration of the racist, xenophobic hate group that today is the one still point in the otherwise changing universe of America's extreme right—the Invisible Empire of the Ku Klux Klan.

The Kluxers actually had started around Pulaski, Tennessee, in 1865, when six young Confederate veterans returned home and decided to start a "club" to cheer up their friends and neighbors who still hadn't shaken off the gloom of Appomattox. As legend has it, the six original Klansmen decided to dress up in costumes because it was faddish at the time to masquerade. With the South ravaged by the war, however, the only costumes they could find were the stiff linen sheets and bedding that their womenfolk had carefully husbanded. When the "pranksters" and their horses—also covered in white linen—rode about the Tennessee countryside on their revels, the racist legend has it, blacks became terrified, thinking they were being visited by the ghosts of rebel war dead.

In 1867, however, General Forrest joined the Klan, took its reins, and transformed the group into a guerrilla cadre dedicated to opposing "Northern oppression." Since the rules imposed for Reconstruction called for granting blacks the vote and allowing majority governments to form, much of the Klan's efforts focused on keeping former slaves from going to the polls. To that end Forrest and his troops developed the tactics of hate that latter-day Klansmen emulate today. Crosses were burned; blacks were told not to vote; lynchings were held in the dark of night.

The Klan was anti-black for obvious reasons. After all, for Klansmen, the Civil War never ended. It also was anti-Catholic because so much of the political power in the North was wielded by the urban Catholic immigrants who had been the targets of the Know-Nothings. Born in the fundamentalist Baptist South, the Ku Klux Klan proclaimed itself a white Christian movement. By the early 1870s the Klan was another template for the modern-day hate groups that are the subject of this book.

Like the neo-Nazi Silent Brotherhood (Bruder Schweigen), the Klan had a complex and highly secret rule book full of hidden meanings. It was called the Invisible Empire, for example, because the day Forrest held his seminal meeting at the Maxwell House he had presented a letter from Robert E. Lee saying that Lee supported the Klan but desired to remain "invisible" in its affairs.

The leader was designated the Imperial Wizard because General Forrest had been nicknamed the "horse wizard" while a cavalry officer. Grand Dragons were named, each to head a different Realm in one of the Southern states. Each Realm or state was divided into Provinces headed by Grand Giants, while each locality in a Province was headed by a Cyclops. Each Cyclops headed a Den composed of twelve Terrors and two Night Hawks, who were couriers and guides. A code of secrecy demanded that no Klansman disclose how the group was structured. While the mumbo jumbo sounds like nothing more than a bunch of schoolboys forming a secret club in their backyard tree house, it has proven to be far more long-lasting— to this day neophytes are given a fifty-four-page Kloran (Klan + Koran) that outlines the elaborate pecking order. Ironically, the Kloran and the Klan's "secret" membership oath were both copyrighted and filed at the Library of Congress, where anybody interested in reading them can obtain a copy.

The original Klan was to continue with its structure largely unchanged down to the present, thanks largely to the efforts of one of America's legendary moviemakers—D. W. Griffith—and the genius of a canny fundamentalist snake-oil seller, Colonel William J. Simmons, who saw that the global tension that gripped Americans on the eve of World War I could be exploited by appeals to the old racial and religious hatreds.

In 1905 Thomas Dixon, Jr., a Southern minister who had grown to manhood during Reconstruction, was so enamored of what he considered the knightly exploits of the Klansmen that he published what turned out to be a best-selling novel, *The Clansman: An Historic Romance of the Ku Klux Klan*. Dixon had captivated oil baron John D. Rockefeller, a fellow Baptist, who offered to build Dixon a church of his own. Dixon's other famous friend was President Woodrow Wilson, the Virginian who had attended graduate school with him at Johns Hopkins University in Baltimore.

The Clansman revolved around two beautiful examples of white Southern womanhood—young girls who were so attractive that animalistic Negroes could not resist the urge to ravish them sexually. Egged on by sneering carpetbaggers, black men surround the first Baptist virgin on a mountainside, giving her the chance to throw herself to death over a cliff rather than be raped by a race mixer. The second belle is trapped in a ramshackle cabin, blocking windows and doors as sexually obsessed black men relentlessly try to invade even as the Klan rides to the rescue.

One of the great embarrassments of Hollywood to this day is the fact that the pioneer filmmaking genius David Wark Griffith chose *The Clansman* as the subject of the first full-length dramatic motion picture ever made. He transformed *The Clansman* into the film *The Birth of a Nation*, the first effort to go beyond the slapstick short subjects that had been the staple of the aborning entertainment medium up to then. It was a success to rival today's blockbusters by George Lucas, Steven Spielberg or Francis Ford Coppola. In 1915, when a nickel bought dinner, a penny bought a daily newspaper and two cents covered a passable breakfast, *The Birth of a Nation* premiered in theaters that charged two dollars for a ticket. It grossed $18 million and was seen by an estimated 50 million people.

Film historians, almost universally a subset of humanity cut from liberal cloth, nevertheless reluctantly rate the movie's climactic scenes a masterpiece both of propaganda and of cinematic dramatic technique. With the theater organ blaring Grieg's "In the Hall of the Mountain King," a posse of white-robed Klansmen rides furiously toward the cabin where the heroine faces imminent rape by a rutting black demon emboldened by his carpetbagger mentors. She swoons; he looms. The camera pans to the crashing hooves of the robed rescuers' horses, then back to the lust-crazed former slave and his trembling victim. The music builds, the black man presses ever harder, the beleaguered virgin's terror grows even as the hooves crash to earth faster and faster. The camera work, the music and the theme were more than many a true-blue son of the South could bear. Movie screens in Knoxville and Greensboro were shot to shreds by audiences who couldn't stand the suspense.

Two weeks before *The Birth of a Nation* opened in Atlanta, William Simmons, a showman and a bitter racist from Alabama, staged a rally just outside of town to mark the revival of the Ku Klux Klan. A professional organizer of fraternal clubs, Simmons saw the Klan as a moneymaking enterprise as well as an ideological goal.

His timing was impeccable. The film was a national box office hit and Simmons's fellow Georgians and Alabamans flocked to join his revived edition of the "Hooded Order." With a ritualistic cross burning in sight of the Atlanta theater where *The Birth of a Nation* played, Simmons wrote the first chapter in the history of the modern-day Klan. It was he who composed the Kloran (and copyrighted it) and outlined the structure of Titans, Kleagles, Cyclopes, etc., that is followed to this day.

Between 1915 and 1920, Simmons became moderately wealthy as membership in his new Klan blossomed. He charged each member an entry fee and monthly dues. He also sold members a group insurance policy and even peddled the requisite white robes, Confederate flags and other regalia. But the organization remained confined to the Deep South. In fact, there was little Klan activity outside Georgia and Alabama until after 1920, when Simmons hired two publicists, Edward Young Clarke and Elizabeth Tyler, to help him take the organization nationwide after membership had reached the saturation point in those two states.

Clarke and Tyler had handled successful membership drives for the Salvation Army and the Anti-Saloon League, which, with their focus on saving humanity from the liquor sold by immigrant Irish and German tavernkeepers, were two of the major anti-Catholic organizations in America at the time. The consultants offered a lopsided deal by which they would get 80 percent and Simmons would get 20 percent of all new membership fees. With new membership virtually at a stop, the racist "colonel" agreed and the savvy, if cynical, public relations wizards went to work.

The Klan needed somebody else to hate, they advised Simmons. It was no longer enough just to target blacks and appeal to people's patriotism. The Klan needed other scapegoats. And they needed to find a conspiracy to attack. Clarke and Tyler explained how World War I had left many people frustrated and frightened. It was clear that it had been far from the "war to end all wars" that President Wilson had promised. The Bolsheviks had seized control of Russia, and once again droves of foreigners were passing through Ellis Island.

Clarke and Tyler went back to the Know-Nothing campaigns for inspiration and advised Simmons to expand his list to include Jews and Catholics to take advantage of the fact that much of the immigration had shifted from German and Irish Catholics to Jews from Poland and Russia as well as Italians and Slavs.

Until the late nineteenth century the Jewish population in the United States had been minuscule, a fact that protected it from much of the outrageous prejudice that flourished in Europe. There were only an estimated 1,000 Jews in the United States at the end of the Revolution, and their numbers only grew to perhaps 200,000 by the late 1800s. Then the wave of emigration from Eastern Europe swelled their numbers to several million and allowed the Klan to bolster its ranks by adopting anti-Semitism.

On the advice of Clarke and Tyler, the Klan declared itself "100 percent American, 100 percent Christian and 100 percent Protestant," and Simmons developed a particularly galling act to open each of his recruiting rallies. He would stride out on the stage, remove a heavy Colt pistol from one pocket and slam it on a table. He would pull an even longer Remington sidearm from the other pocket, toss it alongside the Colt, then draw his bowie knife from a boot and drive its tip into the table between the two guns. With the blade still quivering he would shout, "Now let the niggers, Catholics, Jews and all the others who disdain my Imperial Wizardry come on."

In the first fifteen months of the 1920–21 membership drive, 85,000 people signed up at ten dollars per head. In each town Clarke and Tyler first sent their recruiters to see the local fundamentalist minister and deliver the same Know-Nothing message about the Antichrist prophesied in the Book of Revelation. The recruiters would then make a ten- or fifteen-dollar donation to the church—a windfall for many a hardscrabble-poor country preacher—and ask permission to speak to the congregation.

Recruiters often would pass out broadsides, such as one that read:

> Every criminal, every gambler, every thug, every libertine, every girl ruiner, every home wrecker, every wife beater, every dope peddler, every moonshiner, every crooked politician, every pagan Papist priest, every shyster lawyer, every Knight of Columbus, every white slaver, every brothel madam, every Rome-controlled newspaper, every black spider—is fighting the Klan. Think it over. Which side are you on?

While the Klan never reached the lofty political powers attained by the Know-Nothings in the mid-1850s, it did score some brief triumphs around the country, particularly during the 1920s in Oregon and Indiana, where Klan-backed candidates dominated both state legislatures and Klan forces controlled large numbers of state and local offices as well.

Probably the high point for Klan political power came in July 1923, when 100,000 people turned out in Kokomo, Indiana, for the inauguration of Hoosier Daniel Clarke Stephenson as the group's Grand Dragon, second in command only to the Imperial Wizard himself. It was estimated that at its peak in the late 1920s Simmons's new Klan had raised $75 million and had as many as 4 million members.

But the United States soon was undergoing sea changes that deflated the Klan ranks even faster than they had swelled. Notably, a number of leading newspapers became incensed at the lynchings and cross burnings and launched anti-Klan drives. The legendary

Herbert Bayard Swope of the New York *World* devoted a twenty-one-day series to exposing Klan outrages.

The story of how Clarke and Tyler connived to expand the Klan by adding Jews and Catholics to the list of conspirators came out after it was disclosed by the *World* that both of them had been arrested while "less than fully clad and less than fully sober" in a 1919 police raid on a Birmingham whorehouse.

The sensational disclosures won the newspaper the Pulitzer Prize, and Swope boasted that his circulation jumped 60,000 copies because of the series. Predictably, the *World*'s success led to numerous other newspapers around the country taking on the Klan, attempting to infiltrate its secret ranks and warning about its credo of hatred. In 1985 Roland Wood, an exasperated neo-Nazi Klansman in Greensboro, North Carolina, told the author, "I don't go to cross burnings or rallies anymore because the only people who are there are FBI agents and reporters wearing white sheets tryin' to win the Pulitzer Prize."

But far more devastating to the Klan's prospects for becoming a political force than the antagonistic news media were the two major historical developments of the Great Depression and World War II.

As Fred J. Cook notes in his book *The Ku Klux Klan: America's Recurring Nightmare*, "With banks failing, with millions upon millions unemployed, with factories idle and all business life at a standstill, the Klan's anti-Catholic, anti-Semitic, and anti-black rhetoric seemed unrealistic. It had nothing to do with the great issues of the day."

When the German-American Bund, an arm of Hitler's Nazi Party operating in the United States, became active in the late 1930s, the already beleaguered Klan leadership made the mistake of getting into bed with the Nazis. The two groups shared many of the same ideologies and Klan leaders watched with envy and glee as Hitler's power grew. At an August 18, 1940, rally in a Bund-operated camp near Andover, New Jersey, several hundred robed Klansmen joined a like number of Bundists to hear Arthur Bell, Grand Dragon of the Realm of New Jersey, tell them that "God Bless America" was a "Semitic song fit only for Bowery taverns and brothels" because it was written by a Jew named Irving Berlin.

It is hard to imagine a bigger public relations error at a time when the Nazi blitzkrieg already was moving across Europe and causing great anxiety among Americans. A crowd of angry New Jerseyites gathered outside the Bund camp gates to shout "Put Hitler on your crosses" and sing "The Star-Spangled Banner," and in doing so spoke for most of their fellow citizens.

From the 1940s on, the Klan has declined as any sort of significant national electoral force. Nevertheless, it has had a tremendous impact on the national psyche from World War II to the present. A raft of horrors has been visited upon the American scene by subsequent generations of the "Hooded Order," even while the Klan itself has degenerated into a disjointed agglomeration of feuding splinter groups, an alphabet soup overstocked with K's. There is the United Klans of America Knights of the Ku Klux Klan, Inc.; the Knights of the Ku Klux Klan, Invisible Empire; the National Knights of the Ku Klux Klan; the Knights of the Ku Klux Klan; the Original Knights of the Ku Klux Klan; the Dixie Klans; the National Alliance—and many more.

Yet despite the diversity among the internally warring hate groups, the Klan's connection to Nazism remains firm. Robert Matthews, the commando who founded the Silent Brotherhood, started out as a Klansman before gravitating to the neo-Nazi movement. Robert Miles, one of those who federal prosecutors charged had been sent money from the Silent Brotherhood's armored car robberies, was the Klan's Grand Dragon in Michigan before he joined the neo-Nazi movement and set a half dozen school buses on fire in Pontiac, Michigan, in 1971. Others who allegedly received money from the Silent Brotherhood were the Carolina Knights of the KKK, a splinter group led by Glenn Miller that received national attention after the bloody clash in 1979 in Greensboro when they were filmed shooting five members of the Communist Worker's Party.

J. B. Stoner, who joined the Tennessee Klan in the late 1940s, adopted the Nazi mantle in the early 1950s and in 1983 was sentenced to a ten-year prison term for the 1958 bombing of the Bethel Baptist Church in Birmingham, Alabama. Stoner long has been a suspect in one of the most heinous crimes in civil rights history, the 1963 bombing of Birmingham's Sixteenth Street Baptist Church, in which four young girls were slaughtered as they were getting ready for choir practice. Stoner's National States' Rights Party remains a powerful voice among the Survival Right through publication of its monthly newspaper, *The Thunderbolt*.

In 1985 the researchers at the Anti-Defamation League of B'nai B'rith published the following list of active "neo-Nazi organizations" in the United States:

1. National Socialist Liberation Front
2. SS Action Group
3. Social Nationalist Aryan People's Party
4. National Alliance
5. Euro-American Alliance
6. American Nazi Party (a reconstituted branch of the now defunct National Socialist Party of America)
7. America First Committee
8. National Socialist Movement
9. Universal Order
10. American White Nationalist Party
11. National Socialist League
12. National Socialist Vanguard
13. National Socialist American Worker's Party
14. National Socialist White American Party

These fourteen organizations are located in Cincinnati, Chillicothe (Ohio), Chicago, Columbus, Detroit, Houston, Indianapolis,

Los Angeles, Milwaukee, New Orleans, Philadelphia, Post Falls (Idaho), Salinas (California) and San Diego.

As discussed earlier, the Survivalists who killed Berg emerged from the Hitlerite Identity church movement. Specifically, the Silent Brotherhood emerged from Richard Butler's Aryan Nations compound near Hayden Lake, Idaho, which is owned by his church, the Church of Jesus Christ Christian.

Other anti-Semitic Identity groups include:

William Potter Gale's Ministry of Christ Church in Mariposa, California, which sponsors a paramilitary group called the California Rangers.

James K. Warner's New Christian Crusade Church, which publishes the Identity church monthly *Christian Vanguard*.

Sheldon Emry's Lord's Covenant Church in Phoenix, which is allied with the Citizens Emergency Defense System, a survivalist group.

Gordon Winrod's Our Saviour's Church in Gainesville, Missouri, which operates a radio ministry to broadcast *The Winrod Hour*, in which he has advocated "killing all the Jews."

Dan Gayman's Church of Israel, which operates a compound outside of Schell City, Missouri, and publishes a series of tape cassettes containing Identity sermons. Gayman also is co-founder of the Louisiana-based National Emancipation of Our White Seed.

The Covenant, the Sword and the Arm of the Lord, near Three Brothers, Arkansas, where three members of the Silent Brotherhood were arrested in a dramatic FBI assault in 1985. CSA operates a training compound called Silhouette City, where neo-Nazi commandos work on their urban battle techniques.

The Christian-Patriots Defense League, which operates a compound across the Arkansas state line in Missouri as well as paramilitary training facilities in Illinois and West Virginia.

Rounding out the roll call of haters with this dangerously activist bent is the super-secret tax protest underground called Posse Comitatus, which was formed after the FBI launched an all-out offensive against its 1960s predecessors, the Minutemen. Posse doctrine advises individuals to hoard large amounts of firearms and food to prepare for Armageddon. Because that same doctrine requires Posse warriors to keep their affiliation secret, it is the least-documented facet of the Survival Right, even as many analysts say they believe it also is the largest.

Because Posse dogma views with suspicion organizations that encompass more than a single county—Posse Comitatus means "power of the county"—it is unlikely that its true size will ever be known. Posse units have been organized at the county level in California, Colorado, Delaware, Idaho, Illinois, Kansas, Nebraska, North Dakota, Oregon, Texas, Washington and Wisconsin, according to Anti-Defamation League studies and investigative reports written by agents of the Internal Revenue Service. Posse groups frequently form Identity churches of their own, incorporating dietary laws and health practices as part of their doctrine, as will be seen later in this book.

The Survival Right, then, has come a long way since the days when the late George Lincoln Rockwell appalled mainstream America by renting a shabby house in Arlington, Virginia, decorating it with swastikas and Nazi relics and declaring himself "Führer of the American Nazi Party."

Another of the haters who federal prosecutors believe were sent money by the Berg hit squad, Texas Klan Titan Louis Beam, addressed a Klan rally in New Orleans in 1977 and told anybody who wanted to listen where the Survival Right was heading. Beam explained that the Texas Klan had instituted a "military program" and that its members had been training for the past three years. He told the crowd:

> We are getting ready to reclaim Texas for the white man. So get ready. Get ready for what we know is coming. Everyone talks of a race war. How many guns, bullets, food, training, preparations have you made? Our forefathers built this country with courage and blood. It will take fresh blood, but, by God, a lot of it will be the blood of our enemies . . . Get ready!

They got ready in Hayden Lake, Idaho. They called themselves the Bruder Schweigen in honor of a line in a nationalistic 1814 German poem warning of the dangers *"wenn alle Brüder schweigen / und falschen Götzen traun"* (when all our brothers are silent / and trust in false idols). The federal government simply called them "the Order."

Give your soul to God and pick up your gun,
It's time to deal in lead.
We are the legions of the damned,
The army of the already dead.
—Robert Jay Matthews

2: The Order

On September 12, 1985, ten members of the Order sat in a darkened Seattle courtroom and, along with their jury, watched themselves on the damning videotapes they had let free-lance journalist Peter Lake make two years earlier.

They watched themselves kneeling and being dubbed "Aryan knights" with a swastika-handled sword and then taking blood oaths to kill Jews, blacks and other minorities.

They watched themselves clustered in prayer, arms held stiff in Nazi salutes, venerating Adolf Hitler as a saint and vowing, "I shall never rest until there is created upon this continent a national state for my people. One God, one nation, one race."

They watched themselves taking basic training in an Idaho Survivalist compound called Aryan Nations. Each commando ran through an obstacle course that ended with him firing his automatic weapon into a poster of Menachem Begin and shouting, "For God, nation, race!"

They watched themselves wearing Nazi uniforms while operating the printing press they had used to counterfeit money in a grandiose scheme to bankrupt the United States government, which they called ZOG, for Zionist Occupational Government.

Lake, one of those hungry California filmmakers who fan out about the country seeking to translate news into a salable product, had infiltrated the neo-Nazis in November 1983 while under contract to *The Rebel,* a short-lived muckraking periodical financed by Larry Flynt, the publisher of *Hustler* magazine. The free-lancer wound up with one of the most sensational stories of the 1980s and with a price on his head that stands to this day for any member of the Survival Right who can find and execute him, according to testimony at the Seattle trial.

In November 1983, Lake had stumbled onto the creation of the neo-Nazi commando force called the Order that within weeks was to launch a year-long reign of terror, including assassination, raids on armored cars, counterfeiting and assorted acts of mayhem that ultimately would result in the indictment of twenty-four of its members, ten of whom stood trial in that Seattle courtroom on evidence supplied by most of the others in exchange for their freedom or reduced sentences.

Lake had thought he was merely doing an exposé of the fairly well-known and exceedingly strange neo-Nazi Church of Jesus Christ Christian/Aryan Nations, which was operated out of a fenced-in compound complete with barbed wire and watchtower near the tourist hamlet of Hayden Lake, Idaho. He wasn't to learn until months afterward that what he had filmed was the birth of the now famous neo-Nazi strike force that was started by Aryan Nations members who decided to stop just talking hatred and to live it instead.

Posing as a racist tropical-fish salesman named Peter Palmer, Lake had approached the neo-Nazis and persuaded several of them to let him make videotapes of their lives with the promise that those tapes would only be used to help them recruit new members. "I figured that gun nuts would probably know even less about tropical fish than I do," Lake said, in an interview in explanation of his choice of a cover. To get their cooperation he promised the subjects of the subsequent amazing footage that the tapes would be circulated only among sympathizers in the rest of the Survival Right, such as the extremely active Wisconsin chapter of Posse Comitatus, the Klan in Texas and a group of like-minded bigots called the White Aryan Resistance in California. Unknown to Lake, the men and women he approached were most eager for recruits. They had some very big plans and badly needed more comrades-in-arms to make those plans a reality.

In a single year, this one group of right-wing haters was to strike against society as a whole with what was arguably more bile, more venom and more sheer courage than had been previously observed in a fringe group in all of American history. Within a few months in 1984 this group of Survivalists raised more than $4 million attacking banks and armored car cash shipments. Prosecutors charge that they then sent large amounts of the money to various and sundry like-minded hate groups in Michigan, North Carolina, Idaho, Texas, Washington, D.C., and Arkansas, urging each to use the windfall to continue the fight for racial purity and genocide. They also committed one of the most outrageous anti-Semitic assassinations since the Holocaust and secured themselves a place as martyrs and heroes of the American far right for decades to come.

But, sitting before two large tables in a Seattle courtroom, the nine men and one woman who were the architects of that brief reign of terror fell far short of resembling the noble Aryan warriors they fancied themselves to be.

Bruce Carroll Pierce, thirty, the triggerman who had fired twelve bullets from his Ingram MAC 10 into Alan Berg's body, looked like a bearded forestry student at Montana State University. A strange tic in one eye gave him a demonic air and explained why his racist cronies had given him the code name "Brigham" in honor of the wild-eyed Mormon prophet Brigham Young.

David "Lone Wolf" Lane, forty-six, the hulking Denver Klan leader and small-time golf hustler who was the getaway driver that June night when Berg died, looked even homelier than usual with his jailhouse pallor. Lane considered himself the "Propaganda Minister" of the Order and was active in a Colorado anti-Semitic group that did its proselytizing among farmers and ranchers through a tabloid newspaper called *The Primrose and Cattlemen's Gazette.*

The neo-Nazis' unlikely Brünnehilde at the defendants' table, Jean Margaret Craig, fifty-two, who staked out Berg and followed him for several days to learn his routine, looked very much like the dumpy, graying Wyoming grandmother that she was. They called her "Rainy" because she cried a lot, but they kept her on because, as the group's documents explained, the founder of the Order, Robert Jay Matthews, had "planted his seed in the belly" of her daughter, Zillah Craig. The group spent a lot of time talking about seed. They briefly had called themselves the Emancipation of the White Seed, they called Jews the seed of Satan, and they wrote a paramilitary training manual which offered this advice:

> It is recommended that no kinsman be put in combat situations, i.e. raise their sword against ZOG, until he has planted his seed in the belly of a woman. The same for kinswomen, if possible, they should bear at least one warrior before putting their own life on the line.

Two other members of the Berg hit squad, Matthews, who took the famous terrorist's handle "Carlos" for his code name, and Richard "Mr. Black" Scutari, were not at the defendants' table in Seattle. Scutari, whose nickname referred to his black belt in karate, was at large and on the FBI's 10 Most Wanted list. Matthews was dead, having been left a charred mass of flesh and bone that only a dentist could identify after the dramatic shoot-out on Whidbey Island when an FBI flare touched off his cache of thousands of rounds of ammo, hundreds of grenades and other ordnance.

The most striking of the Seattle defendants was Gary Lee Yarbrough, who became the favorite of the news media courtroom sketch artists with his constantly moving green eyes and flowing red beard that led to his code name "Yosemite Sam," after the famous cartoon character.

It was Yarbrough who made the fatal mistake of starting a gunfight with two federal agents who came by his house looking for Yarbrough's brother on a completely different matter that allowed the FBI to establish the links that helped them uncover the Order. Two FBI agents posing as Forest Service employees had approached Yarbrough's house in Sandpoint, Idaho, in an effort to arrest Yarbrough's younger brother on a fugitive warrant from Arizona. The younger brother was not in Idaho, but "Yosemite Sam," thinking that the FBI was after him, pulled out one of his many handguns, fired at the agents as they sat in a borrowed Forest Service pickup in front of his gate, then fled into the trees.

When the agents searched Yarbrough's attractive A-frame home they found a small shrine dedicated to Hitler along with a staggering cache of weapons, explosives, money, survivalist gear and the notorious MAC 10 that killed Berg. As a result of that find, forty-two people would be arrested in seventeen states and charged with crimes attributed to the Order. Another twenty people were arrested for related crimes, such as persons in the Deep South and the Midwest who helped hide Order members once police began their manhunt.

Sitting next to Yarbrough at the defendants' table was balding Randolph "Luke" Duey, who looked like a meek accountant rather than the murderous criminal who prosecutors charged—and the jury agreed—had participated in two commando raids against armored cars and personally executed one Order member, Walter West, who got weak-kneed and wanted out. Duey and an Order member from Philadelphia named James Dye lured West into an Idaho forest. After a third comrade knocked West to the ground with a ball peen hammer, Duey calmly pumped a round from the victim's own Ruger Mini-14 into West's forehead. His nickname, given to him that afternoon, came from the Paul Newman movie *Cool Hand Luke*. Before he entered the violent netherworld of the Survival Right, Duey had been a U.S. Postal Service letter carrier.

The hammer man was another of the defendants, Richard "Jolly" Kemp, a baby-faced racist who at the age of twenty-two specialized in armored car robberies and was prone to giggling. After the West murder, Kemp was known by a new code name—"Hammer."

The other "baby" of the Survivalist commandos was Andrew V. "Closet" Barnhill, twenty-eight, a onetime member of the Survivalist group the Covenant, the Sword and the Arm of the Lord before taking up arms to fight ZOG for Matthews. He and Kemp became fast friends and were arrested together in Kalispell, Montana, where they had taken part of the Bruder Schweigen's loot and opened a legal poker parlor.

Randall Evans, twenty-nine, sat alongside Barnhill and Kemp throughout the lengthy legal proceeding, listening as prosecutors described how he had joined the Klan in California and then helped Matthews formulate the intricate and cheeky plan to isolate an armored car on a remote mountain highway and loot it of more than $3.5 million.

Perhaps the quietest of the defendants was Frank Silva, a leader in the California Ku Klux Klan whose major role in the crime wave had been operating a message center behind the front lines where he helped the true warriors keep in touch with one another.

Most out of place of all was Ardie McBrearty, the fifty-seven-year-old "Professor" for the Order, who was recruited out of the Arkansas tax protest movement, where he belonged to the Posse Comitatus. While the other defendants wore casual dress, McBrearty arrived each day during the four-month trial wearing an ill-fitting suit, a starched white shirt and a necktie. Like most Posse figures, McBrearty had spent a large amount of time reading lawbooks and filing a steady succession of "pro se" lawsuits to press for right-wing causes everywhere, from the county courts of Arkansas to the United States Supreme Court. The aging racist had been recruited at his home in Gentry, Arkansas, for his expertise with computerized voice-stress analyzers, which he had used to spot enemies who tried to infiltrate the Arkansas tax protest movement. During the long Order trial McBrearty continually argued with his lawyer over legal points.

Those are the players. During a dramatic presentation before the jury in the Order trial on September 12, 1985, Robert Ward, United States Attorney for the state of Washington, spent five hours explaining how they fit together. Ward turned to the jury and in typically stilted prosecutorial prose began: "Ladies and gentlemen, in 1983 Robert Matthews was a person who was living in Metaline Falls, Washington. Robert Matthews had become a strong believer in white supremacy and perhaps an equally strong believer in the theory that the Jewish people were responsible for the problems that the white race was encountering . . ."

It starts, indeed, with Matthews.

When he died, Robert Jay Matthews was a handsome, trim, clear-eyed man of thirty-one. There was a magnetism about him, friends recalled, that inspired the anti-establishment types he associated with to stop whining and do something about their hatred.

Matthews was born in 1953 in the border town of Marfa, Texas, but moved about the Sunbelt between Texas and Arizona as an Air Force brat every time his father was transferred. Even among his blood brothers in the Aryan Nations he was circumspect about his past, although he did complain that he had been rejected by West Point after a routine FBI security check found that he had—through his father—joined a tax protest unit in Arizona at the age of fifteen. So, at the age of twenty-one, Matthews joined another military outfit or, more precisely, a paramilitary outfit, called the Sons of Liberty, in Phoenix, Arizona.

The Sons, like virtually every other member group of the Survival Right, adhered to a complex philosophy based on the key concept that the Jews had foisted the income tax on God's chosen people as part of a plan by the hidden "Elders of Zion" to capture the world's economic order. The Sons held that the Elders of Zion had made American currency worthless by removing all the gold in Fort Knox decades ago. Since the currency is worthless, there can be no tax levied, the rationale holds. And so the tax protesters, particularly those in the quasi-religious Posse Comitatus, simply do not fill out the forms sent them each year by the IRS.

Details of Matthews's next moves are scant, but one letter he left behind alludes to being shot at by an IRS agent and quarreling with FBI personnel in Arizona. He next appears as a member of the

National Alliance in Washington, D.C., a Klan and Nazi hybrid group that had evolved from the Youth for George Wallace for President campaign of 1972.

At the National Alliance, Matthews was totally captivated by another charismatic denizen of the Survival Right, tall and Lincolnesque William Pierce, the National Alliance's director. Pierce, a former physics professor at Oregon State University, had written a book, *The Turner Diaries*, which was to become for Matthews what the golden plates from God were to Mormonism's founder, Joseph Smith.

Pierce, not related to the Order's Bruce Carroll Pierce, had started out in the far right as a disciple of John Birch Society president Robert Welch before hooking up with George Lincoln Rockwell, the Kennedy-era neo-Nazi who along with his band of brown shirts lived in a shabby house in Arlington, Virginia, that they called "the Barracks." Rockwell's strange cadre of misfits became the first post-World War II Americans to openly strut the streets in Nazi regalia.

Pierce told the author in an interview that during his Birchite years he had been exposed by Welch to an apocalyptic novel, *The John Franklin Letters*, in which the narrator describes an America of the 1950s "Sovietized" by the Communists to the extent that a Yugoslavian inspector for the United Nations World Health Organization is granted powers by the President to invade any house in the land and check to see if its water is being properly treated with mind-sapping fluoride as ordered by the global Communist conspiracy. In the Eisenhower-era novel, the United States joins a World Authority controlled by the Soviet-Asian-African bloc, and Red Chinese administrators are sent to Washington to rule. In Harlem triumphant Negroes rise up and loot the liquor stores while mobs of public housing residents move into the suburbs, where they take over homes and subject their owners to torture by blowtorch and televised rock-and-roll music in their own Levittown two-car garages.

But John Franklin and his friends have been preparing for the Reds for a decade. They have stockpiled weapons in a remote rural compound along with enough food to sustain them during a pitched battle. These latter-day Minutemen move against the godless Communists and in the course of a climactic chapter perform fourteen patriotic murders: one by hammer, two by fire, one by strangling, two by bow and arrow, one by throwing the victim out of a high-rise window and the other seven by gunfire. Despite the use of atom bombs by the Soviet overlords, Franklin's revolution prevails.

Inspired by *The Franklin Letters*, Pierce two decades later wrote *The Turner Diaries*, which was to become Robert Matthews's bible. Like John Franklin, Pierce's hero, Earl Turner, has prepared for years while the Jewish international conspiracy took power in the United States, forcing whites to intermarry with other races until the population becomes "a swarming horde of indifferent mulatto zombies." In Pierce's anti-Utopia, banks are required to give low-interest loans to racially mixed couples who want houses in white neighborhoods. All guns are outlawed by the "Cohen Act" and black members of each city's Human Relations Council are deputized to search whites' houses seeking illegal weapons. The Supreme Court rules that rape laws are unconstitutional because they imply a difference between the sexes, leading to a massive upswing in rapes by black men against white women.

To resist the international cabal that has taken over the United States in the early 1990s and implemented all these laws, Turner joins a group called the Order, which wages its guerrilla war by attacking banks and Jewish-owned stores for funds. This fictional Order also murders numerous Jewish conspirators as well as blacks and law enforcement officials, striking fear in the hearts of America's Zionist overlords. One of Turner's first projects is the destruction of the FBI's national headquarters with a truckload of homemade explosives.

Soon after killing seven hundred people in the FBI attack, the Order launches a barrage of mortar shells at Capitol Hill in Washington, killing sixty-one lawmakers and aides. That is followed by a grenade attack on *The Washington Post* and assorted other guerrilla actions. Much of the early activity centers on bombings of synagogues, pornographic bookstores, adult movie outlets and places where homosexuals congregate. Throughout the narrative, Turner finds himself obliged to execute several teenage "sluts" whom he finds openly cavorting with black boyfriends.

Turner and company wreck the American economy by flooding the nation with counterfeit money before taking control of a nuclear arsenal and using it to attack both Israel and selected targets where the Zionists have taken over in the Soviet Union. Turner's followers cache a vast stockpile of weapons near Bellefonte, Pennsylvania, and when the revolution arrives, they take up these arms and attack the Pentagon, where Turner dies a martyr in a suicidal attack using a nuclear weapon against the gigantic building.

The parallels between the plot line of *The Turner Diaries* and the description given on the opening day of the Seattle trial by U.S. Attorney Ward are striking. Matthews had gathered together a band of the most committed among the nation's Survival Right and led them on a crusade, during which they waged a war of terror against ZOG using *The Turner Diaries* as a blueprint. The counterfeiting, the assassinations, the bomb attacks, the raids against banks and armored cars, even McBrearty's voice-stress tests, all were inspired by Pierce's novel, Ward said. Peter Lake recalled in an interview how Frank Silva had asked him during one videotaping session whether he had read *The Turner Diaries*. "You gotta read it," said Silva. "Everything that's gonna happen is in there."

Matthews had left the National Alliance in the late 1970s and moved to Metaline Falls, Washington, where he attempted to create a new all-white society. Armed with an ax and a chain saw, he cleared a swatch of forest and built a log home for his wife, Debbie, and their adopted child, an infant son, Clint. Nearby he erected a "Barracks"—named after George Lincoln Rockwell's quarters in Virginia—for the Aryan warriors he hoped to recruit. For the next few years Matthews divided his time between working at a mine and then later at a cement factory in the remote community near the Idaho and Canadian border.

And he read. He immersed himself in the literature of the Survival

Right, a far larger library than most Americans realize. There were the innumerable tracts about tax code nuances by the various segments of the Posse Comitatus and other like-minded sects. There was *The Protocols of the Elders of Zion*, the old standby document forged by nineteenth-century anti-Semites in Czarist Russia and adopted by every anti-Jewish hate group ever since. There were the numerous volumes sold by the Liberty Lobby claiming that there never was a Nazi Holocaust in which six million Jews died, that *The Diary of Anne Frank* is a forgery and that most cases of missing children occur during the periods when Jews celebrate their satanic holidays of Purim and Passover, during which they sacrifice Gentile virgins.

In a letter he wrote the day before he died in his own holocaust of illicit ammunition on Whidbey Island, Matthews described his self-education as a racist warrior:

> I soon settled down to marriage, clearing my land, and reading. Reading became an obsession with me. I consumed volume upon volume on subjects dealing with history, politics, and economics. I was especially taken with Spengler's *Decline of the West* and Simpson's *Which Way, Western Man?* I also subscribed to numerous periodicals on current American problems, especially those concerned with the ever increasing decline of White America.
>
> My knowledge of ancient European history started to awaken a wrongfully suppressed emotion buried deep within my soul. That of racial pride and consciousness.
>
> The stronger my love for my people grew, the deeper became my hatred for those who would destroy my race, my heritage. And darken the future of my children.
>
> By the time my son had arrived, I realized that White America, indeed my entire race, was headed for oblivion unless White men rose and turned the tide. The more I came to love my son, the more I realized that unless things changed radically, by the time he was my age, he would be a stranger in his own land, a blond-haired, blue-eyed Aryan in a country populated mainly by Mexicans, mulattoes, blacks and Asians. His future was growing darker by the day.
>
> I came to learn that this was not by accident, that there is a

small, cohesive alien group within this nation working day and night to make this happen. I learned that these culture distorters have an iron grip on both major political parties, on Congress, on the media, on the publishing houses, and on most of the major Christian denominations in this nation, even though these aliens subscribe to a religion which is diametrically opposed to Christianity.

These are the same people who ex-Senator William J. Fulbright and the late General [George] Brown [Chairman of the Joint Chiefs of Staff during the Ford administration] tried to warn us about. Henry Ford and Charles Lindbergh tried vainly to warn us also. Had we been more vigilant, my son's future would not be so dark and dismal.

Thus I have no choice. I must stand up like a White man and do battle.

A secret war has been developing for the last year between the regime in Washington and an ever growing number of White people who are determined to regain what our forefathers discovered, explored, conquered, settled, built and died for.

The FBI has been able to keep this war secret only because up until now we have been doing nothing more than growing and preparing. The government, however, seems determined to force the issue. So we have no choice but to stand up and fight. Hail Victory!

Matthews began waging that secret war against the FBI, the IRS and the rest of officialdom after encountering a fairly large number of men and women who shared his mind-set, whom he met through a powerful figure who would complete the education of this particular radical. That man was Richard Girnt Butler, pastor of the Church of Jesus Christ Christian in Hayden Lake, Idaho, whose association with Matthews would lead to his own indictment on sedition charges in 1987.

William Pierce's novel about ZOG provided Matthews with an action plan, but Butler's Identity church supplied the philosophical and theological underpinnings, as is dramatically portrayed in Lake's videotapes of Butler's liturgy, in which the Hitlerite "pastor" dubbed each member an Aryan knight while backlighted by his church's stained-glass window with its stylized blue swastika on a field of red. Identity Christianity as preached by Butler allowed Matthews to kill, steal and terrorize in the belief he was doing God's will. Further, it was through Butler's network of cronies in Survivalist training camps around the nation that Matthews and company learned many of the skills that they were to use on their brief but stunning crime wave.

Each summer, Butler invited racists from around the country to a gathering called the World Aryan Congress at his Hayden Lake compound. The only year he missed was that of the Order's trial (1985), when intense federal investigations of many figures inside the movement made a session impossible. A broad spectrum of the Survival Right turned out at each of these meetings—Klansmen from several sections of the country, shadowy Posse Comitatus leaders, tax rebels, a number of the sundry National Socialist groups, a dozen or two Identity church delegations and a goodly number of lone wolves, right-wingers too cranky to join any group but fully in accord with the Aryan Nations' theology of hate. Butler's get-together was the most popular of several national gatherings held throughout the year by elements of the Survival Right. Another popular meeting is held each year near Nashville, Tennessee, hosted by the National Pistol and Rifle Association, which, as the name implies, focuses more on firepower than theology. A third annual hate group gathering is the Freedom Festival hosted under circus tents in downstate Illinois by the Christian-Patriots Defense League.

Like any other conventions, these Survival Right sessions include speeches, workshops and, of course, numerous tables where members try to sell other members literature and products dealing with the attendees' interests. The speeches focus on such typical messages as how the Jews are responsible for the raft of missing children now advertised throughout the country on the sides of milk containers or how blacks are simply members of a race descended from creatures God made but rejected while working toward making the perfect Aryan, Adam.

Workshops often teach such survival skills as how to obtain the best sort of fake identification cards or how to immobilize a city by pouring gasoline into the sewer systems, poisoning the water supply with cyanide and blasting phone lines with dynamite. Many of these tactics were demonstrated once the Silent Brotherhood swung into action. Matthews's band, for example, made extensive use of the fake ID technique taught at one Hayden Lake session. Attendees had been told to find the names of children who died in infancy at their local cemetery and then send away for copies of their birth certificates. One book sold at virtually all these sessions is *Privacy?* (published by Eden Press), which for $18.95 promises to teach a survivalist how to:

> Become "Invisible" to Investigators
> Stop Generating Financial Records
> Stay Out of Government Files
> Begin Eliminating Negative Records
> Create Helpful New Records
> Hide Your Assets
> Find Privacy from Taxes
> Discover Banking Alternatives
> Live Nomadically
> Obtain Multiple Addresses
> Use Hideouts, Deep Cover

Bruce Carroll Pierce made repeated trips to the Missoula, Montana, cemetery to find the names of dead infants which ultimately were used to create identities complete with social security cards, Costa Rican and Montana driver's licenses and voting cards. These identities were used to buy autos, rent safe houses and make other arrangements during the armored car attacks and the Berg murder.

Another example of putting the theory taught at Aryan Nations workshops into practice surfaced when two members of the Order were captured during a dramatic federal raid on the compound of the Covenant, the Sword and the Arm of the Lord in Arkansas in

1985. A massive quantity of cyanide, suitable for poisoning the water supply of an entire city, was confiscated.

The dean of Survival Right paramilitary training instructors, Randall Rader, a member of the Covenant, the Sword and the Arm of the Lord, attended Butler's Aryan Congresses and taught Matthews, Pierce and company there. Ultimately Rader joined the Order, where he trained the members like some sort of Olympic coach, working with them on marksmanship and commando tactics. It was Rader who converted the MAC 10 used against Berg and gave it to Pierce. The Order's first code name for him was "Field Marshal." Then one day Rader killed and ate his pet dog to make a point about how tough a Survivalist must be. After that they called him "Big Boy," a lame reference to the cuisine in a restaurant where Yarbrough had been a dishwasher.

Other major assets that came to the Order at the Hayden Lake sessions were the contacts made among top leaders of the Survival Right. These were to come in handy—at least for a while—after members were forced to go on the run. Of particular importance were several movement stalwarts who commonly attended Aryan Congresses and apparently became heroes to Matthews. These leaders play the role of highly visible elders in the Survival Right while most ordinary movement insiders remain highly secretive about their ties. Federal prosecutors charged that many of these leaders were sent money taken in the crime wave. Among those named as benefiting from Matthews's hero worship were:

—Thomas Metzger, a former leader of the Ku Klux Klan in California who went on to head a neo-Nazi group called the White American Resistance. Metzger won the 1980 Democratic nomination for the seat in Congress representing California's 43rd District and attended the Order trial to express his support for the "Aryan warriors being persecuted here by ZOG."

—Louis Beam, former Grand Titan for the Texas Ku Klux Klan and a leader of the Klan's violent protests against Vietnamese immigrants who fled their homeland to become shrimpers on the Texas

Gulf coast. By 1987 Beam had created at least a dozen racist computerized bulletin boards—some ultrasecret, some relatively public—which members of the Survival Right use to communicate via telephone and modem through software supplied by Beam.

—Glenn Miller, head of the Carolina Knights of the Ku Klux Klan and the neo-Nazi White Patriots Party, whose associates in Greensboro, North Carolina, were to shelter Lane until his arrest. It was members of Miller's Klan unit who killed five anti-Klan demonstrators in the so-called Greensboro Death to the Klan massacre of 1979.

—Robert Miles, former Grand Dragon of the Michigan KKK and, along with Butler, one of the country's leading Identity preachers, operating out of his Cohoctah, Michigan, Mountain Church. He is considered one of the most effective speakers and writers in the movement, and his words are uncompromising in their demand for violence. Miles wrote, just before the Order started its wave of terror, that it was crucial that he and a few others serve as spokesmen for the Survival Right and not personally engage in further violent activism:

> The point is that no racist leader or spokesman can suffer talk, discussions or even mention of illegal acts in his presence. Those who talk seldom act; those who act seldom talk. The talkers should be suspect from the git!
> Our fight, at this stage of the game, is psychological in nature. We are the Johnny Appleseeds, broadcasting the seed. The seeds must be given priority. The hour for the Armed Party will come. As surely as the nuclear fire comes. When the central government implodes from its own corruption and decadence, then the original Ku Klux Klan will rise again. It will be the Posse Comitatus . . .

In April and May of 1987 many of these Survival Right elder statesmen were arrested as part of a Justice Department operation code-named Clean Sweep. Fourteen neo-Nazi figures including Miles, Butler, Beam, Pierce, Lane, Scutari, Barnhill and McBrearty were charged with engaging in a "seditious conspiracy" to overthrow the government by plotting such crimes as poisoning urban water supplies with massive amounts of cyanide and conducting widespread counterfeiting. That indictment described a Survival Right summit meeting in July of 1983 at Butler's compound when the movement's patriarchs launched the multipronged attack on what they call ZOG.

An FBI report given to the Seattle jury said that, after he was arrested, Bruce Carroll Pierce told agents that the Order had sent between $250,000 and $300,000 of its loot to Metzger, $100,000 to Beam, $300,000 to Miller and $15,300 to Miles. Pierce also said Butler got $40,000 and that the Order members sent William Pierce of the National Alliance $50,000 in recognition of his authorship of *The Turner Diaries*, which had so inspired them. Each of these men denied in interviews—most of them very brief—with the author that they had received any money.

During his opening remarks and throughout the trial, prosecutor Robert Ward and his colleague Gene Wilson hammered away on the point that Matthews and his followers dreamed of the day when the money would allow the Metzgers, the Mileses, the Millers and all the rest of the Survival Right to come to a vast tract of land they would purchase in the Pacific Northwest to form the ultimate Survivalists' compound, a city-state within the mongrelized U.S.A., which they would call the White American Bastion.

And so the groundwork was laid for that brief reign of terror in 1984 that would cost Alan Berg his life and directly benefit the future activities of the racist movement. The motive was to create a neo-Nazi homeland, the blueprint was *The Turner Diaries*, and the rationale was the racist theology of Identity Christianity.

With motive, blueprint and theology in hand, the Order went to work in earnest.

Much now is known about the inner workings of the neo-Nazi commandos because several of their number, including Rader, Denver Daw Parmenter II and Thomas Martinez, turned on their comrades in exchange for leniency.

In *The Turner Diaries* the heroes made a point of robbing and bombing immoral places such as pornographic stores, synagogues and gambling dens because it served the dual purpose of financing the movement and "eliminating the vermin." The first attack the group was charged with was the April 1983 strong-arm robbery of a pornographic bookstore in Spokane, where Pierce, Duey and Matthews accosted a man and a woman who were clerking the night shift.

Meek-looking Duey slugged the male Spokane porn clerk in the mouth, then, visibly flustered, used up all the tape they had brought binding the clerk's hands and feet. They left the woman untied and ran out the front door with a paltry $369 from the till.

At Metaline Falls the outlaws resolved to do better the next time. They decided, for instance, to start out each future criminal exercise with a prayer whereby they reconsecrated themselves to their white God. Standing and holding hands in a circle around one of their babies, who represented the "future of the Aryan race," they recited, "From this time on I have no fear of death. I know that I have a sacred duty to deliver our people from the Jew, the mud people [blacks] and all who would dilute our Aryan race. One God, one race, one nation."

The first time they pledged this oath, there were only six of them. They drove off to Seattle and were so short of funds that all six men had to stay in a single room at the Golden West Motel. They had planned to rob an armored car at one of the city's larger discount stores but, after five days—and nights—crowded into the cheap motel room, they lost their nerve and went back to Metaline Falls.

By the time the net closed in on the Order a year later, they were a group of at least twenty-three battle-tested hard-core commandos driving about in fleets of new $50,000 recreational vehicles bristling with enormously expensive firearms, and their hidden caches were bulging with cash. When arrested, most of them wore a heavy solid-gold medallion or belt buckle that Matthews had custom-minted with the words "Bruder Schweigen" in the center. (Earl Turner had been given a gold medallion with a suicide pill in a secret compartment when he was initiated into the fictional Order.)

In November 1983, when Lake visited Butler's compound in

Idaho, the Order would have been more properly named the Gang That Couldn't Hate Straight. By a fluke, Pierce, Matthews and Duey had moved into the compound that month to launch their first effort to emulate the counterfeiting scheme carried out in *The Turner Diaries*. But while Earl Turner masterfully forged hundreds of millions' worth of $10, $20, $50 and $100 bills, which he spread in black ghettos so that the residents would flock to the liquor stores, Matthews and his cohorts tried to produce greenbacks on the same presses that Butler used for his Sunday church bulletins. The result was so sloppy that they even tried rubbing coffee grounds into individual bills to make them passable. They printed more than $200,000 worth of the sleazy counterfeit, but when Pierce and Lane went to Union Gap, Washington, to attempt to pass it, Pierce was promptly arrested. The real Order was still a long way away from its fictional counterpart.

Enter Yarbrough and David Tate, a twenty-two-year-old martial arts expert from Athol, Idaho, who passed up the chance to inherit his father's dairy farm in order to pursue the Aryan dream in Butler's seedy dormitory for hired help. Tate and Yarbrough were in charge of running Butler's press as well as providing security for the evangelist. Butler had recruited Yarbrough through one of his "outreach" programs while "Yosemite Sam" was an inmate in Arizona.

For the first time the Order was about to acquire some good old-fashioned criminal expertise. A career criminal who had served time for everything from marijuana selling to armed robbery, Yarbrough had been a particularly unruly inmate at the Arizona State Prison just before coming north to Hayden Lake. He had been sentenced to serve between five and eight years for grand theft and wound up serving the whole eight years after a series of reprimands for assaulting guards, assaulting other inmates, possession of marijuana, possession of homemade knives and possession of Nazi literature.

Yarbrough was a member of one of the most notorious families in Pima County, Arizona, the red-haired clan of Red and Rusty Yarbrough, a husband and wife whose own knife fights in the family kitchen were part of their children's growing up. Three sons went bad, a fourth, Robert, went to Nashville to become a popular disc jockey. A sheriff's deputy in Tucson once told the *Arizona Daily Star*, "When anything went wrong down there we'd just go down and arrest one of the Yarbroughs and chances were we'd be right."

After Matthews hooked up with Yarbrough, the Order grew bolder. Soon the real mayhem was to begin.

But first they had to endure a final gaffe. On December 20, 1983, Matthews held up a branch of Citibank in Seattle with a handgun and was given $25,900 in cash by the teller. But as Matthews ran down the sidewalk, an explosive "dye pack" included with the bills detonated with such force that it threw him to the ground. Nevertheless, Matthews escaped the scene and took the money back to Metaline Falls, where Lane helped him remove the dye from the bills. First, of course, they tried coffee grounds. Then they tried turpentine, alcohol and several other solvents before finding the answer in a type of furniture paint remover called Zip Strip, which allowed them to salvage part of the loot.

It would be a long time before the Order had another such failure. After the botched bank job, Yarbrough's addition to the Gang That Couldn't Hate Straight and Rader's patient commando training sessions soon turned them into the crack squad of racist warriors they had dreamed of being from the start.

First, in March 1984, Yarbrough took the Order back to Seattle to show them how to properly rob an armored car. After the group spent a few days watching the movements of a targeted cash shipment, Yarbrough drove them to the same store, a Fred Meyers discount chain outlet, that they had staked out while the six of them were crammed into a single motel room. This time Duey, Pierce and Matthews went inside with specific instructions about what each was to do while Yarbrough acted as lookout and getaway driver.

When George King, a guard for Continental Armored Transport Service, came wheeling a cart of money down an aisle in the store, he was stopped by Pierce, who pulled a gun. Duey came up behind King, shielding the scene from customers, and ordered him to lie on the floor. Matthews scooped the money out of the steel cart in seconds. They left with $43,000 in cash and slipped away from the scene and into rush-hour traffic without a hitch. It was their first successful hit and the Silent Brotherhood was ecstatic.

The next outing was to put them in the big leagues.

In mid-April, less than a month after the Fred Meyers caper, the Order returned seven strong to Seattle, where, financed by the earlier raid, they each took a separate room at the Motel 6 in suburban Issaquah. They bought a van and a Chrysler automobile for their getaway vehicles and got down to the serious business of master crime. This time the target was a Bon Marché department store in Seattle's affluent Northgate Mall. Those in on this strike were Matthews, Yarbrough, Pierce, Duey, Barnhill, Kemp and Denver Daw Parmenter II, the racist with a drinking problem and a Hitler-like mustache who was to become the government's key witness and supply many details of the reign of terror that followed.

The Northgate Mall robbery was right out of prime-time TV. Yarbrough was in charge of diversionary tactics, Pierce was in charge of acquiring the getaway cars and Duey had been assigned to find the safe house where the gang would hole up after the heist. Taking a page out of *The Turner Diaries* for his diversion, Yarbrough bought a ticket to see *Wet Nurse* and *Data Girl*, the double bill at a porn house called the Embassy Theater in Seattle's notorious Third Street red-light district, the day before the robbery. He left a bomb under his seat, went to a pay phone and called the box office. "The place is going to go sky high," he told the ticket seller. She called the police and the bomb went off just as the first squad car arrived at the theater.

As it was designed to do, the black-powder bomb caused minor damage and inflicted only a few slight injuries to the twenty persons in the audience who fled the smoke-filled building. The next day, April 23, 1984, just before the robbery, Yarbrough called the same box office and said, "It's going off again," hoping to draw police attention away from the nearby mall. Kemp, meanwhile, tossed dozens of roofing nails onto the roadway leading into the mall to stop any police cars called to the scene.

When the armored car they had targeted pulled up to the Bon Marché and began loading, Barnhill and Parmenter drove the newly purchased Chrysler in front of the truck to block its passage. Yarbrough pulled the van to the rear of the armored vehicle. Pierce and Duey, who had been posing nearby as window washers, stepped over and pulled handguns on the guards who had left the truck. Kemp, Barnhill and Yarbrough jumped out of the vehicles brandishing automatic weapons, and Matthews held up a sign to the two guards still in the truck that read: "Get Out or Die."

The crew left the truck and Pierce recognized one of them as George King, the victim of their first big robbery at Fred Myers. "You know the score, George," said Pierce. King nodded and meekly sat down on the sidewalk.

They loaded the contents of the truck—except the coins—into the van and drove off to their own cars, which were less than a mile away. Abandoning the two getaway vehicles, they drove to Newport, Washington, where Duey had rented a house with funds from the earlier success, using identity papers that Pierce had obtained in a name taken from a child's tombstone in the Missoula cemetery.

In the rented house they put all the food stamps, checks and money wrappers in one pile and all the cash in another. There was $500,000. They burned the food stamps, checks and paper money wrappers and jubilantly paid each other $24,000 "salary" apiece. Then they chatted happily into the night about which hate groups they would send donations from the haul. According to Pierce's statement to the FBI, they decided to give Butler $40,000 and to use the rest of the money to finance another armored car strike to raise funds for other hate groups.

Flushed with success, the Order members did a little free-lance hating in the next few days. Pierce and Kemp drove to Boise, Idaho, where they planted a dynamite bomb in the crawl space under the synagogue of Congregation Ahaveth Israel. Other than causing anger and sorrow among the small congregation, the bomb did little physical damage except to the facility's kitchen. Duey and Barnhill, who had the code name "Mr. Closet" because he liked to ferret out homosexuals and hurt them, took to cruising the tougher sections of Portland, where they stopped to beat up people who looked like gays or pimps to them.

Parmenter and several other Order members who later made plea bargain deals told how after the Fred Meyers and Northgate robberies, the group established elaborate plans for its own structure as well as for future paramilitary exercises. Matthews called the agenda "The Six Steps":

> Step 1—Military training
> Step 2—Fund-raising
> Step 3—Purchase of supplies
> Step 4—Donations to other groups
> Step 5—Security (assassination)
> Step 6—Expansion

Under heated questioning by FBI agents, Parmenter outlined how the master plan called for the original group to continue with its commando strikes until the pressure from law enforcement became too intense. Then they were to break up into "seed cells," with one or two members of the original group fanning out in different directions equipped with a minimal amount of guns and other supplies needed to found a new Order somewhere else.

This indeed happened after the law caught up with and killed Matthews on Whidbey Island. Lane, Pierce and Tate all were eventually arrested with stockpiles of weaponry and equipment to start a new cell. Each carried computers for tapping in to Beam's system, police scanners, voice-stress analyzers (to spot potential infiltrators during recruiting drives) and other paraphernalia.

One Order document, written by Lane, specified that each "seed carrier" tote these weapons to supply his recruits:

> Two .308 caliber assault rifles
> Two .223 semiautomatic rifles

Two 12-gauge riot shotguns

Twelve 9 mm sidearms, one for each member

But in May and June of 1984 the time had not yet come to fan out across the nation. Instead, the group decided to find their first assassination victim.

From the beginning the Order had been based on an initiation rite in which members were required to acquire "points" in order to stay in good standing within the group. Points could only be earned by committing a violent crime against the targeted minorities or ZOG. A key facet of this requirement, Matthews had explained from the start, was to make each member vulnerable to being turned in for a serious crime if he or she ever betrayed the others.

The gang established a decimal system in which members won points by committing various violent acts, and each member was supposed to eventually accumulate a score of 1. Although none of the documents or testimony in the Seattle trial ever stipulated just how many points a given crime would bring, it was clear that a member would have to kill more than one person to reach a whole number. But whether an Alan Berg was worth two-tenths or nine-tenths of a point wasn't stated. Targets for which Order members could earn points included "federal judges, FBI agents and other federal officials and employees as well as the murder of Jewish people, black people and others," according to a federal complaint filed in the case. Pierce's bombing of the Boise synagogue and the hooliganism of Barnhill and Duey in Portland's tough neighborhoods apparently were efforts to gain these points, according to the prosecutors. But nobody had yet pulled off an assassination.

Star prosecution witness Parmenter told how the Order had met repeatedly after the second Seattle armored car strike to discuss the target for their first assassination. Numerous prominent names were discussed—Henry Kissinger, David Rockefeller, the Baron Elie de Rothschild, oil magnate Armand Hammer, etc. They settled on just three names with which to start; the bigger fish would come later. That first list included television producer Norman Lear, Morris Dees, the old-guard civil rights attorney who headed Klanwatch in Montgomery, Alabama, and Berg, who had taunted at least two members of the Order on his talk show.

Dees made the first cut because he had a long-running feud with Louis Beam. The computerized "Aryan bulletin boards" run by Beam around the country frequently carry a lengthy message that one can call up under the heading "Morris Dees Queer." In that message the civil rights activist is condemned to death because his Southern Poverty Law Center helps finance an abortion clinic and because Dees is "queer," both capital offenses in the eyes of much of the Survival Right. Not surprisingly, no mention is made of the fact that Dees has repeatedly denied being homosexual. In a world of blood oaths, assassinations and storm-trooper-style armored car raids there is little cause to fret over something as mild as mere slander.

The Silent Brotherhood singled out Lear because he made the sort of TV shows that they just couldn't tolerate, Parmenter told the jury from the witness stand. In addition to *All in the Family* and *Maude*, Lear brought to TV such shows centered on blacks as *The Jeffersons*, *Good Times* and *Sanford and Son*. Said Parmenter of Lear, "He was a Jew, and all of his programs were thought to be anti-white. We thought they were attacking what we thought to be white moral principles."

But Dees was all the way across the continent in Alabama and Lear lived in bicoastal circles of New York and Los Angeles that were hard for the small-town racists to fathom, so they turned to Berg down in Denver.

Lane had pressed hard to make Berg the Order's first target anyway, prosecutors showed. A sullen introvert, as his code name "Lone Wolf" indicates, Lane had had only two sources of income in Denver before moving off to join Butler's Hayden Lake church— hustling golf on the links of Denver's city course, and selling ads for the ultraright tabloid *The Primrose and Cattlemen's Gazette* in the suburb of Brighton, Colorado. Being a golf hustler in the Mile-High City, with its long winters, is of course highly seasonal work at best.

The Primrose and Cattlemen's Gazette devoted virtually all of its editorial space to various Survival Right stands, such as urging farmers to stockpile arms, to hoard gold instead of cash, and to blame Jewish international bankers for the agricultural depression. Berg had attacked the newspaper by name for its anti-Semitic tirades, and Lane as well as the publisher, Roderick Elliott, had called in to debate on the air.

At the trial, Lane's fellow ad salesman, Richard Konopa, said, "When they got finished discussing Jews and Nazis [in front of Berg's large radio audience], most of our advertisers canceled out. They just called up and said they didn't want anything to do with us."

The boycott cost Lane his job. He told Konopa and anybody else who would listen, "I was run out of Denver by the Jewsmedia." For months afterward Lane would lie in bed listening to Berg's show, seething with hate but incapable of getting up and turning the radio off, Konopa told police.

For the same months Lane also had carried a tape recording of himself on Berg's KOA show, according to trial witness Elizabeth Dracon, a onetime friend of Lane. At one point Lane played that tape and several others of Berg to the Church of Christ congregation in La Porte, Colorado, she said. Another tape that Lane carried was an exchange between Berg and Jack Mohr, a general in the Survivalist Christian-Patriots Defense League.

"He's a filthy Jew," Lane told the congregation, referring to Berg. "Somebody ought to shoot that guy." In June 1984, flush with their success, the Silent Brotherhood agreed. And, they decided, Lane could drive the getaway car.

In 1987 a federal grand jury indicted Lane, Pierce, Scutari and Craig on charges that they deprived Berg of his civil rights by killing him. The indictment charged that Matthews pressed Craig into action to lay the groundwork by trailing Berg about his Denver haunts to find the best time and place for the assassination.

On the road to founding the Silent Brotherhood, Matthews had left his infertile wife, Debbie, and their adopted son, Clint, behind to take as a mistress Craig's twenty-year-old daughter, Zillah. "Planting his seed" was very important to Matthews, and the liaison with Zillah just as the Bruder Schweigen was forming had forged a bond between Matthews and Jean Craig. He kept Jean actively engaged from the start despite the fact that she was clearly out of place and unpopular among the others. Nevertheless, by June, Zillah was carrying Matthews's daughter and Jean was a full-fledged member of the Order.

After following Berg from his job at KOA in downtown Denver to his favorite restaurants, nightclubs and other haunts, Craig called the hit squad of Lane, Scutari, Matthews and Pierce, who were waiting in Laramie, Wyoming. Strike him at home, she suggested, adding that she had thrown her "runes"—medieval Nordic seer stones—to confirm the advice.

On the night of June 18, Berg pulled up to his town house. Fumbling, as he often did, with his car keys, a lighted cigarette and a paper sack filled with cans of dog food, Berg stepped out of his Volkswagen at 9:20 p.m. as Pierce stood in the bushes holding the MAC 10 that Rader had converted into a rapid-firing machine gun in his church's gun shop.

The silenced weapon emitted thirteen pops, sounds about as loud as striking a heavy dictionary against a desk. On the fourteenth round, the gun jammed, a fact that Matthews found mystically significant, according to later testimony by his friends. Twelve of the .45 caliber slugs made thirty-four different wounds as bits of Berg's own bone and shattered bullets churned about his body. His spinal cord was severed, his brain destroyed and the atrium, an upper chamber in his heart, was obliterated. "He didn't make a sound. He just went down like I pulled the rug out from under him," Pierce later told another Order member, the gang's banker, Kenneth Loff.

Pierce jumped into the getaway car driven by Lane and sped off into the night. Both Matthews and Scutari had been waiting nearby, each in a backup vehicle financed by the Northgate Mall robbery. All four drove off to Laramie to relive their moment of glory when they butchered a man armed, as federal prosecutor Gene Wilson was to tell the jury, "with a lighted cigarette and a can of dog food."

Once again the Order had borrowed a page from *The Turner Diaries*, in which the guerrillas frequently declare a given day to be the "Day of the Rope" and hang somebody from the news media, preferably a Jew. With their "Day of the Rope" past them and each in possession of an unknown number of decimal points for killing Berg, the murderers headed northwest to resume their efforts to flood ZOG's Federal Reserve with bogus currency.

Stung by the problems they encountered when they made bills on Butler's press, the now plush Order members brought in some expertise. They found Robert and Sharon Merki, two friends that Scutari had made in Costa Rica when he had been briefly hired in 1981 as a mercenary to guard a gold mine secretly owned by the Covenant, the Sword and the Arm of the Lord. At the time, Merki and wife were hiding in Costa Rica, where they had fled counterfeiting charges. Now they were back in the United States, where Robert had a job printing and selling advertising for bowling alley score sheets.

Merki bought a proper press for making U.S. $10s and $20s and set up a counterfeiting center in Boise. In short order he ran off 4,000 sheets, each with four bills, and Lane took off in his yellow Volkswagen for Philadelphia, where the Order planned to start flooding ZOG's banks with boodle. To this day it remains unclear how much of Merki's phony money was passed off by the Order, but the decision to expand the project to Philadelphia was to cost Matthews his life.

Matthews made the fatal mistake of trusting someone with the unlikely name—for an Aryan Nazi supremacist—of Martinez to run his counterfeit-passing scheme in Pennsylvania.

Thomas Martinez, unlike most Order members, who tended to

be rural Westerners or Southerners, was a creature of the urban Northeast. He grew up in the tough Fishtown neighborhood of Philadelphia and had trouble with authority figures from the start. His formal education ended when he spent two and a half years in the tenth grade before dropping out. He tried to join the Army but was given an honorable discharge during basic training—the Army will not say why. His girlfriend got pregnant in 1973 and, at the age of nineteen, Martinez was desperate to find a job. He looked for months and was turned down repeatedly. Many of the jobs he didn't get went to blacks and women under affirmative action rules, and Martinez was later to tell reporter Kitty Caparella of the Philadelphia *Daily News* that this experience turned him into a bitter racist. Why, he asked himself, should his black inferiors be employed while he, with his superior brain power and abilities, remained jobless?

Martinez began reading racist tracts and joined a local Nietzsche book club. He sent away for literature from the Klan, the Posse and, of course, William Pierce's National Alliance, where Matthews was a rising young leader.

Then Martinez was given a job with the Philadelphia Housing Authority as a maintenance man. He took the job and kept it for almost a decade, but he did so by swallowing his outrage. Martinez decided that the only reason he was hired by the housing projects was that somebody had made a "mistake" and decided he was Hispanic because of his surname.

Even at the Order trial, when he was trying to convince the judge and jury that he had rejected the hatred of the neo-Nazi movement, Martinez was painfully troubled about his ethnic heritage, insisting under cross-examination that his father had been a "pure-blooded" Castilian from Spain and his mother a Swede. He most decidedly was not a Hispanic, he retorted. No, he said, Martinez was every bit as Aryan a name as Matthews, Pierce, Duey or McBrearty.

After Martinez joined the National Alliance he met Matthews at several of the Survival Right conventions and a friendship was born. Both men distinguished themselves as public speakers at these sessions by their glib mastery of neo-Nazi rhetoric. Together they enlivened many a workshop at Butler's World Aryan Congresses or the Christian-Patriots' Freedom Festivals. Martinez told the *Daily News* reporter, in the only interview he gave before being hidden by the government under its witness protection program, how he was so taken by the movement after he became popular there that he bought anti-Semitic and racist literature with his own funds and handed it out for free on Philadelphia street corners. Later he would recall of his days in the movement—including while he was part of the Order—"You talk to people who feel like you do, and you don't want to talk about anything else. You don't read sports. You don't watch TV. All you do is read about Israel and race. It's race, race, race."

When Lane dropped by Martinez's house on Matthews's instructions six days after the Berg assassination, Martinez agreed to pass Merki's crisp, professional-looking bills in Philadelphia and New Jersey. Lane and Martinez worked for several days to cut the individual bills out of the sheets printed by Merki. Then Lane left after telling Martinez to cash the bills in New Jersey or else pass them out in Philadelphia's black neighborhoods to cause havoc, as prescribed in *The Turner Diaries* and *The Franklin Letters*.

Martinez did as he promised, but he also got greedy and kept some of the money for himself. It was quickly noticed in the working-class Kensington neighborhood where he lived that the Martinez family suddenly had a new video recorder, a whole set of spanking-new lawn furniture, and that they were driving about town in rental cars instead of the old family heap.

On June 28, Martinez tried to buy a lottery ticket at a neighborhood Beerland store with one of Merki's $10 bills and got caught. In July, Matthews and Zillah, just beginning to show her pregnancy, went to Philadelphia to urge Martinez to simply plead innocent to the counterfeiting charge and then go underground as a member of the Order. Matthews told him there were great things brewing in the future, including a really big armored car raid and other adventures. Martinez agreed and told Matthews he would join up just as soon as formal charges were lodged against him. In the meantime, he said, he would keep passing counterfeit in the Northeast.

The next day, however, Martinez went to the FBI and sold Matthews out in exchange for a berth for himself and his family in the protected federal witness program. In FBI files Martinez became CS (confidential source) 1 in the Order case.

Meanwhile, back in Metaline Falls, not suspecting that Martinez had turned color, Matthews and his commandos were planning the most spectacular of all their crimes, the strike against a Brink's armored truck just outside Ukiah, California, which would net the Silent Brotherhood a staggering $3.6 million and secure their status for a long time to come as legends of the Survivalist movement.

Just as they had used the $43,000 taken from the relatively small-scale robbery of the Fred Meyers store to buy equipment and other resources needed for the $500,000 Northgate Mall heist, they now were using proceeds from that half-million-dollar strike to finance a commando raid on a major Brink's shipment. This time they decided they would need much more gear, so they established a dummy company, Mountain Man Supply Co., to buy it.

There had been four commandos on the first hit at Fred Meyers and seven at Northgate. For Ukiah the neo-Nazis employed a strike force of fourteen armed participants and several support personnel, such as Jean Craig and Frank Silva, who maintained message centers in Boise to coordinate the getaway and arrange the post-robbery meetings to split the loot. The actual robbers gathered at Santa Rosa, about fifty miles north of San Francisco, a week before the raid, which took place on July 19.

On the morning of the attack they assembled in a room at the Santa Rosa Motel 8, said yet another of their Aryan prayers, then went to a staging area along Route 101 where they knew the targeted truck must pass. Merki, dressed as an old woman, was assigned to drive a quarter mile ahead of the Brink's truck on Route 101 so that when the strike force saw him pass by they would be ready to swing out into the roadway.

They did just that. Merki in a gray wig and black dress drove by, and Yarbrough, in a pickup truck, pulled out in front of the Brink's truck while another pickup pulled in behind the armored shipment. When, after a few miles, the truck began to slow on a steep grade, Yarbrough slowed up in front of the laboring armored vehicle and forced it to stop. The men jumped out of the rear pickup and calmly began directing traffic on the busy highway around the robbery.

One of the commandos, Bill Soderquist, jumped out of Yarbrough's pickup and held up a sign reading: "Get Out or Die," just as Matthews had done at Northgate Mall. Matthews approached the truck, and when the crew inside didn't immediately open the doors, he sprayed a clip of ammunition into the bulletproof windshield. The two men in the front promptly piled out, but the woman guard in the back refused until the commandos had shot both rear tires out with their shotguns and the always trigger-happy Duey had fired a round directly into the steel compartment where the terrified woman huddled as the slug ricocheted off the walls. She then relented and opened the door.

Matthews jumped into the back and began throwing money bags to the men in the beds of the two pickups. As the robbery proceeded, Scutari continually listened to police radio monitors and kept shouting out the elapsed time—". . . forty-five seconds, one minute, one minute fifteen seconds . . ."

As soon as Scutari heard on the radio that one of the passing motorists who had been waved around the crime scene had called the police, he sounded the warning and the band fled.

A few miles down the road they abandoned the two pickups for two "switch" vehicles they had purchased, a white Buick Riviera and a new Ford Econoline van. They took these vehicles to their own personal cars and split up.

Afterward, coordinating their appointments through the message centers run by Craig and Silva, they congregated in Reno, Nevada, where they discovered that they had stolen a staggering $3.6 million in cash. Each armed participant was given $30,000 as a "salary" and each unarmed associate received $10,000. The rest of the money

was earmarked either for a future attack or for Step 4 and Step 6—
donations to other hate groups and plans to fan out around the
country and start new cells of the Silent Brotherhood.

A large amount of that money eventually was channeled through
the Mountain Man Supply Co. to buy military gear to train other
right-wing commandos at two Survivalist boot camps set up in Idaho
and Missouri. FBI agents traced 137 separate shipments via United
Parcel Service of military-type gear to the camp that Rader established at Priest River, Idaho, on 110 acres purchased with funds
from the armored car robberies. The receipts were for everything
from cases of Army K rations to three-wheel motorcycles designed
for off-road use. There were hundreds of guns and thousands of
rounds of ammunition purchased along with numerous voice-stress
analysis machines and dozens of Apple computers for hooking up
to Beam's bulletin boards. Pierce even bought Rottweiler guard dogs
with the funds.

Parmenter testified in the Seattle trial that another Order member,
Daniel Bauer, was given $100,000 to spend on recruiting and sup-
plying "high-tech scientists to develop weapons for the Order." He
said the money was spent on unnamed scientists to produce lasers
that could be used as assassination weapons. Parmenter said that
this scheme—there is no evidence it was carried out—was inspired
by a memo from Matthews passed along on the computer network
telling his followers that if the Order were ever disbanded they should
"strike back in a well-thought-out manner that would inflict maximum damage to ZOG—go for the brain, not for the throat—get
many bastards with one stone."

But while it uncovered these expenditures the FBI ultimately had
to admit that it could account for less than $600,000 of the enormous
Ukiah take. The rest, prosecutors speculated in the courtroom,
could have been donated to any of hundreds of Identity Christian
churches, small Klan and Nazi splinter groups, Posse chapters or
whatever.

That money may to this day be financing further growth among
the Survival Right, according to both the Seattle prosecutors and

their colleagues in other jurisdictions like Fort Smith, Arkansas, where the fourteen Survivalists were indicted in 1987 and charged with an ongoing seditious conspiracy.

Even while he was playing financial angel and sending funds from the Ukiah haul to other Survivalist leaders, the net was tightening around Matthews. The feds, with Martinez under complete control, simply waited until Matthews contacted his friend in Philadelphia.

The call came shortly after Yarbrough had been accosted by two FBI agents at his Sandpoint, Idaho, home and been forced to flee. He left behind the Berg murder weapon and tens of thousands of dollars' worth of property, including dozens of pistols and rifles, hundreds of sticks of dynamite, $35,000 in cash, a Harley-Davidson motorcycle, a four-door Pontiac Phoenix hatchback, a three-wheel all-terrain motorcycle, a $20,000 Jeep Wagoneer and a new Chevy Vega.

When it was disclosed in the news media that the Berg murder weapon had been discovered in the possession of one of Butler's neo-Nazis, Matthews became the most wanted man in the Western United States. Nevertheless, he had great plans for expanding the Silent Brotherhood and felt he needed his glib young friend Martinez as a new recruit.

Matthews told Martinez how he and Jean Craig had attended Zillah at the October 4 birth of his daughter—Survivalist style, without any outside help from ZOG medicine with its poisonous fluoride treatments, circumcisions and other Jewish-inspired mischief. Now, he told Martinez, Matthews was ready to resume the war in earnest.

Martinez agreed to fly to Portland on November 23 and meet Matthews at the airport. Wary of likely gunplay, the FBI decided to let the meeting go off without a hitch and not strike until Martinez called them to say where he and Matthews were staying. The two men wound up at the Capri Motel in Portland, where Yarbrough too was a guest. Yarbrough and Matthews stayed in room 42 and Martinez in room 14. The next morning, after Martinez had turned them in, FBI agents raided the motel and took Yarbrough captive.

Matthews, however, shot his way out and ran down a driveway with FBI agent Arthur Hensel in pursuit. A few hundred yards down the street there was a gunfight in which Hensel was wounded in the leg and foot while a second agent, Kenneth Lovin, managed to fire a single shotgun round at the fleeing Matthews, striking him in the hand.

As Matthews later told it in a letter:

> I rounded the corner of the motel and took off down the hill into a residential area. After running for two blocks I decided to quit being the hunted and become the hunter.
>
> I drew my gun and waited behind a concrete wall for the agents to draw near. When I aimed my gun at the head of the closest agent, I saw the handsome face of a young white man and lowered my aim to his knee and his foot. Had I not done so I could have killed both agents and still had left the use of my hand which is now mangled beyond repair and which I might well lose altogether. That is the last time I will ever give quarter.
>
> As for the traitor in room 14, we will eventually find him. If it takes 10 years and we have to travel to the far ends of the earth, we will find him. And true to our oath, when we do find him, we will remove his head from his body.
>
> I have no regrets or apologies for Gary or myself. In fact, I am proud that we had the courage and the determination to stand up and fight for our race and our heritage at a time in our history when such a deed is called a crime and not an act of valor.
>
> . . . I am not going into hiding, rather I will press the FBI and let them know what it is like to become the hunted. Doing so, it is only logical to assume that my days on this planet are rapidly drawing to a close. Even so, I have no fear. For the reality of life is death, and the worst the enemy can do to me is shorten my tour of duty in this world. I will leave knowing that my family and friends love and support me. I will leave knowing I have made the ultimate sacrifice to secure the future of my children.
>
> As always, for blood, soil, honor, for faith, and for race.

On Friday, December 7, the FBI's newly established hostage and terrorism commando SWAT team located Matthews, Duey, Merki and Merki's wife, Sharon, in three houses rented on Whidbey Island in Puget Sound. Federal officials closed the entire Sound to boating and flights to Seattle-Tacoma International Airport were rerouted well away from the area. More than two hundred combat-equipped agents surrounded the small compound of houses. When they announced their presence with bullhorns, the ever-pugnacious Duey stormed out onto the porch of his house brandishing an Uzi machine gun. Then, as Wilson and other prosecutors tell it, Duey did a thunderstruck double take and said, "You're all white men," threw down the automatic and surrendered. Merki and his wife stalled for a few hours, apparently to give them time to burn counterfeit money and other documents before they too surrendered. Matthews spoke to the task force by phone but refused to come out.

Toward dusk, the commandos fired tear gas into the house and waited for hours in the ensuing silence. Then, under cover of darkness, four agents slipped through the kitchen door and Matthews greeted them with a burst of fire from an automatic weapon. Then the firefight began in earnest. Matthews ran up and down the stairs of the two-story building, firing from windows to keep the SWAT team from approaching the house and sending up repeated fusillades at the FBI's helicopter, which was trying to bring searchlights to bear. The chopper then fired a magnesium illumination flare, and the white-hot metal burned through the roof of Matthews's barricaded house and touched off his cases of ammunition, grenades, plastique explosives and other ordnance, incinerating Matthews in the fire of his own engines of hatred.

Living, Matthews had given the Survival Right money. Dying, he gave it another martyr. Today his picture often hangs alongside that of Hitler in the churches of the next element we will examine, the Identity Christians.

*It ain't so much from not knowin' that causes the
trouble, as it is in knowin' so much that ain't so!*
—*A proverb from the Arkansas Ozarks
often quoted by Survivalist preachers*

3: Identity Christians

Clint Matthews, the four-year-old son of the late Robert Jay Matthews, clasped his pastor's leg with one small arm. Then the little boy bravely extended his other arm in a stiff Nazi salute as the flames started to die down on the cross his minister had just burned in an Idaho mountain meadow as part of a church service.

Pastor Richard Butler, spiritual leader of the Church of Jesus Christ Christian, softly removed the small arm from about his leg and stood back so that the television cameras from all four major networks could record Clint standing in his tiny camouflage uniform and swastika armband saluting the ultimate American symbol of racial and ethnic hatred. It was a warm summer night in 1986 at Butler's Survivalist compound north of Coeur d'Alene, Idaho, and the Christian Identity movement had just staged the major event of its liturgical year—the annual cross burning and anointing of new members as "Aryan warriors."

As Clint and three other preschool boys stood before cross and cameras, Robert Miles, preacher from the Identity Mountain Church of Cohoctah, Michigan, decked out in the purple and black robes of a Klan Grand Wizard, chanted over the children, "Dragon of the Night, bring forth the hope of our future. For these we go to prison, for these we fight. For these, if necessary, we die."

On the Sunday morning following the Saturday-night cross burning, Butler and Miles anointed nearly two hundred new "warriors." Each filed down the church aisle bearing thirty-three cents in copper pennies—"no Jew alloy coins allowed"—to symbolize the biblical soldier's ransom of one shekel which tribal chieftains extracted from their warriors, to be used to buy them back if captured in battle. Otherwise sane-looking men filed down the aisle in ranks of two abreast. One wore the dress blues of the United States Marine Corps. Another wore the badge of the Pennsylvania highway patrol. Others wore the blue shirts with red swastika arm patches of Butler's Aryan Nations compound. Some were dressed in camouflage jackets with the "drop of blood cross" favored by the Klan. Others wore uniforms they had designed in their kitchens specially for the event. There were black shirts, brown shirts and the Sam Browne belts so favored by the late George Lincoln Rockwell, the first neo-Nazi to step fully uniformed out of the closet in post-World War II America.

Each communicant was handed the same sword which Butler had used two years earlier to dub Matthews, Pierce, Lane—and, of course, the hated undercover journalist Peter Lake—as warriors in the founding days of the Order. The new recruits at the 1986 service held the sword toward the stylized swastika in the large stained-glass window over Butler's altar and took an oath to fight for racial purity. Miles and Butler then made the sign of the cross in oil mixed with water on each man's forehead and said, "I anoint thee as a soldier of Jesus Christ."

Behind the men came a dozen women dressed in their Sunday finery to take the same oath. As Jean Craig's lawyers had pointed out during the Order trial in Seattle, the neo-Nazi movement is utterly sexist as well as racist. Women do not get to wear its uniforms, and they file down to the altar behind their men. Their role is to serve as planting ground for the "white seed" so their warrior husbands can propagate the race before they raise their swords against

ZOG. Plural marriages are encouraged so that a warrior can plant many seeds before risking his life.

The principal reaction a person with relatively mainstream political views experiences when attending an Identity church service is anger, a tumbling in the gut that comes as virtually every example of bigotry, whether those of Hitler's Nazis or those of the American KKK, is praised as virtue while virtually every decent expression of human tolerance is castigated as the work of the Jewish Antichrist.

For an outsider, the experience of sitting through such sessions quickly degenerates from amazement at what one is seeing and hearing into loathing. After a few hours of hearing Identity sermons outlining how the international Jewish conspiracy manufactured the lie about six million people dying in Hitler's Holocaust, how Anne Frank's diary was a "Jew forgery" and how "Negroes have their particularly bad smell because of the way the beasts' body oils accumulate in their unnaturally thick skins," it is tempting simply to hate these "Christians" right back. It's easy to fall into the spirit of hatred in a church with romanticized portraits of Adolf Hitler and Rudolf Hess on the wall in place of saints, with pamphlet racks in the back offering *The Holy Book of Adolf Hitler; The Negro: Serpent, Beast and Devil*; and *The International Jew*. Indeed, few people in America today know anything at all about this dangerous religious movement for the simple reason that the mass media have been understandably reluctant to waste space and time on it. Simply quoting Identity sermons can be construed as an exercise in tastelessness.

But, for current purposes, to gloss over this "theology of hate," as the Anti-Defamation League of B'nai B'rith calls Identity, would be to ignore what the ADL's own leaders claim is nothing less than "the glue that binds together" the otherwise widely dispersed elements of the Survival Right. There are strong indications that these leaders are correct, and that the Identity movement has in recent years provided the framework for a sea change on America's radical right. The bizarre religion unites numerous segments of the Survival

Right that in the past had been so inclined toward internecine squabbling that the prospect of joint action was remote. Further, the doctrine of hatred preached from Identity pulpits transforms the sort of violence advocated by the fringes of the Survival Right from furtive sin to virtue praised by one's congregation.

Under Identity, common ground is established for the first time between such normally antagonistic segments of the far right as the violently anarchistic Posse Comitatus, which is out to end all governments, and the neo-Nazis, with their complex formulae for an extremely intrusive new government. Espousing Identity, Posse members and Nazis can join forces to oppose the ZOG establishment that each hates so thoroughly.

Before Identity came along, students of the radical right such as writer Phillip Finch had noted what they called the "circular firing squad" phenomenon whenever similar groups tried to join forces. Each special-interest group was so utterly obsessed with its own cause—tax revolt, racism, anti-Semitism, fluoride in the water supply or whatever—that it was unwilling to collaborate with groups that otherwise would have been natural allies. Indeed, single-cause right-wingers usually took as many shots at fellow radicals with a different single cause as they took at those on the left. The violent early Survivalists in the Minutemen feuded with the John Birch Society for being Milquetoasts eager to curl up in some Jewish-controlled conservative politician's pocket, while the Birchers castigated the Posse for being anti-Semitic when it should have been anti-Zionist instead. The hooded Klan, imbued with small-town patriotic values as well as its racial hatred, found brown-shirted neo-Nazis to be a bunch of un-American "queers" dressed up in strange clothing. Now they sit on folding chairs in dozens of churches like Butler's rubbing armbands (Nazi swastikas against Klan crosses) while listening to the sermons of men like Thom Robb, self-styled national chaplain to the Ku Klux Klan and an Identity preacher in Harrison, Arkansas.

"There is war in America," Robb told the congregation in Idaho, "and there are two camps. One camp is in Washington, D.C., the federal government controlled by the Antichrist Jews. Make no mistake about it—their goal is the destruction of our race, our faith and our people. And our goal is the destruction of them. There is no middle ground. We're not going to take any survivors, any prisoners. It's us or them."

In addition to being the great unifier of the radical right, Identity also is the great rationalizer for the Survivalists. Because it is a religion with all the traditional trappings, preached by Bible-quoting pastors from pulpits in churches very much like those most Americans grow up in, Identity allows its born-again men and women to practice with suddenly clear consciences the bigotry, hatred and even criminal violence that they had been taught from childhood were sinful. When Bruce Carroll Pierce, Robert Matthews and company cut Alan Berg down with their machine gun, they were acting in the role of saints in the Identity church.

Matthews gave up his life for that faith, and dozens of its members have gone to prison for acting on their beliefs. By their actions they have dramatically shown just how powerfully Identity has gripped the fringes of the radical right.

So with apologies in advance for the content of what is to follow, it becomes necessary to examine the cosmology, theology and distasteful rhetoric of hatred that its advocates call Identity Christianity.

Identity is a relative newcomer on the landscape of the Survival Right, but it has been around for more than a century as a full-blown, if exceedingly small, religious sect.

In 1871, Identity's founder, Edward Hine, published and sold 250,000 copies of *Identification of the British Nation with Lost Israel*, a book that in its day gave Jules Verne's *Twenty Thousand Leagues under the Sea* a run for its money as a best-seller. Hine's book was brought to the United States during the late nineteenth century by two followers, G. W. Greenwood, who published *Heir of the World*, a monthly in New York, and the Reverend W. H. Poole of Detroit, Michigan.

The crux of this movement's holy book by Hine can be stated briefly:

For two thousand years the world has mistaken the true identity of the Jews. The true Jews, the actual descendants of Moses, Abraham and Jesus whom God called his Chosen People, are the people of the British Isles. The people known today as Jews are actually a race of Mongolian-Turkish "Khazars"—read Ashkenazim—who are descended from the seed that Satan planted in Eve's belly right along with the seed planted there by Adam. Nine months after eating the apple, Eve bore two sons. Adam's son was Abel. Satan's was Cain. Cain killed Abel. Cain's descendants killed Jesus. Now, under the banner of world Jewry, they're trying to kill all white Christians.

Starting with this interpretation of the Eden story, Identity then offers a convoluted account of the origin and role of Jews in human history.

According to a voluminous body of Identity literature, the people in the Bible whom God described as his Chosen Ones, the House of Israel, had left the Middle East hundreds of years before the Messiah's birth. These true Jews, sons of Isaac (Isaac's sons, Saxons), crossed the Caucasus Mountains (they are called Caucasians today) and founded the new Israel in the British Isles, the "British Israel."

In common with Mormonism and many apocalyptic religious sects, Identity reaches its strange end point by dwelling on the biblical mystery of the Lost Tribes of Israel. There is no dearth of Identity literature describing the movement's unique blend of Scripture, pop archaeology and old-fashioned racial and ethnic intolerance. What follows is a synthesis of four Identity tracts: *Still 'Tis Our Ancient Foe* by Kenneth Goff of Aurora, Colorado, *Know Your Enemies!* by Jack Mohr of the Survivalist Christian-Patriots Defense League, *End Time Revelation* by William V. Fowler of Mission Hills, California, and a striking pamphlet, *Identity—Under This Sign You Shall Conquer,* written from federal prison by David Lane after he was convicted of being the getaway driver in the Alan Berg assassination and of other crimes.

Identity, writes Goff, looks back two thousand years before the birth of Christ to a Chaldean moon worshipper named Abram who was accosted by the God of the Old Testament and ordered to call himself Abraham. ("This man was not a Jew.") In their old age, Abraham and his wife, Sarah, were given a son, Isaac, who had two sons, named Jacob and Esau. Esau lost out to Jacob and Jacob left his parents and took two wives, Leah and Rachel. From these two wives, and from two concubines—Zilpah and Bilhah—were born twelve sons, each of whom became the head of one of the twelve tribes of Israel. They were: Judah, Reuben, Simeon, Levi, Dan, Naphtali, Gad, Asher, Issachar, Zebulun, Joseph and Benjamin. Stripped of its anti-Semitic asides, much of the Identity account of early Israelite tribal history conforms with mainstream Jewish and Christian Bible scholarship.

Writes Goff:

> God blessed Jacob, who was not a Jew, and changed his name to Israel (Gen. 32:38), and here begins the story of the Israelites and the Twelve Tribes of Israel, which sprang from the loins of Jacob through his twelve sons. Let us be reminded again that these were not twelve Jewish tribes but they were tribes of Israel, and the word Jew does not come into being until II Kings 15:5–6.

Soon after they were formed, all twelve tribes were placed in bondage by the rulers of Egypt, where they remained for 430 years, until two members of the tribe of Levi—Moses and his brother, Aaron ("neither one a Jew")—led the Exodus, Goff writes.

Once the tribes were in the Promised Land, God parceled out the ground to each of the twelve. But the tribe of Levi was named to a priesthood and assigned to service each of the other tribes instead of being given land of its own. God then gave the twelfth parcel of land that the Levites would have received to the descendants of Joseph's son Manasseh, creating the legendary thirteenth tribe of Israel. This wrinkle is exceedingly important to the Identity movement, because the church teaches that this Manasseh tribe ultimately moved into Europe, then across the Atlantic on the *Mayflower* to America, where God gave them such sacred documents as the Declaration of Independence, the Constitution and the first ten amendments, known as the Bill of Rights. Subsequent amendments, holds much of the Identity movement, are blasphemous additions dictated by Satan's Jewish forces and designed to bring down the white race.

Meanwhile, back in the Holy Land, a few centuries passed during which the dramas of such figures as Saul, Solomon and David were played out, until the tribes ultimately aligned themselves into a northern and a southern branch. Those of the south were Judah, Benjamin and the Levites. They became known collectively as Judah, a word that Goff grudgingly admits is sometimes translated as Jews. The other ten tribes made up the northern branch. In roughly 721 B.C. the Assyrian armies of Sennacherib invaded and took into captivity the ten northern tribes, who are never again seen in Scripture.

Fowler's amazing book, *End Time Revelation*, which is replete with accounts of the hidden messages that the Egyptian stonemasons left in the Great Pyramids about the Jewish menace, outlines Identity's view of where each of the ten northern tribes wound up after crossing the Caucasus Mountains. Manasseh, of course, became the United States. The tribe of Zebulun became France; Ephraim (of the younger son of Joseph) became Great Britain; Issachar became Finland; Asher was Sweden; the tribe of Gad became Italy; Simeon's descendants settled Spain; the people of Naphtali became Norway; the tribe of Reuben settled Holland; the people of Dan settled Denmark.

In 586 B.C., roughly a century and a half after the Assyrians placed the ten tribes in bondage, the Babylonian tyrant Nebuchadnezzar seized the tribe of Judah, killed most of the Jews, sacked the temple at Jerusalem and took the survivors into captivity. It was during the years of Babylonian captivity that the tribe of Judah became the evil force in global affairs known as Jewry. Babylon, according to Identity, was the kingdom of Cain, who, after killing Abel, fled eastward to reign under the name Sargon the Great. In Babylon, the tribe of Judah was introduced to the black magic of Satan. Writes Goff:

In Babylon the whole character of Judaism was changed, for when they left Babylon they no longer had priests but in their place rabbis, and rabbis were never ordained of God . . . In place of the temple and tabernacle they instituted a congregational worship called the synagogue . . . In place of the Old Testament teachings they came out with the Babylonian Talmud, which became the new religion of Judaism from that day, and has no part nor parcel with our Christian faith . . . One needs but to browse through the Babylonian Talmud to find within its pages the most filthy sewer of all human thinking. No human could conceive that a religious book would take up such a tremendous amount of space to discuss in lewd details the right of a rabbi to seduce a three-year-old baby girl. No other religious teaching has ever condoned sexual relations of a mother with her own son. No other religious teaching has endorsed the cursing of one's own parents or the burning of one's children to the god of Moloch. No other religious teaching has underwritten and subscribed to lying, cheating and murder as a means of promulgation of its faith. No other religious teaching has called a woman outside of its faith "cattle," and has dealt with a woman in such filthy language. No other religious teaching has allowed sexual relations with a dead woman. No other civilized religious teaching underwrites superstition and black magic such as carrying pulverized manure from a white dog around one's neck for certain cures, and many other forms so vulgar that they would be nonpermissible to print on these pages.

The question of how accurately the backwater Colorado Identity preacher Goff reflects issues raised in the sixty-three volumes of the Babylonian Talmud which have been the subject of twenty-four centuries of rabbinical scholarship is less important than the rampant paranoia with which he and his fellow Identity zealots view the period of captivity.

In fact, the attacks against the Talmud espoused by the Identity Christians are ancient hand-me-down materials that have been used by anti-Semites for centuries. The Talmud (Hebrew for "study"), like the Old Testament, is a hodgepodge of songs, laws, prophesies and other material that, as a whole, defines Jewish religious life. It consists of three parts: the Mishnah, a compilation of oral tradition regarding Scriptures, and two Gemaras, rambling commentaries on everything from sexual etiquette to property law. The Palestinian Gemara was produced in the third and fourth centuries A.D.; the Babylonian Gemara was, as its name implies, produced largely during the Babylonian captivity. Historical anti-Semitic drives often focused on the allegations that the book contains various heresies and atrocities. In 1242, for example, twenty-four cartloads of Talmud manuscripts were burned in Paris, and similar Talmud burnings were staged in the streets of Germany seven hundred years later by Hitler's Nazis.

Like the bigots they venerate, Identity scholars find the hidden hand of "the Jew" in human history from the time the Babylonian Talmud was written. Post-Talmud Jews taunted Jesus and crucified him. They took control of the monetary system of the Roman Empire and goaded Nero into the slaughter of tens of thousands of Christians in the hated Colosseum. They moved into the Iberian Peninsula, where they inspired the Grand Inquisitor Torquemada to new heights of cruelty. They brought the Black Plague to Europe and were expelled from each country they entered after native peoples noted that their children started vanishing at those times of year when the Jewish holidays called for blood sacrifices. They undermined Napoleon's drive for a world French empire and they inspired a Jew named Karl Marx to produce the literature that brought the globe the hated Jewish curse of Communism. They promoted the Bolshevik Revolution in Russia and the formation of the Federal Reserve banking system in the United States. It's a bewildering panoply of accusation, but the common denominator is simple indeed—anything that has gone wrong in the affairs of humankind since the fifth century before Christ has been the work of Jews contaminated by the devil himself during the Babylonian captivity.

In his 1982 Identity treatise, *Know Your Enemies!*, Jack Mohr, a self-described "Identity Baptist" and a onetime leader of the Christian-Patriots Defense League, writes:

For centuries the Shylocks of International Jewry have sat in their "counting houses," of Europe and America, while a horde of sweating mankind has labored in their factories, under the constant threat of Jew-led strikes and dissensions . . . All of America's wars have been instigated and financed by Jewish bankers with enormous profits for them and a terrific bloodbath for us. The German war factories of 1914 and 1939 were, for the most part, Jewish owned. . . . We fought two wars with our mother country [England], both instigated under pressure from International Jewry. We have fought two great wars with a great Christian White country named Germany, this in spite of the fact that 25 per cent of our American people were of German heritage. . . . If [a coming limited nuclear war] escalates into an "all-out nuclear war," what will happen? The surviving Jews better look for holes to hide in, whether they are guilty or not. The homeless, the starving, the nuclear sick, the mobs of survivors, will be roaming the countryside, looking for two things, food and loot, and someone to blame. The Jews who supported the Israelis, and the Christian dupes who supported them, will feel the full anger of a terribly enraged people.

Lane, the lanky Denver racist whose talents ran to counterfeiting and murder—he didn't participate in any of the Order's armed robberies—outlined the entire Identity anti-Semitic bill of particulars in his bitter pamphlet *Identity: Under This Sign You Shall Conquer*, written in the federal prison in Terre Haute, Indiana, and passed out at Butler's 1986 World Aryan Congress.

Lane's original obsession, like that of so many Identity followers, had been racial hatred more than anti-Semitism. He had been a Klan follower, then a Klan leader in Denver for a decade before discovering Identity in the late 1970s. Once exposed to it, Lane quickly latched on to the movement's teaching that race mixing is just another facet of the unrelenting Jewish conspiracy against Christians or, more specifically, against white Christians. In 1981 Lane wrote a lengthy Identity pamphlet called *The Death of the White Race*, which he attempted to pass out on the streets of Denver, only to find himself arrested and featured in articles in both of the city's newspapers. Berg read those articles and sought Lane out for his talk show, a move that proved to be the worst mistake he ever made.

A loner obsessed with fears about his own health, Lane was even more pessimistic than other Identity followers. His brother-in-law, Carl Franklin, Sr., wrote in a 1986 Survival Right hate sheet tabloid called WAR [White Aryan Resistance] that Lane grew up in the Denver suburbs and attended a community college there, where he enrolled for a single semester, earned straight A's, but then dropped out "in disillusionment over the prostitution of higher education." In 1973 Lane passed the examination to become a real estate broker but abandoned a business called Lane Realty after Butler's sermons convinced him that real estate sales amounted to the Jewish-inspired sin of usury. Lane quit selling real estate and took a job as a clerk in a Denver title insurance company that paid a fraction of his former income. Then, again with Butler's help and that of Texas Klan leader Louis Beam, Lane wrote *The Death of the White Race* and took to the streets with his warnings about race mixing. After his 1981 arrest, Lane's wife of fourteen years left him and he became a pitiful, lonely, sexually frustrated figure at neo-Nazi meetings, a trait that gave him the nickname "Lone Wolf" while in the Order. At a memorial service held for members of the Order at the Idaho compound in 1986, Butler told the congregation that one day the Identity movement would prevail, "and there will be many wives waiting for Brother Lane when he walks out of ZOG's prison."

Carl Franklin's defense of Lane is an excellent example of how so many Identity adherents use their belief in an Antichrist conspiracy to justify their own shortcomings. Lane's failure to complete more than a single semester at a junior college becomes a noble protest against the "prostitution" of truth to the Jewish conspiracy. His failure to sell real estate becomes a praiseworthy decision to reject Jewish-inspired usury. His wife's abandonment of him is explained as her failure to cope with the barrage of attacks by a hidden foe.

Obsessed with sex and his impending death, the childless Lane's writings dwell on Jewish efforts to dilute his sacred white seed. The

Jews, in Lane's scenario, focus each of their schemes on turning the Aryans into mongrels. This is accomplished by promoting homosexuality and abortion, as well as by tinkering with the global economy to make it ever more difficult for white people to reproduce, and ever more easy for other races to do so.

Some excerpts from *Identity: Under This Sign You Shall Conquer* sound themes that show how the Identity philosophy uses character assassination and paranoia to flow smoothly from anti-Semitism to racism. Lane wrote from prison:

> At the time the Jews took over our monetary system via the Federal Reserve, and instituted the income tax in 1913, the White Race constituted about 40 per cent of the Earth's population. Since then, the Jews have instigated two World Wars and fomented the Russian Revolution. These three events alone resulted in the death of over 80 million White Christians, most of them being young males and the genetic cream of our race.
>
> Next they laid such heavy taxes on the White workers of the world that it became, if not impossible, very financially impractical to have children. At the same time, the Jews took the taxes stolen from the labor of productive Whites and gave it to non-Whites, both here and abroad, encouraging them to have from 10–20 children. They used their media to insult and emasculate the White man while depicting non-white males to be heroes so White women would desert their Race by the millions.
>
> The result is that the percentage of child-bearing women in the world today who are White and married to White men is at best four per cent. Add to this the fact that we have no nation or territorial imperative of our own where we can propagate, promote, and protect our own kind, and you can begin to see what a hill we have to climb if we are to preserve our existence as a race.

While the Lanes, Mohrs, Fowlers and Goffs make their secular arguments for anti-Semitism and race hatred, the Butlers, Robbs, Mileses and other Identity pastors chime in from the pulpit with their sermons that the day of Apocalypse is upon us, and that the events foretold by St. John in the Book of Revelation are being played out on the six o'clock nightly news.

"People are afraid today," said Miles at a church service just before the 1986 Idaho cross burning. "They are so afraid that there is going to be a nuclear war . . . the culture distorters are out to see that we all have become mongrelized mud people before the missiles come over the poles with white Russians killing white Americans while the Jews move south. It's time we stop worrying about the 'Boys from Brazil' and start looking at the Boys going to Brazil." (The reference was to Ira Levin's novel about the cloning of dozens of boys from Hitler's genetic material in postwar Brazil.)

A few hours after Miles's sermon, Butler took to the same pulpit to preach that the American grain belt is the "field of Armageddon" that the Book of Revelation prophesies will be the scene of the final battle between Gog and Magog, between the Seed of Light and the Seed of Darkness. "Those fields would make an ideal place for a tank battle between the United States and the Soviet Union," Butler said. "And it will be a great battle between two white armies."

That theme underscores the key facet of Identity that has enabled it to unite so many of the normally warring far-right fringes—its hatred for blacks and other people of color. Whether castigating the global Communist conspiracy, deriding homosexuals or campaigning against abortion, the movement repeatedly cites the same dire consequence of whatever plot is at hand. In each case, the unseen enemy is out to mix the races, to dilute the white seed with the "colored" seed and create a world populated by "mud people."

Attacking blacks along with Jews ingratiates Identity everywhere from the rural Posse Comitatus backwaters of Nebraska to the Klan sessions in the embattled Marquette Park neighborhood on the South Side of Chicago. Survivalist Posse members, awaiting Armageddon with their stockpiles of ammunition, food and other gear, are receptive to Identity's message that a coming race war will signal the final battle for which they have waited so long. Klansmen are attracted by the Identity teaching that the tool the Jewish conspiracy will use in the final confrontation between good and evil will be the selfsame hordes of black people that have always been the Klan's target. Anti-Semites such as Butler's neo-Nazis share this view, as do the Survivalists of such groups as the Christian Defense League, the Christian-Patriots Defense League and others. In the bizarre world of Christian Identity, black people themselves become a Jewish plot.

The Identity justification for color hatred against blacks, Asians, American Indians or any other group they choose to target comes by rewriting the Book of Genesis to read that God created all races except the white one on the third of the six days. These races were experiments that didn't quite work. It wasn't until the final day of Creation that God succeeded in making the perfect man, the white Adam, and then formed a woman from his rib before blowing life into each.

In one sermon, Butler asked his congregation of swastika wearers the rhetorical question: "Do you suppose that all that walk this earth on two legs are human? But this is not true," he answered. "God breathed the spirit only into white people. Human comes from the Sanskrit which means ho-man or spirit man. And when we trace down the roots of the people, it is the ho-man people, the fair-haired white people, to whom they referred. We can also find that in the Vedas of ancient India."

To promote its hatred of blacks and its belief in their inferiority, Butler's church circulates a thick pamphlet written by "Philip Jones, B.A." titled *The Negro: Serpent, Beast and Devil,* which quotes the relevant parts of Scripture that Identity claims prove that blacks are a subhuman race created early on to serve as "attendants to the White Man." Included are such items as a poster outlining numerous common links which "science" has established between "The Negro and the Ape." Among them: "animal wool, melon shaped head, small brain, animal smell, long arms, black ape color, weak lower limbs, everted lips, forward slanting ape pelvis and large feet."

The day he was sentenced to sixty years in the federal penitentiary for his part in the Berg murder and other crimes, Lane told the Seattle jury, "If it seems that some members of the Order emphasized the race issue, it is for good reason. First, it is the primary aim of the people who control the United States government and the media of the United States to mix and destroy the race of Washington, Jefferson, Franklin; the race who created Western civilization and on whose existence it depends. Second, it is one evil which cannot be reversed. Morality can be returned. Economic, political and religious systems will be changed, but when the blood is mixed it is forever."

Gordon Melton, an expert on extremist movements affiliated with the Institute for the Study of American Religion at the University of California at Santa Barbara, said in a 1986 interview that Identity is "a religion by sociopaths, for sociopaths. It turns their sickness into virtue." Indeed, perhaps the most striking quality displayed by those linked to violent crimes committed in the name of Identity is a lack of any sense of guilt, a pride, in fact, in the crimes for which they were jailed.

During his speech to the Seattle jury, Lane said, "I have no quarrel with my fate. Throughout history when little men have rebelled against tyranny, they have faced two possibilities. The few who are successful become the patriarchs of new nations, and the rest suffer imprisonment and death." Alluding to the Berg murder, Lane said, "A few years ago a black Communist by the name of Angela Davis smuggled guns into a courtroom to kill a federal judge. The media made her a hero and soon she was spouting Communism and hate-whitey rhetoric in the universities across the land. Will the media demand such justice for a white man who resisted the murder of his race? Will I be made a hero to speak in the universities across America next year?"

A similar remorseless tone was sounded in a letter written from prison by Richard "Mr. Black" Scutari to his wife, Michelle, and passed along to the news media by Butler's press aides.

"Many have disagreed with the methods of the Bruder Schweigen. I offer no apologies except for having failed to meet our goals. At least we were not afraid to take on the Beast," wrote Scutari. "For those of you who truly believe in Yahweh our God and our King, Jesus the Christ, it is time to follow our example. The Bruder

Schweigen has shown you the way. Learn from our mistakes, succeed where we failed."

And so a religion dreamed up in the slums of Victorian England has become the rock upon which is built the foundation of the Survival Right. A major study of the Identity movement by the Anti-Defamation League in 1983 traced how its proponents have slowly built bridges between their religion and major American hate groups.

In the late 1940s and 1950s, Identity was promoted in Massachusetts by Howard B. Rand, an eloquent anti-Semite who was particularly outraged by the events that led to the formation of the infant state of Israel. It was Rand who coined the term "Identity" to describe Hine's concept of Anglo-Israelism, in which Jesus was not a Jew of the tribe of Judah but an Aryan of the ten lost tribes of Israel and an ancestor of the present British, Germanic and Scandinavian people, who therefore are God's chosen people.

Rand's followers viewed Hitler as a prophet and circulated *The Holy Book of Adolf Hitler*, a lengthy tract written in 1951 by James Larratt Battersby of Southport, England. This "holy book" became the basis for Identity zealots' elevating Hitler to sainthood. Sold in virtually all Identity churches, it stands today as one of the more blatant statements of the movement's obsession with sexuality. Wrote Battersby on the topic of "Population and Race":

> Every healthy Aryan woman is expected to bear children. This is the woman's supreme and holy task. There is shame only in deliberate childlessness.
>
> Aryan man, especially in the higher categories, is accorded freedom in sexual life; but this is conditioned by a high eugenic and procreative purpose. Such freedom is only for the pure in blood and noble in character.
>
> Marriage and monogamy will no longer be insisted upon. All children born Aryan and healthy are considered legitimate.

Under the heading of "Woman," he continues:

> Every child that an Aryan mother brings into the world is a battle waged for the existence of her people.
>
> Aryan woman is honored in that Adolf Hitler declared, "Had

it not been for the constancy and really loving devotion of woman, I should never have been able to lead the Party on to victory." . . .

All across the landscape of the Survival Right are examples of true believers running afoul of one another trying to practice the polygamy advocated in *The Holy Book of Adolf Hitler* and other movement literature.

After Randolph Duey and company executed Order member Walter West in the Idaho forest, another Order leader, Thomas Bentley, took West's widow, Susan, as his second wife. Matthews maintained his plural marriage with Clint's adoptive mother, Debbie, and Zillah Craig. Polygamous arrangements were recorded when police raided communes everywhere, from the Nebraska–Kansas border area to the property of the Covenant, the Sword and the Arm of the Lord.

The matrimonial rules for preserving the "white seed" have been with the movement at least since the time of Dr. Wesley Swift, who was the first to move the teachings of Identity into the world of the Klan, the neo-Nazis and other right-wing fringes in the early 1960s. Swift, originally ordained a Methodist minister, had started his Identity career in Arkansas as the chauffeur for Gerald L. K. Smith, the driving force behind the post-World War II Christian Defense League, an anti-Semitic and racist spin-off of the Ku Klux Klan. Swift simply incorporated the Hine text about Identification into Smith's teachings. Smith was publisher of *The Cross and the Flag*, a tabloid that under Swift's influence came to employ religious justifications for its attacks against targeted minorities that were virtually identical in style to the literature being passed out today, three decades later, by his successors.

In the late 1950s Swift parted company with Smith and moved to Los Angeles, where he joined forces with Bertrand Comparet of Metairie, Louisiana, who had been Smith's attorney, to start the Anglo-Saxon Christian Congregation and preach their creed before an "Anglo-Israel Bible Class." This became the bridge between the

Victorian proponents of the British Israel and the Hitlerite Identity establishment of today.

With Americans obsessed by the prospect of atomic war, Swift melded nuclear anxiety, pseudoscience, biblical fragments and hatred into a single credo. An oft-quoted 1949 sermon entitled "Dwelling on Two Planes" ably illustrates Swift's fusion of these disparate elements. Noting that the same scientists who had just built the atom bomb had found evidence of an "aura" surrounding certain people photographed by new infrared techniques in their laboratories, Swift explained that this aura was simply an indication that the people photographed were whites of the "Adamic race." Other photographic subjects who didn't produce an aura were either subhuman members of colored races or white-appearing creatures whose blood actually was mongrelized through the Jewish conspiracy, living proof that "the original violation of God's law by the Adamite race was intermingling through mongrelization with decadent civilizations."

Swift told his congregation that "the aura of Spirit was the secret of Christ's power of resurrection," explaining that this spiritual power was akin to the atomic power that had just been so dramatically introduced at Hiroshima and Nagasaki. When Jesus rose from the grave after his crucifixion and rolled the heavy rock away from his tomb's entrance, he was utilizing the power of the atom bomb and of his Aryan race. Recalling that Jesus told Mary Magdalene not to touch his body after she came to the tomb with spices to embalm him, Swift said that Jesus was charged with radiation. "Celestial power had raised his physical body out of the tomb . . . had rolled away the blocking stone at the door of the sepulcher. It had enveloped him, and this field of energy was of such intensity that Mary could not have reached over and touched him without placing herself within the field of such consuming force that chain reaction would have been destructive to her body, which was not yet spiritually adjusted to such an experience."

Asserting that Identity was God's way of helping his chosen people to cope with the terrors of the new technology, Swift argued that "a 'horse and buggy' religion will not take you through the atomic age. You have moved into the atomic age of wisdom and knowledge which science has discovered, and your spiritual understanding must keep pace with it or else your civilization is doomed."

Swift, who died in 1970 of diabetes in a Mexican clinic where he had hoped to avoid the Jewish-dominated medical establishment of the United States, laid the basic underpinnings of Identity as it is known today. One of those who heard the Swift sermons and was moved to action was a young engineer for the Lockheed Company named Richard Girnt Butler who was assigned to help build the company's Tri-Star jet aircraft. Butler had been drawn to Swift by William Potter Gale, a retired Army colonel who had been a fixture among American right-wing groups ever since leaving General Douglas MacArthur's staff after the war. Gale had organized guerrilla operations in the Philippines and directed the clandestine fighting against the Japanese while MacArthur marshaled his forces for his triumphant return to Corregidor. Throughout the 1970s and early 1980s, Gale, although his vigor was declining due to age, preached about how the next generation of patriots must use the guerrilla tactics he developed in the Philippines to "survive the coming anti-Christian bloodbath." Quoting his friend Wesley Swift, Gale assured his listeners that the bloodbath would be nuclear in nature and directed by the Jewish conspiracy.

In the 1960s Gale and Butler organized the paramilitary California Rangers, a group that affiliated itself with the right-wing Minutemen and advocated stockpiling vast supplies of survival gear—food, guns, water, medical supplies, etc.—for the coming final battle. As late as 1983 Gale was preaching over a Kansas radio station:

> Yes, we're gonna cleanse our land. We're gonna do it with a sword. And we're gonna do it with violence. "Oh," they say, "Reverend Gale, you're teaching violence." You're damn right I'm teaching violence! God said you're gonna do it that way, and it's about time somebody is telling you to get violent, whitey.
>
> You better start making dossiers, names, addresses, phone num-

bers, car license numbers, on every damn Jew rabbi JDL [Jewish Defense League] leader in this land, and you better start doing it now. And know where he is. If you have to be told any more than that, you're too damn dumb to bother with. You get these roadblock locations, where you can set up ambushes, and get it all working now.

Like sinister Johnny Appleseeds, Gale and Butler carried the Identity germ into numerous camps of the Survival Right that were aborning throughout the 1960s and 1970s. They joined forces with the New Christian Crusade Church in Los Angeles, and they preached frequently in the Midwest before the Christian Conservative Churches of America, a forerunner of the Klan-affiliated Christian-Patriots Defense League, which now runs Survivalist compounds in Missouri and Illinois. Gale also associated himself with the Posse Comitatus in the early 1980s, and law officials determined that he had established the U.S. Christian Posse Association, a West Coast branch of the religious and political movement that teaches that the Constitution is a divinely inspired document commanding all true believers to refuse to recognize any form of government higher than that of county sheriff. In early 1987 Gale was among seven leaders of the Posse Comitatus indicted in Nevada for threatening IRS agents with assassination by mailing them "constructive notices" advising them that they faced indictment and "maximum penalties" for pursuing Gale's followers.

In the early 1970s, Butler left Southern California and moved his operation to the Idaho panhandle, where he built the armed camp, complete with guard tower, gatehouses, German shepherd patrol dogs and armed sentries, that has become, by far, the best-known chapter of the Identity church.

Another Identity leader was Sheldon Emry, who established the Lord's Covenant Church in Phoenix and hosted a long-playing radio program called *America's Promise* to promulgate Identity hatred. Emry, who died in 1985, became one of the most widely published of all Identity figures. Among his books and tracts are *The Old Jerusalem Is Not the New Jerusalem* and *The Jews That Aren't*.

After several decades of radio preaching and pamphlet writing, Emry joined forces with the Illinois-based Christian-Patriots Defense League and its armed group, the Citizens Emergency Defense System. He became a favorite of the editors of the most widely circulated of all Survival Right publications, *Spotlight*, the weekly published by the Liberty Lobby and distributed in boxes right alongside *USA Today* and *The New York Times* in much of rural America. One of *Spotlight*'s most popular reprints is "Billions for the Bankers, Debts for the People," a special section Emry authored outlining his view of how a Jewish conspiracy has seized control of the world economic order through the international banking system and the U.S. Federal Reserve.

Another large Identity following surrounds Gordon Winrod, "the Jayhawk Nazi," who operates out of Our Saviour's Church in Gainesville, Missouri, and conducts a radio ministry. A defrocked minister in the Missouri Synod of the Lutheran Church, Winrod served as national chaplain of the racist, anti-Semitic National States' Rights Party in the early 1960s.

Likewise, Dan Gayman, a former Missouri high school principal who now heads the Church of Israel in Schell City, Missouri, is known for his popular series of audio and video cassettes pushing the Identity credo. He also heads a subset of Identity called the Emancipation of the White Seed, which publishes a tabloid called *The Battle Axe News*. In an essay called "For Fear of the Jews," Gayman warned: "Today every word that is printed in America's newspapers, slick periodicals, and over radio and television is censored by the psychological Fear of the Jews." His book *The Two Seeds of Genesis*, according to Gayman, "proves incontestably that the Jews are Satan's seed."

James K. Warner of Metairie, Louisiana, also hometown to Identity pioneer Bertrand Comparet, is head of yet another paramilitary "church," the New Christian Crusade Church of the selfsame Christian Defense League that was founded by Gerald L. K. Smith in the days he and Swift shared the podium. Warner also proselytizes Identity hatred through his publishing concern, Sons of Liberty.

(Robert Jay Matthews told his comrades that he found his way into the movement by joining a chapter of Warner's Sons of Liberty while growing up in Arizona.)

Warner's operation also issues *Christian Vanguard*, one of the most venerable of the newsprint tabloids, published all across the spectrum of the Survival Right under mastheads such as *The White Patriot*, *WAR* and *The Torch*. A sampling of headlines from a half dozen issues more than suffices to set their tone: "New Research into Jewish Ritual Murder," "Queer Seeks Legion Post," "American Jews are Khazars, Not Israelites," "Happy Mud Flood Day, America" (commemorating the 1986 Statue of Liberty celebration), "Inequalities of the Negro Race" and "Michael Jackson's New Nigger Nose." Perhaps the most obscene of all was this one from *The White Patriot* in August 1986: "The Klan Reaches Out to America with Love."

The greatest impact of Warner's long ministry came in 1978, when he led forces on the extreme right opposing the CBS television docudrama *Holocaust*. He stunned nationwide audiences by expressing the prevalent belief among Identity followers that the international Jewish conspiracy manufactured the false accounts of Nazi extermination in order to win global sympathy for Jews.

But the Warners, Butlers and Gales are old men today. Representing a fresh new generation of Identity leaders is Thom Robb, the Harrison, Arkansas, preacher whose thundering sermon of hatred opened Butler's 1986 World Aryan Congress. Self-billed as the national chaplain of the Ku Klux Klan, Robb was a major organizer of an outbreak of Klan violence during the summer of 1986, when a crowd of several thousand whites and blacks clashed over a KKK White Pride rally in Chicago's racially charged Marquette Park neighborhood. The day after the White Pride violence, Robb and his followers triggered another riot in the city's lakefront Lincoln Park when they staged an "Anti-Queer" rally. The twin events represented the worst outbreak of racial violence in Chicago since the 1966 rioting that erupted when the late Martin Luther King, Jr., marched on the suburb of Cicero.

With a personal style not unlike that of many other Protestant preachers, Robb has built a fairly large church following that apparently includes many people who share his faith but are reluctant to dress up in camouflage colors or Klan robes and play the activist role Robb advocates. In a 1985 open letter to his flock Robb chastised members for hiding their Identity affiliation from their neighbors and employers out of fear for reputations and jobs. "You are fearful that someone might find out that you are one of those Identity people," Robb wrote. "Shame on you." That sort of complaint suggests that far more people are being swayed by the religious arguments of Identity in this fundamentalist era than are willing to visibly put on the robes or take up the weapons of the more vocal among their ranks.

The letter sent by Robb to his church mailing list in 1985 reads in part:

> During recent months the media has attempted to totally smear the Christian Identity message and all those who rise up against Jewish terror and oppression. But why are you so shocked! Did you think this was a game! Have not all the reading, listening to sermons and watching world events told you that it is us or them? The anti-Christ Jews want to kill you and your children in a gigantic genocidal bloodbath such as they put upon the citizenry of old Russia. They want to steal the souls and to destroy the minds of your children with their hell-inspired teachings of Secular Humanism.
>
> Because some men have stood out boldly for our faith they have been the first to receive the lies and slander of the media. There has been nothing material to gain, only the satisfaction that they have served God well and seek to hear "well done, thou good and faithful servant" when they come to the end of their days. And yet, while they are willing to suffer the lies of the media, all many of you can think of is that you might lose one of your precious friends. Shame on you . . .

It is difficult to estimate the number of Identity adherents in America today, but surveys by such groups as the Anti-Defamation League have estimated that there are roughly fifty major Identity preachers operating throughout the country. Estimates of Identity congregations following these fifty range between 7,000 and 20,000, although the movement's significance is greatly amplified because of its adoption by larger groups, including the various Klans, Posse chapters and other fringe elements.

In 1985, when Butler and his associates were unable to hold their annual World Aryan Congress in Idaho due to the pressures from the federal investigation into the Bruder Schweigen crime wave, Robb hosted a national Identity convention in Harrison that virtually all the leading movement lights attended, including Butler and Miles.

No listing of major Identity leaders is complete without Miles, who has become the elder statesman and leading showman of the Survivalists. Miles's brand of Identity—he calls it "Dualism"—is somewhat more exotic than that practiced by most of the movement's preachers. While Miles shares the view that two seeds parted ways in Eden and that the true Israelites are the British and the Americans, he also incorporates large helpings of primitive Nordic mythology into his religion, quoting Druidic writings, Viking sagas and Norse verse in his sermons and writings to justify the Identity white supremacist credo.

Miles's Dualism holds that God and Satan are super-beings of nearly equal power, and that they have waged a war in outer space since before Creation. Both the United States and the Soviet Union have joined this fray—on the side of Satan, according to Miles, who says the two countries are nothing more than "twin sisters of hell." Both countries soon will fire nuclear weapons at one another over the North Pole, leaving the world to Jews who in recent years have migrated southward in anticipation of Armageddon, Miles teaches.

Handsome in a grandfatherly way, Miles circulates among Survival Right crowds—where the most common garb is camouflage colors or a T-shirt and baseball cap—wearing a coat, tie and wing-tip shoes. A veteran of hundreds of press conferences, street rallies, public cross burnings and court proceedings, Miles is a glib spokes-

man always willing to spend time with any news media representative who asks. His cross-burning ceremonies—from Texas to Idaho,
from North Carolina to Michigan—have been transformed into
media events in recent years as Miles implements a strategy to seek
publicity for the Identity movement after decades of deliberate secrecy.

Miles operates his Mountain Church of Jesus Christ the Saviour,
which he calls the Mountain Kirk, out of Cohoctah, Michigan.
When Robert Matthews was still in diapers, Miles had been joining
such fellow racists as J. B. Stoner on midnight Klan rides against
civil rights workers in the South. "Sometimes I still feel good, like
I did when we were young, it was midnight and we were riding
again," he told one audience. His monthly newsletter, *From the
Mountain*, has long been one of the most virulent—and most ar-
ticulate—espousals of Identity hatred.

In the early 1970s Miles was convicted in the Klan burning of
several school buses in Pontiac, Michigan, and served six years in
the federal penitentiary at Marion, Illinois, one of the most racially
tense penal institutions in America. During his prison stay, Miles
organized what has proven to be the single most potent recruiting
operation of the Identity movement, its prison ministry.

Toughened by his half dozen years as a convicted white racist in
one of America's meanest black-dominated prisons, Miles has chided
the Survival Right for holding its training sessions in public. He
noted that on one occasion a Klan group actually invited the FBI
to attend one of its survival training camps. He told Survivalists,
"If one wants real guerrilla training, let them enter the armed forces,
keeping their racial beliefs covered. . . . If you need practice in
surviving in the wilderness, why not obtain it through outdoor sport
and hiking associations? Penetrate these. Join accepted clubs and
camps. Keep your racial attitudes concealed while building your
skills for the day we all know lies ahead."

Urging the Survival Right to stay underground, Miles argues that
open revolution is impossible:

Soldiers must be rewarded, traitors punished. Can you pay such a price now? Can you support one soldier in the terror army? It takes $15,000 a year to support one in Italy, according to the Red Brigades. Are you able to really support armed action today?

Can you build your chain of safe houses across this land before you move? Are there fifty such families who can be trusted and who have never subscribed to any racialist paper or publication, never been on any list or attended any racialist meetings?

How many lawyers are there who are eager to defend your cause in court? Can your group arrange a war chest of $1 million to serve as a retainer for such a nationwide group of legal defenders? It had better have these before armed action begins, for if it tries to gain it after such action begins, it is doomed to failure.

Do you have the doctors and nurses recruited, with medical facilities set up either in homes or inside actual hospitals used as covers? Your soldiers will need fifty such medical facilities. Not just for wounds, but for the regular daily illnesses which strike anyone . . .

Where do your soldiers go for rest once the armed action begins? To which nation can your hunted ones flee when the heat is too much to stand for them in their own land? Where indeed is a sanctuary for a white racist?

It is folly . . . nay, it is treason, for any leader to enter into an armed action until the preparatory work has been done . . .

Everything has to have its time and its season. Do the work which is required of you in this season. Prepare for the work ahead. Know that the hour of the harvest comes. In the right time, more than just the moon shall rise.

Today, an unknown number of Survivalists are taking Miles's advice. They live largely clandestine lives, their basement storerooms stocked with food and weaponry to tide them over the coming nuclear holocaust. They wait on farms and ranches and even in many cities for the cleansing war that will leave them the heirs to the scorched New Israel that will follow Armageddon. Meanwhile, they wait and take their inspiration—and order their lives—as followers of the Posse Comitatus.

These enemies of Christ have taken their Jewish Communist Manifesto and incorporated it into the Statutory Laws of our country and thrown our Constitution and our Christian Common Law (which is nothing other than the Laws of God as set forth in the Scriptures) into the garbage can.
—Gordon Kahl

4: Posse Comitatus

Sitting at the kitchen table in the fortified farmhouse just outside Smithville, Arkansas (pop. 113), on the muggy night of June 3, 1983, Gordon Kahl, sixty-three, knew that the federal authorities were closing in. He hadn't paid any income taxes since 1970 after undergoing a religious conversion that told him that paying the IRS was sinful, and four months earlier he had killed two federal marshals in North Dakota when they tried to serve him a warrant. Kahl's convoluted moral code held that to pay taxes would be to acknowledge the authority of the Jewish-dominated federal government, while God's law clearly states in the divinely inspired Constitution of the United States of America and in the equally sacred Articles of Confederation that a man should heed no authority higher than that of the county sheriff.

This born-again blend of Identity faith, Survivalism and reactionary politics called Posse Comitatus takes its name from the Latin for "power of the county." Investigators for the U.S. Treasury Department have traced its formation to Portland, Oregon, in 1969, when a retired dry-cleaning executive named Henry Lamont Beach formed the first Posse chapter, called the Sheriff's Posse Comitatus (SPC) or Citizens' Law Enforcement Research Committee (CLERC). Beach had been a controversial Pacific Northwest right-winger ever since the early 1930s when he was a leader in a group of American supporters of Hitler who called themselves the Silver Shirts.

According to a 1986 report by analysts for the Treasury's Internal Revenue Service, in the first manual for the Posse, Beach wrote: "In some instances of record the law provides for the following prosecution of officials of government who commit criminal acts or who violate their oath of office . . . He shall be removed by the posse to the most populated intersection of streets in the township and, at high noon, be hung by the neck, the body remaining until sundown as an example to those who would subvert the law." The 1986 advisory to federal law enforcement agents about the Posse advised that "members associated with some of the Posse groups wear tiny gold hangman's nooses on their lapels."

Beach, Kahl and their followers based much of their strange ideology on an interpretation of the legal doctrine surrounding the congressional Posse Comitatus Act passed in the wake of the Civil War specifically to bar the federal military from intervening in local police matters. In response to President Grant's post-Civil War efforts to use troops to guard ballot boxes and prevent election fraud, Congress had ordered that such police powers rest only at the county level. Federal troops were barred from enforcing domestic laws.

The legal doctrine established by the Posse Act has become a hallmark of American democracy, keeping Presidents from sending soldiers, banana republic style, to implement policy or enforce domestic laws. When Richard Nixon's top aides suggested the use of troops to round up left-wing protesters, for example, the FBI director, J. Edgar Hoover, who held such people in ultimate contempt, nevertheless hotly told his Commander in Chief that such a move would violate the Posse Comitatus doctrine. Likewise, it is the Posse principle at work when state governors call up the National

Guard to quell civil disorders or cope with natural calamities instead of asking for help from the active military. Posse Comitatus, then, is a significant part of the American fabric.

However, modern-day Posse adherents, a group of ultra-right-wingers distinguished by their curious zeal for amateur lawyering and Survivalism, treat as a matter of religious faith that the Posse Comitatus principle means that no citizen is bound to obey any authority higher than that of the county sheriff. Paying income taxes, making social security payments, even purchasing license plates and acquiring a driver's license violate this principle, according to this major subset of the Survival Right. Many, but not all, Posse followers take matters even further and hold that the Posse doctrine was divinely revealed by God and therefore to pay taxes is not only illegal but sinful.

Such a man was Gordon Kahl, who had killed for this faith.

Now the balding and grandfatherly-looking tax protester was in hiding, protected by two fellow Posse adherents, Leon and Norma Ginter, whose farmhouse resembled a wartime bunker with heavily barricaded doors and windows and an underground larder well stocked with ammunition and crates of freeze-dried food, all held in readiness for the coming of Armageddon. As Kahl sat before a kerosene lantern and ate a last meal of hot dogs and green beans, the Ginters gazed nervously out the rifle slits that covered their farmhouse windows. They had noticed an inordinate number of out-of-town cars on the roads all day in the nearby Arkansas mountain hamlet of Smithville, 125 miles northeast of Little Rock. Some of the vehicles carried police equipment—shotguns, bullhorns, billy clubs, etc. Clearly, trouble was on its way.

In a letter sent to Richard Butler's Aryan Nations but addressed to the world at large, Kahl described the foggy February night in North Dakota just six months earlier when he and his son, Yorivon, twenty-three, and a companion, Scott Faul, twenty-nine, had taken on four carloads of federal marshals who tried to arrest the Posse patriarch on tax charges near his own farm outside the farming town of Medina. Kahl's letter read in part:

I Gordon Kahl, a Christian patriot, and in consideration of the events which have taken place within the last few hours, and knowing to what lengths the enemies of Christ (who I consider my enemies) will go to separate my spirit from its body, wish to put down on paper a record of the events which have just taken place so that the world will know what happened . . .

We had just finished our [Posse] meeting in Medina, concerning how we could best implement the proceedings of the third Continental Congress, which was to restore the power and prestige of the U.S. Constitution up to and including the 10 articles of the Bill of Rights, and put our nation back under Christian Common Law, which is another way of saying God's Law as laid down by the inspiration of God, through his prophets and preserved for us in the Scriptures, when word was received from someone whose identity I am not able to give, that we were to be ambushed on our return to our homes . . .

As we came over one of the hills, just north of Medina, I saw on the top of the next hill what looked like two cars parked on it. About this time they turned on their red lights and I knew that the attack was under way . . .

I picked up my Mini-14 and got out and got myself and my weapon ready as the vehicle coming from behind skidded to a stop about 20 feet away . . . there was a lot of screaming and hollering going on [and] a shot rang out.

Utilizing the commando training he and his family had undergone at several Posse training camps, Kahl, a decorated and twice-wounded World War II veteran of the campaigns in India and Europe, engaged the federal officials in a firefight as his son and Scott Faul ran for cover in some nearby trees.

One federal marshal's shot struck the handle of the .45 caliber MAC 10 that "Yorie" Kahl wore in his shoulder holster and he shouted out, "I'm hit, I'm hit!"

Enraged, the elder Kahl responded by pouring dozens of rounds from his automatic military-style Ruger Mini-14 rifle into the vehicles behind which the officers huddled. Two marshals died in the fusillade, and the others fled, dragging four wounded comrades and seeking reinforcements. Incredibly, Kahl had won an all-out gunfight with ZOG. He then took his injured son to the same nearby clinic where the wounded marshals were being treated and fled the state a hero to the Survival Right and the FBI's most wanted fugitive.

For nearly four months Kahl had eluded his pursuers with the help of Posse members scattered throughout rural America. Now the hiding would stop. Five days earlier, on May 28, Yorie Kahl and Scott Faul had each been convicted on two counts of second-degree murder and six counts of assault, and both faced lengthy prison terms. Now the feds were coming down the dirt road to the fortified bunker that the Ginters had erected outside Smithville and called their "earth home."

With the farmhouse surrounded, the law officers demanded their surrender. The Ginters complied immediately, but Kahl refused to come out. Then Sheriff Gene Matthews led three federal agents up to the door in hopes that Kahl would be consistent in his Posse belief that the only recognizable legal authority was the county sheriff. Instead, as Matthews stepped inside the Ginters' kitchen with his gun drawn, Kahl stepped out from behind the refrigerator and fired a round from his Mini-14 into the lawman's armpit. A flash of lightning illuminated the scene as the fatally wounded sheriff's comrades dragged him off the porch.

The next hour was a nightmare of rifle fire and crashing thunderbolts as Kahl and the surrounding force exchanged rounds in the middle of a howling storm. Then one of the commandos outside lobbed a smoke grenade into a stove flue and the device set off several cases of ammunition, killing Kahl instantly. Police were later to estimate that more than 100,000 rounds had been stored in the heavily fortified Arkansas bunker.

By his death Kahl drew attention to what is the least known but, in terms of sheer numbers, probably the most significant segment of the Survival Right, the Posse's strange blend of Identity religion, dietary laws, polygamy and jailhouse lawyering.

For nearly a decade Gordon Kahl had traveled about the country giving low-keyed speeches in his slow North Dakota accent, explaining to small audiences gathered in rented motel rooms the complex code of Posse ethics. Patiently he had urged his listeners to adopt the Posse tactics of attacking the federal government through its own courts and legal system, of filing nuisance lawsuits and not paying taxes.

Taking a page out of the Identity Christian textbooks, Kahl explained that the founding fathers of the American republic were actually members of the lost tribe of Israel known as Manasseh. Just as God had handed Moses—"who was not a Jew"—the sacred tablets containing the Ten Commandments, so had Yahweh dictated the Constitution and the earlier Articles of Confederation, a document that Posse preachers favor because of its tendency to state repeatedly that all rights are given only to white males.

Like so many other rural Americans, Gordon Kahl had been a victim of the crisis in agriculture that had surfaced as early as the mid-1970s. Kahl's fortunes plummeted even as many urban people were enjoying unparalleled prosperity by exploiting the then rampant inflation rates. In common with his neighbors in the fertile wheat country outside Medina, Kahl had built a fortune—at least in the books of the First National Bank of Medina—by doggedly bringing in his crops each year. He nurtured an abiding faith in technology, and every time the experts at International Harvester or the John Deere Company suggested a new piece of hardware they found a willing customer at the Kahl farm. But things had taken a turn for the worse as each year feed costs rose while prices for the cattle that consumed that feed dropped. Wheat prices fell until it cost more to plant than could be earned by selling the harvest. As costs exceeded income, farmers started to buckle under and acknowledge defeat. And they cast about for an explanation for why they had failed.

Kahl found that explanation by blaming an international Jewish conspiracy—bankers who had extended all those loans for modern, air-conditioned farm equipment knowing full well that the poor clod doing the borrowing would soon be back, hat in hand, begging for his farm. When the debts became too much to handle, Kahl declared himself retired and went on the road to preach the Posse message he had learned through his contacts with the ultraright.

The Posse's conspiracy theory was derived from an earlier group of gun-toting haters from the 1960s who had called themselves the Minutemen, after the colonial American patriots who had taken up arms and wrested the nation from its British overlords. In their heyday the Minutemen sought out publicity to promote their position that whites should arm themselves, practice urban combat and otherwise prepare for a dismal future that promised extensive race riots at best and all-out thermonuclear war at worst. Minuteman leaders like Robert DePugh opened the doors to their compounds to allow newspaper photographers—TV cameras still were too bulky to take into the field—to take pictures of extensive arsenals filled with automatic weapons, hand grenades, silencers and other military paraphernalia.

The Minutemen soon gained the attention they sought. The spate of urban rioting that followed the 1967 assassination of Dr. Martin Luther King, Jr., had made the prospect of urban guerrilla warfare a reality that few could deny. As President Lyndon Johnson and the Democratic-controlled Congress pressed into law their raft of civil rights and Great Society anti-poverty legislation, reactionary forces on the far right grew in influence. The John Birch Society flourished, and Alabama's black-baiting governor, George Wallace, became a significant national political figure. George Lincoln Rockwell and his neo-Nazis decked themselves out in Nazi regalia and marched in the streets of Washington. And the Minutemen made the six o'clock news.

But the tide turned rapidly. Impeccably conservative Richard Nixon replaced Johnson. Rockwell's confidant, John Patler, gunned him down in an Arlington, Virginia, laundromat with a .30-06 hunting rifle. Wallace was rendered a paraplegic by an assassin named Arthur Bremmer in a Maryland shopping mall. The FBI incorporated the far right into the lists of targets for its illegal COIN-TELPRO dirty tricks project and, throughout the country, federal attorneys and state and local officials began cracking down on the right-wing zealots with their illegally converted automatic weaponry and equally illegal silencers. DePugh was indicted on weapons charges and went underground; he was ultimately arrested and imprisoned for four years.

The publicity-seeking Minutemen disappeared from the scene just as quickly as they had surfaced, but their ideology survives in the form of the Posse Comitatus. And nowhere on the landscape of today's ultraright is the demand for secrecy more intense than among these well-armed and ardent tax protesters. Unlike the shadowy Posse, for example, the neo-Nazis are easy to find. Likewise, Identity preachers are listed in their local phone books. But phone bills mean records are kept and Posse members are loath to leave any sort of paper trail. You can send away for a staggering amount of literature from most of the Survival Right, but not from the Posse. And therein lies its strength.

Paranoically secretive—with good reason—and recruited largely by word of mouth, the Posse typically exists as cells made up of seven white males along with their families in a given area who operate independent of any national leadership. But this loosely affiliated conglomeration of Survivalists appears to be the largest single element of the Survival Right now operating on the American scene.

In the mid-1970s the Internal Revenue Service assigned a number of its best agents to a newly formed Illegal Tax Protester Program to seek out Posse members and bring charges against them. In 1980, the IRS was able to identify 17,222 tax protesters who either stated their views on tax forms or did not file forms as a specific protest. (These numbers did not include people who didn't file for non-ideological reasons such as simple greed.) By 1982 the figure for protesters had nearly tripled to 49,213 and it jumped again to 57,754 in 1983. Despite vigorous prosecution by the new unit, the number of protesters had only declined to 52,000 by 1986, according to the General Accounting Office. To cope with the flood of protests, the IRS bureaucracy assigned two hundred auditors full-time to deal with Posse cases. Sixteen workers were assigned in each of the agency's ten regional centers to pursue forms filed by protesters.

Additionally, a "protest coordinator" was named in each state to direct investigations.

One of the most fruitful of these IRS protester investigations focused on a fairly typical Posse-affiliated group that called itself the Virginia Patriots. This organization was part of a nationwide group, the Patriots Network, led by a now disbarred South Carolina lawyer, Robert Carlson. In 1985 the federal government brought the Virginia Patriots' leader, Charles Shugarman, and two associates to trial on charges that they had recruited several hundred residents of the Virginia tidewater area surrounding the naval facilities at Newport News to file protest forms on which they illegally demanded $430,000 in improper deductions. IRS agents testified that they had infiltrated the group by attending tax seminars at which, for two hundred dollars per person, Shugarman outlined his tax protest philosophy and tactics. These prosecution witnesses told how Shugarman began each meeting with a prayer and the Pledge of Allegiance. He then passed out copies of the Constitution highlighting the Tenth Amendment, which gives police powers to the individual states instead of to the federal government. Shugarman, then thirty-nine, was convicted along with the two associates on federal conspiracy charges for running what the prosecutors described as "tax-fraud mills."

A former music student who once was a drummer in the band for television evangelist Pat Robertson's 700 Club, Shugarman told the jury he had been converted to the protest movement after hearing the arguments made by Kahl and others that income taxes were part of the *Communist Manifesto*. He told the jury he had been "startled" to find that the Sixteenth Amendment allowing income tax collections was in keeping with the "plank" in Karl Marx's *Communist Manifesto* calling for a progressive income tax. "Most of us have been brought up to believe there are two things in the world you have to do: to pay taxes and die," Shugarman said. "But when I read more, I learned that the intent of the Sixteenth Amendment was not to tax wage earners. It was supposed to be a tax on corporate privilege and wealth . . . a tax to soak the rich. That's how it was sold to the people."

Shugarman explained that the Virginia Patriots believe that the payment of wages is actually barter, an equal exchange between an employer and a worker. Therefore, a worker's paycheck is not "income" that the government can tax legally. "Income," he argued, pertains to things like rent from property one owns or interest on stock market investments.

Barter is a key Posse concept. In 1985 a federal task force operating out of Minneapolis conducted raids in Colorado, Minnesota, South Dakota and Iowa against five "warehouse banks" where Posse-affiliated tax protesters had been persuaded by movement leaders to convert their money into gold and silver to avoid paying income taxes. Denver Posse figure John Grandbouche, who died in 1986, had drafted the scheme in the late 1970s as part of his tax protest plan shortly before his unsuccessful run for the Colorado governorship in 1980. Under the barter scheme, participants turned all of their wealth over to a group that Grandbouche had formed called the National Commodities and Barter Association. The association would then convert the money into bullion—gold and silver bars or coins—and store it in heavily guarded warehouses. In exchange for the money, barter groups like the NCBA would pay all necessary bills for enrolled people, most of whom tended to be farmers, ranchers or self-employed individuals whose main income was not subject to immediate federal withholding at the workplace. Doctors, dentists, chiropractors and even lawyers were among the customers. All transactions were conducted without paper receipts.

The raid by the IRS on the five barter banks resulted in the seizure of a staggering ten tons of silver bullion, and James M. Rosenbaum, the U.S. attorney in Minneapolis who coordinated the exercise, told *The Wall Street Journal* that officials believed the scheme was laundering as much as half a million dollars in cash per day for as many as 20,000 participants. Much of the appeal of the scheme— and the trust on the part of those who turned over their life's savings—apparently derived from the nature of the barter bankers' sales pitch, which was based on the religious cant frequently spouted by Posse recruiters, Rosenbaum speculated. He noted that his raiders had confiscated along with the bullion such Identity tracts as "Bible Law on Money" and "Billions for the Bankers, Debts for the People," by the late Identity leader Sheldon Emry.

Over eight tabloid pages, Emry blames international bankers "of Eastern European ancestry" for everything from the creation of the U.S. Federal Reserve System in 1913 to both world wars, the Vietnam War and the assassination of Abraham Lincoln. By issuing all the paper currency they want, "for nothing more than the cost of paper, ink and bookkeeping," the bankers have been able to extract "interest (usury)" and drive both individuals and nations hopelessly into debt. Without the interest system, individuals and nations always can flourish:

> Germany issued debt-free and interest-free money from 1935 on, accounting for its startling rise from the depression to a world power in five years . . . Abraham Lincoln did it in 1863 to help finance the Civil War. He was later assassinated by an agent of the Rothschild Bank. No debt-free and interest-free money has been issued in America since then.
>
> . . . With debt-free and interest-free money, there would be no high and confiscatory taxation, our homes would be mortgage-free with no $10,000-a-year payments to the Bankers, nor would they get $1,000 to $2,500 per year from every automobile on our roads. We would need no "easy payment" plans, "revolving" charge accounts, loans to pay medical or hospital bills, loans to pay taxes, loans to pay for burials, loans to pay loans, nor any of the thousand and one usury-bearing loans which now suck the life-blood of American families. There would be no unemployment, divorces caused by debt, destitute old people, or mounting crime, and even the so-called "deprived" classes would be deprived of neither job nor money to buy the necessities of life.

So, praising Hitler and quoting from the biblical text where Nehemiah persuades the moneylenders to abandon usury, Emry crafted an argument that convinced hundreds of highly suspicious people, who didn't even trust their own government's money, to deposit their wealth in Grandbouche's "debt-free, interest-free" barter bank.

A year before he died, Grandbouche told the author in a brief interview, "We simply advocate lawful and legal ways to have private banking." Instead of discussing the project further, he offered to sell numerous Posse pamphlets outlining the barter rationale.

When the agents raided Grandbouche's offices in April 1985, they came armed with shotguns, pistols and bulletproof vests. Holding several clerks at bay, the agents confiscated an estimated $250,000 in gold bullion and thousands of documents. Lawyers for the barter association successfully argued in court a few weeks later that the raid had been heavy-handed and that confiscating the gold had deprived more than 250 participants of their legally held property. A federal judge ordered Grandbouche's bullion returned.

Further hampering the IRS investigation into this particular tax protest was the fact that one of the group's executives had been a highly trained computer programmer who had rigged the computers which held the records with a "self-destruct virus," so that when the government prosecutors tried to read the files of those whose bills the barter group was paying, the files were erased.

Grandbouche's barter association was only one of several similar groups operating out of Denver in the mid-1980s. A second, and perhaps bigger, operation came to light when a local coin dealer named Larry Martin committed suicide after a Posse barter fund he was managing came up short.

Mark Finlayson, a lawyer who tried to recover some of the money that had been entrusted to Martin, told the author in 1984 how his client's father, the late Roy Dickson, had put his ranch, cattle and money into a trust and then turned it all over to Martin. Dickson, a crusty eighty-one-year-old rancher, liked to quote the Identity credo about Jewish bankers and made a point of announcing to all concerned that he did not perform ranch chores on the "sacred" holidays of July Fourth and Armistice Day, Finlayson recalled. Dickson had turned over his wealth to Martin for a share of the hoard of silver and gold bars and coins he had deposited in a Denver bank and in the heavily fortified vaults of Silver Towne, a gigantic Indiana-based coin store operated in the town of Winchester. Complaints filed in U.S. District Court in Denver by the IRS charged that Martin had been actively engaged in the Posse Comitatus and had control over the assets of people ranging from Colorado rancher Dickson to farmers in Indiana, doctors in Oklahoma, military officers in Colorado and chiropractors in Washington State.

Finlayson explained that Dickson's bills, as well as those of other depositors in what Martin called the National Commodities and Exchange Association, were to be paid in exchange for his continuing deposits, all without a paper trail. When Martin died, there were 400 members paying into his barter association, and since then they have filed a barrage of lawsuits trying to regain their wealth while the IRS tax protest task force urges the courts to turn the funds over to the U.S. Treasury.

As the failed barter ploy shows, Posse zealots looking for loopholes to avoid the federal tax collector often wind up as victims of plain, old-fashioned fraud.

In July 1986, for example, Roderick Elliott, fifty-eight, onetime employer and mentor of Order figure David "Lone Wolf" Lane, was convicted on theft charges for embezzling funds that farmers around the Midwest had loaned him as part of a barter plan offered by his newspaper, *The Primrose and Cattlemen's Gazette.* (The tabloid's name referred to Elliott's charge that Jewish-controlled banks were leading American farmers "down the primrose path.") Elliott had traveled about holding seminars on Survivalism and tax protest. Most of his seminars cost $135 to attend and focused on advising attendees how to file lawsuits to avoid repaying federal loans. Using a thick book of laws—Title 15 of the U.S. Code—as a textbook, Elliott would walk his farmer audience page by page through the sections dealing with truth-in-lending regulations. His point was that every loan contract signed by farmers since 1968 was void because the contracts lacked basic truth-in-lending protections enacted by consumerist legislation in that year. He encouraged his audiences to jam the courts, Posse style, with "pro se" lawsuits, all filed without the aid of lawyers, to slow the progress of foreclosures and thus buy their brother farmers some time.

In 1984 Elliott boasted that his followers had filed 1,200 of these "pro se" suits with claims totaling more than $1 billion. Despite repeated victories by federal lawyers who argued that the truth-in-lending laws cited by Elliott did not cover agriculture loans, Posse members continued filing the suits, using forms drafted by Elliott, even after he was convicted on the theft charges. Elliott also promoted his schemes through *The Primrose and Cattlemen's Gazette*, telling his subscribers that they could obtain the same privileges that members of the Jewish-dominated news media get with their press credentials by joining his National Agricultural Press Association. Members received a press card, a news media sticker for their cars and a deluge of mail describing a raft of loan schemes.

Dan Levitas, research director for Prairiefire, an Iowa-based rural advocacy group that opposes the Posse, said of Elliott, "He's giving bad information, useless advice and distorted conspiracy theories—motivated by racial hatred." At its peak, prosecutors stated at Elliott's trial, the tabloid enjoyed a circulation of 20,000.

Ultimately Elliott was convicted on fourteen counts of theft, each charging that he had secured loans from farmers promising to use the money to help others in dire financial straits and then to replace the loans with interest-free loans that he claimed were forthcoming from an unidentified friend in the Caribbean.

The various Posse-related frauds prompted a number of clergy leaders to warn that the embattled state of the agricultural economy was allowing opportunistic right-wingers both to pull off con schemes and to acquire previously unattainable political power.

The Reverend Donald Manworren of Des Moines, Iowa, executive coordinator of the Iowa Interchurch Forum, told a press conference in late 1985: "I believe that if we do not speak now, speak forcefully and speak together, we will be inviting the continued rise of a movement which is demonic and capable of undermining, if not destroying the fundamental values that allow this nation to be a land that prizes justice and freedom."

At the same session in New York, Leonard Zeskind, research director of the Center for Democratic Renewal, warned of the Posse: "Most successfully of all, they sell farmers a faulty understanding of legal procedures, and before long, while convincing farmers that they are offering them a simple way out of their legal problems, they have moved to talk of impending Jewish destruction of Western and Christian civilization."

Indeed, despite its general penchant for secrecy, the Posse has surfaced publicly as a political force from time to time, notably in Wisconsin, where James Wickstrom described himself as "national director of counterinsurgency for the United Posses of America." Wickstrom, openly espousing Posse tax revolt and violence, has run for both the Senate and governorship in Wisconsin. Along with Posse sects in California, Missouri and Oregon, Wickstrom's followers frequently form "Christian grand juries" that issue indictments against local officials to dramatize a central Posse point that both the Sixteenth Amendment, which authorizes the income tax, and the Seventeenth Amendment, which calls for the popular election of senators instead of having them chosen by members of the House of Representatives, are illegal.

The Posse differs from the Identity movement in one key way. While Identity zealots derive their ideology from religion and urge communicants to prepare for the impending Apocalypse, the Posse focuses on legal technicalities while warning of imminent collapse either from nuclear attack or from economic disaster. Posse members are entranced by legal questions, pore over lawbooks and dream up myriad ways to tackle the system they hate. Law, in fact, becomes another aspect of Scripture, and the Posse adherents pursue it with the gusto of rabbinical scholars. Many a county clerk looks up and winces when a Posse believer like Randy Geiszler of Milwaukie, Oregon, walks up to the counter with the latest batch of lawsuits.

Frequently Posse members like Geiszler will send the government back its various legal documents—birth certificates, driver's licenses, social security cards, marriage licenses, etc.—to dramatize their belief that they need not adhere to any government beyond that of the county sheriff.

Geiszler and several colleagues, including Richard Butler's close associate Paul Wangrud of Oregon City, Oregon, a leading Posse writer, prepared a do-it-yourself kit titled "Republic Redress vs. Democracy" for Posse members eager to flood local courts with lawsuits. Much of this fifty-page pamphlet consists of sample legal forms for Posse members to file in their local courts demanding that they be allowed to operate automobiles without either driver's license or registration. The document tells far more about the Posse mind-set than it does about the issues of jurisprudence its amateur lawyer authors discuss. The Survival Right is a very authoritarian place, and its denizens love the idea of rules. The more rules, laws, court precedents and footnotes, the better. Beating the system by seizing upon a legal technicality has great appeal. John V. Staffen, a deputy county prosecutor in Yakima County, Washington, once told the Seattle *Times* that Posse members "want to take every parking ticket to the Supreme Court."

The IRS report on the tax protesters described how a favorite Posse tactic has become to file "lien cases against the personal property of judges, Court Commissioners, District Attorneys, Assistant Attorneys General, Clerks of Courts, and newspaper publishers in an effort to clog the court system and to embarrass, impede, and obstruct the trial courts in the administration of justice." The report noted that in 1980 more than a hundred such cases had been filed in a single week in Wisconsin as Posse members placed liens against the houses, autos and other property of targeted officials. Eventually, the Wisconsin legislature passed a measure to bar such frivolous liens.

The streak of jailhouse-lawyer meanness illustrated by the deluge of liens in Wisconsin comes out dramatically in many of the books popular at Survival Right gatherings. Typical titles include: *I Hate You: An Angry Man's Guide to Revenge; Get Even: The Complete Book of Dirty Tricks; Techniques of Harassment; Up Yours: A Guide* to *Advanced Revenge Techniques*; and *The Revenge Book*, which promises on the dust jacket to supply "the meanest and nastiest tricks for all those people you love to hate—snakelike salesmen, crooked landlords, bungling bureaucrats and nosy neighbors."

And if the Posse legal arguments seem like so much mumbo jumbo to most, they can have a deadly effect when adopted by people who find in Posse rhetoric comfort and deliverance from their economic woes. Gordon Kahl was one American whose encounter with the Posse credo was to prove fatal. Arthur Kirk was another.

On October 23, 1984, Kirk died in a gunfight with a Nebraska state SWAT team after he attempted to turn his farm into a sovereign county under Posse dictates. Obviously demented, Kirk had rushed from his farmhouse brandishing an M-16 rifle and screaming "Fucking Jews!" at the state troopers, who, a subsequent investigation determined, he thought were agents of Mossad, the Israeli secret service.

The death of Kirk became a political crisis for Nebraska governor Robert Kerrey, whose naturally conservative farm constituency tended to sympathize more with Kirk than with the SWAT team that shot him down in a dispute over a farm loan. So Kerrey persuaded Samuel Van Pelt, a retired district court judge, to investigate the case and determine why Kirk had acted as he did.

In an interview with the author, Van Pelt told this story:

At the age of forty-nine in the fall of 1984, Kirk was typical of many Nebraska farmers badly strapped by the crisis in the agricultural economy. His small acreage near Cairo was heavily indebted to the bank in nearby Grand Island, and the harvest that October had been a poor one.

Hoping to stave off foreclosure, Kirk had sold about fifty cows to raise money for a loan payment, but these animals had already been pledged as collateral for that loan's principal. The bank complained about the matter to the county sheriff, and officers notified Kirk that they would have to seize his remaining cattle as collateral for the bank. Kirk warned them not to try.

Kirk had picked up the Posse credo after joining Roderick Elliott's National Agricultural Press Association, and Van Pelt found papers in the Kirk farmhouse indicating that Kirk had hoped Elliott would get him a low-interest loan from the Bahamas that would get him out of his current troubles.

Extensive Posse literature was found inside Kirk's house, including documents outlining how a farmer could under common law, as suggested by Geiszler and Wangrud, post his property in such a way that law officials could not enter. Kirk had indeed tacked on his fence posts all around the farm twenty signs with this Posse "Notice to Post" legal form advising all law officers that they couldn't trespass.

Also found inside the farmhouse was *Why "They" Wanted to Get Gordon Kahl,* a pamphlet written by Posse leader Len Martin that says, in part: "I don't think the CIA or the FBI is part of the U.S. Government. I think it is part of the Mossad, the Jewish Police. In fact, I think the Mossad is world-wide and that all police organizations like the CIA and FBI in all countries are under the Mossad . . ."

Martin's strange writing also told Kirk, who had been raised a strict Lutheran before adopting the Identity and Posse teachings, that the members of the Masonic Lodge in Cairo and Grand Island were controlled by "the Jews."

Banned from joining the Masons because of his Lutheran roots, Kirk now had reason to fear most of his neighbors as well as the Masons at the banks where he got his loans. Further, noted Van Pelt, Kirk had told a reporter from the Grand Island *Independent* that he was afraid of the highway patrol because they were controlled by the governor and Kerrey at the time was getting a lot of national publicity through his courtship of Jewish actress Debra Winger.

Like other Posse members, Kirk maintained a substantial arsenal, including military-style M-16s and an elephant gun equipped with armor-piercing ammunition. Clearly, the Nebraska highway patrol's task of helping to serve a warrant to take the rest of this man's cattle away from him was a dangerous mission.

SWAT members donned bulletproof vests and a state airplane was dispatched to watch the barricaded farm as the sheriff drove down the dirt road past the "Notice to Post" signs and onto Kirk's farm.

For unknown reasons, Kirk had built a bunker around his windmill instead of fortifying his house. At the foot of the windmill he had laid down an enclosure made of thick cottonwood logs that would have stopped an antitank round. When he ran out to meet the approaching law officers, he dived into the fortified windmill and started screaming at them to leave.

"He thought they were the Mossad," said Van Pelt.

Then Kirk stood up, losing his cover, and fired as many as sixty M-16 rounds before being hit himself. He bled to death beneath his windmill.

Ultimately, Van Pelt's investigation concluded with a 300-page report that found no fault with the way the police had acted. But in the interview Van Pelt sadly noted that despite the dead farmer's racist dementia inspired by the Posse, the Kirk case still boils down to one of "a farmer shot for not paying his debt to the bank."

From his Lincoln, Nebraska, law offices just across the street from the State Capitol, Van Pelt has become one of America's leading students of the Survival Right as a result of his work for Kerrey in the Kirk investigation. In the summer of 1985, Van Pelt found himself deeply involved in an effort to understand an even more dangerous subset of the movement than the virulent and legal-minded members of the Posse.

Sam Van Pelt encountered the compound dwellers.

Something there is that doesn't love a wall.
—Robert Frost

5: The Compound Dwellers

The hamlet of Rulo, Nebraska, perches alongside the Missouri River where the borders of Kansas, Nebraska and Missouri converge like the cross hairs on a telescopic rifle sight. A rusting Eaton Metals Co. grain silo stands at one end of Rulo's short main street and an abandoned A&W Root Beer drive-in sits at the other end. Just outside Rulo, up the dirt road that heads north toward Omaha through the rolling scrub oak and cropland along the wide Missouri, sits the fortified compound where Michael ("Archangel") Ryan ruled over his sodomist neo-Nazi commune of four "queens," twenty servants and one very nervous goat.

When he was arrested at the Rulo compound in 1985 on charges of murder, torture, theft and scores of federal firearms and explosives violations, Michael Ryan wore a crew cut, an Old Testament prophet's beard and farmer's high-bib overalls with a swaggering charisma that belied his background. Until he embraced the Survival Right, Michael Ryan had been just another farm boy, a native of Anthony, Kansas (pop. 2,600), one more broken-down farm town with an economy depressed by sluggish crop prices. He ended as the patriarch of a bizarre Survivalist clan of men and women who treated his every whim as a divine proclamation ordered personally by the angry God of the Old Testament.

123

According to trial testimony in the Nebraska courtroom where prosecutors brought the tragedy of Rulo onto the public record in 1986, Ryan had been a dull boy. His teachers recalled that he had managed to raise his high school D's to low C's only by applying maximum effort. He needed the C's to get on the football team; but earning them required so much concentration that Michael Ryan didn't have anything left to devote to football. Grudgingly accepted by his teachers, Ryan was rejected by his coaches.

Ryan dropped out of high school in 1968, less than two credits shy of a diploma, and went to Vietnam, where he learned the rudiments of military weaponry but apparently never participated in battle. Afterward, with the help of his father, Gene Ryan, a lineman for the Southwestern Bell Telephone Co., Michael found work first as a menial laborer and later as a long-haul truck driver moving loads of hogs, veal calves and other livestock to markets in Omaha and Chicago. After he was married in 1970, Ryan and his wife, Ruth, lived in working-class anonymity in and around Whiting, Kansas, where they raised two sons, Dennis and Alvin, and a daughter, Mandy.

As a knockabout blue-collar worker in small-town America, Ryan heard the Posse doctrine repeatedly as he plied his trade. At his subsequent trials, local prosecutors outlined how Ryan's personal road to Damascus led to a Hiawatha, Kansas, motel room in 1982, where he went to shake the hand of Wisconsin Posse leader James Wickstrom, who was in town on a recruiting swing through Kansas and Nebraska.

Wickstrom, one of a handful of open leaders in the super-secret organization, had his own Survivalist compound in the sleepy town of Tigerton Dells, Wisconsin, where he operated an Identity sect called the Life Science Church and a "pro se" law school called the Christian Liberty Academy. After a 1983 conviction for impersonating a government officer, Wickstrom served a short prison term, then won parole in exchange for a promise to stop his political organizing activities. But in the early 1980s, James Wickstrom, onetime candidate for the Wisconsin governorship and its Senate seat, was the most visible Posse leader in America. His revival-meeting-type shows of anti-Semitism and Identity sermonizing received extensive coverage in small-town farm belt newspapers, which frequently sent reporters because such large numbers of local residents were going to the sessions.

Like Robert Miles, Richard Butler and the rest of the Survival Right's leaders, Wickstrom urged his followers to call God "Yahweh" because that is the name he had told the true Jews to use in the Old Testament. Using the word "Yahweh," Wickstrom told his often rapt audiences, serves as a constant reminder that they are the true Jews, who were claimed by the Creator as his chosen people instead of the satanic "Khazars" who are called Jews by virtually the entire world today.

Yahweh sent to earth his only begotten son, Yoshua, "Jesus the Christ, who was not a Jew," and whose name too must be spoken in the ancient Hebrew. Wickstrom advised his farm belt audiences on ways to file Posse-style "pro se" lawsuits, without using lawyers, to declare their independence from any government higher than that of the county sheriff. Mail back your driver's licenses, Wickstrom encouraged them. Repudiate the social security system. Reject your obligation to pay back farm loans. Post your land with signs forbidding entry to any outsiders under power of the same common law that God gave to his white Anglo-Saxon chosen people along with the Magna Carta. Refuse, in the name of Yahweh and Yoshua, to pay your federal income taxes. And above all, he exhorted the farmers, prepare for Armageddon. This is the End Time Generation, the cleansing battle is at hand.

In that Hiawatha motel room in 1982, Wickstrom had looked at the 6 foot 2 inch, 235-pound Ryan and told his new Posse disciple about "the power of the Arm Test." To demonstrate, Wickstrom told Ryan to hold one arm up at a forty-five-degree angle from his shoulder. Wickstrom then grabbed the burly man's wrist with one hand and clasped Ryan's shoulder with another.

"Yahweh," asked Wickstrom, "does Brother Ryan have the Power?" With that, Ryan's arm moved slightly but remained upright, even though Wickstrom pulled downward on the wrist.

Wickstrom explained that those with the Power were, like himself, able to ask God for advice on matters from the most trivial to the most profound and obtain an immediate answer using the Arm Test. If the person being tested dropped the arm, it meant that Yahweh said no. If the arm stayed erect even while the tester pulled downward on the wrist, the answer was yes. No mention was made of the fact that the person holding the shoulder was in total control of whether the arm stayed or fell.

Ryan walked away from the motel convinced that he could administer the Arm Test to others and, incredibly enough, this one strange bit of third-rate stage magic, when wielded with the personal force Ryan was to muster, allowed him to set up his own Survivalist society.

During Ryan's trials, witnesses told how he applied the Arm Test throughout each day at virtually every decision. "Yahweh," he would ask while clasping the arm of his original wife, Ruth, "should we eat rice instead of beans?" Yahweh, of course, would respond according to whether Ryan wanted rice or beans for his dinner.

Women who had served as Ryan's concubines testified during subsequent trials that the Arm Test was used in the kitchen to determine what food to fix, how to prepare it, when to serve it and how much to give to each person.

The Arm Test was used for far more important matters as well. Starting with the Identity tenet that the best of the Aryan race should plant their seed as often as possible, Ryan used the Arm Test to satisfy his need for the commune's women. At the same time he cemented his leadership by sexually humiliating the males about him, forcing them to sodomize the pet goat and one another while he bedded their wives, mothers and daughters.

Kevin Penrod, an Omaha television reporter who covered the Ryan case, told of going to the farm after the arrests and recalled, "That goat was really something. It clearly had adopted a taste for humans. It was embarrassing the way the thing would follow you around that farmyard."

The testimony about the inner workings of the Survivalist compound that Ryan established was given by his followers after Ryan and his fifteen-year-old son, Dennis, were charged in the murders of five-year-old Luke Stice and twenty-seven-year-old James Thimm, whose bodies were found in shallow graves on the farm when police came in armed with warrants to search for illegal weapons and stolen farm equipment.

Ryan had been introduced to the complex Posse politico-religious rap during the early 1980s after a back injury forced him to lay off as a truck driver and go on welfare. He sat around the house reading Identity tracts and listening to audio cassettes of various Survival Right sermons, which are easily obtained through ads in publications like *Spotlight*. He also acquired several of the private videotapes of Wickstrom's most virulent sermons, which the Posse leader circulated among the faithful.

In 1982, his back injury on the mend, Ryan got a job as a feed salesman for Norbert Haverkamp, a farmer who lived in Mercier, Kansas, a short distance from Whiting. Haverkamp's son, James, who was to become one of Ryan's most devoted commune members, shared Ryan's fascination with the Posse ideology to the point that at Christmas 1983 he came to the dinner table carrying a Bible and a Ruger Mini-14 combat rifle. After the gifts had been opened and the turkey was back in the refrigerator, the younger Haverkamp showed his family some of Wickstrom's videotapes railing against Jews, blacks and the Federal Reserve Board and warning that the advent of Armageddon was imminent.

Among James Haverkamp's listeners was his mother, Maxine, and his sister, Cheryl Gibson, who lived with her husband, Lester Gibson, and their five children in Highland, Kansas. Trial witnesses later were to recall how Cheryl too was enraptured by the Posse/ Identity spiel and abandoned both her Catholic Church and her husband to embrace Identity and eventually become one of Ryan's polygamous wives.

The bizarre story of Ryan's Survivalist compound came out because of Lester Gibson's efforts to find his wife and their five children, who had secretly moved onto the Rulo farm. After Cheryl Gibson disappeared, Lester hired an Omaha private detective named Denny Whelan, who traced her to Ryan's commune, then kept pressing skeptical local law enforcement officers until they conducted a raid and uncovered the horrible story of the Rulo commune.

After that fateful Christmas of 1983, Cheryl had begun telling her husband that she had accepted the Identity credo and was preparing for Armageddon. Cheryl told Lester that Michael Ryan had used the Arm Test with her and had found that she and Lester were not married in the eyes of Yahweh. She continued her job at a local grain elevator but began stockpiling large stores of vitamin pills and reading the Book of Revelation long into the night.

Lester Gibson was put off by the Posse from the beginning. He told friends how he first encountered the movement when he took his chain saw to a nearby blacksmith and noticed that the man was playing Wickstrom tapes over speakers in his shop as he repaired farm machinery. The tapes, recalled Gibson, warned listeners that they must learn "who's who and who's Jew" or face the consequences. Gibson said the blacksmith urged every one of his customers to join the Posse.

By the spring of 1984 Cheryl Gibson had filed for divorce and won a court order giving her primary custody of the couple's five children and only limited visiting rights to Lester. She and the children first moved in with Ryan and his wife, Ruth, in a two-story farmhouse they rented in Whiting, Kansas.

Meanwhile, using the Arm Test, Michael Ryan had found another disciple in Rick Stice, a young hog farmer from Rulo who had attended several Wickstrom sessions while looking for a faith healer for his fatally ill wife, Sondra. In 1982, facing the same economic squeeze that beset his neighbors, Stice had decided he must economize or lose the eighty-acre farm where he raised hogs alongside the Missouri just outside Rulo. Among the economies he took was to cancel the family's health insurance for himself, Sondra and their three children, Luke, Ora and Barry.

Sondra Stice's mother, Garneta Butrick, later told the author how, within weeks of canceling the policy, the family learned that Sondra had contracted Hodgkin's disease, a form of cancer that, while deadly, can often be forestalled for many years through draconian and expensive medical treatments. With his insurance canceled and with income virtually nonexistent at the hog farm, Rick Stice began seeking a solution in faith healers. He described in an interview how that quest led him to the same session in Hiawatha where Michael Ryan met Posse patriarch Wickstrom and learned the Arm Test.

At Wickstrom's urging, said Stice, the couple tried many of the medical practices that, like the use of the words "Yahweh" and "Yoshua," are part and parcel of the Identity/Posse ideology. The couple traveled to Wisconsin, where they consulted an "iridologist" recommended by Wickstrom. Iridology holds that an initiated practitioner can look at the patterns of lines extending from the pupil to the edge of the iris in a person's eyes and learn such things as what sort of disease that person might have and what sort of treatment might be effective. Stice said the Wisconsin iridologist recommended a regime of massive doses of vitamin pills and a strict diet for Sondra in accordance with the rigorous Posse dietary code.

As a logical extension of the Identity belief that the white people who settled the Americas are the true Jews of biblical lore, Posse members are urged to keep the same strict dietary laws as do Orthodox Jews. Pork is forbidden to orthodox Posse members, as are shellfish and all other foods deemed not in keeping with their brand of kosher. One popular Identity audio cassette sold by Heirs of the Blessing in Herrin, Illinois, is "The Dangers of Eating Pork! Worms, Cancer and God's Judgment." Additionally, the Posse/Identity movement often bars its members from eating fish that lack scales, because such fish, like swine rooting in the mud and shellfish in the sea, often feed on the detritus at the bottom of the river. It is a sin, therefore, among orthodox Identity adherents to eat catfish, one of the traditional delicacies for people living on the banks of the Missouri in and around Rulo.

Sondra Stice took the massive amounts of vitamins prescribed by the Posse doctors. She also kept the sect's bizarre anti-Semitic kosher diet and attempted numerous other alternative health solutions with faith healers, naturopaths, chiropractors and others not associated with what the far right considers to be the Jewish-dominated American Medical Association.

Spotlight is packed each week with ads for various folk remedies which adherents believe are being concealed from whites by race-mixing enemies. A Special Health Supplement published in *Spotlight* and distributed to many new subscribers charges that a conspiracy by the American Medical Association and the federal Food and Drug Administration keeps most Americans from benefiting from the ancient wisdom of folk medicine, because folk remedies are usually derived from plants and animals, whereas most modern drugs are "synthesized from petroleum products" and sold by international bankers.

"Should you make the decision as to what—if any—treatment you receive for any disease or condition?" one article concluded. "Or should that decision be made in the boardroom of Standard Oil of New Jersey?"

On April 24, 1983, sitting in a rocking chair in the farmhouse not fifty yards from where police later were to exhume the battered body of her five-year-old son, Luke, Sondra Stice died without having consulted a mainstream doctor about her disease. She was buried in the Rulo cemetery in a plot overlooking the rolling Missouri. Embedded in her headstone is a picture of Sondra Stice wearing one of her high school prom gowns. Rick Stice buried his wife, erected that tombstone and then took his three children back to the hog farm and, briefly, tried to rebuild his life.

But Michael Ryan was waiting in the wings to fill the void left by Sondra's loss. Within days of her burial, Ryan administered the Arm Test to Rick and told him that Yahweh disapproved of his raising hogs on the Rulo farm. The flesh of swine, he thundered, was declared unclean by Yahweh. Stice acquiesced and shut down the hog pens. The hogs had been the farm's only source of profit, however, and the decision quickly forced the property into foreclosure.

Once the property was foreclosed by the Richardson County Bank, Ryan's disciple, James Haverkamp, and another sect member, Lynn Thiele, bought the Rulo farm and Ryan moved his band of followers onto the grounds to establish his compound. At its peak there were an estimated twenty-five people living in the strange commune.

Ryan brought his wife, Ruth, along with their children, Alvin, Mandy and Dennis.

James Haverkamp brought his cousin Timothy, his father, Norbert, his mother, Maxine, and his seventeen-year-old sister, Lisa. Within the year Lisa bore a child in one of the farm's crude buildings.

Lynn Thiele and his wife, Debra, Timothy Haverkamp's sister, moved onto the Rulo farm from a similar armed compound they had established on their own farm just outside Norton, Kansas. When police raided the Thieles' property they found an underground bunker with an estimated 85,000 rounds of ammunition of various calibers, some armor-piercing ammo and an assault rifle. The bunker had its own water supply, a generator and a large store of freeze-dried food. It was unclear whether the Thiele bunker was built as a fallback for the Rulo commune or whether the family had simply been deeply involved with the Survivalist movement even before they joined up with Ryan.

Joining the Thieles on the trek to Rulo was Cheryl Gibson, who brought her five children: Melissa, ten, Michael, nine, Nicholas, six, Brandon, four, and Tamara, two.

James Thimm, twenty-five at the time, and John David Andreas, two friends from the Mennonite community around Beatrice, Nebraska, also joined Ryan's cult.

Finally, there was the Stice family: Ortho Stice, Rick's father, who had operated the farm for decades before turning it over to his son; Rick himself; Rick and Sondra's nine-year-old daughter, Ora

Dawn Stice, and their sons, Barry, seven, and Luke, who was three years old when the Rulo commune began.

In trial testimony, Cheryl Gibson, Andreas and others told of a daily routine in which Ryan required members to sit in a cramped living room and watch incessant rescreenings of Wickstrom's Identity videotapes. Often they also would watch videotapes of the movie *Red Dawn*, a thriller in which Soviet troops take over a small farm town in America only to be routed by local high school students who take up arms and wage a guerrilla war from the surrounding hillsides.

Sometimes Yahweh would tell the group to smoke marijuana via the Arm Test and a protracted drug binge would follow. At such times, members would mill about the farmyard watching flashes of light in the sky and speak of the coming of Armageddon. Frequently on these occasions neighbors would hear the crackle of automatic-weapon fire in the night.

Ryan would open his Bible to the Book of Revelation and tell his followers that the place called Armageddon was nothing more than a wheat field. And, he would add, the Rulo farm was surrounded by wheat fields. Ryan insisted that the final battle of Armageddon will happen, not in some exotic place in the Middle East, but right there outside Rulo. The Battle of the Wheat Fields was imminent, he would warn. Citing passages from Revelation where God raises up an army of 144,000 soldiers—12,000 from each of the twelve tribes of Israel—he boasted that the Rulo group would lead "one of the 12,000."

To prepare for Armageddon, the Rulo commune raised large amounts of money by stealing cattle and farm machinery from farms in Iowa and Kansas, targeted so that the group could avoid law enforcement efforts from the two neighboring states in the sanctuary of their Nebraska compound. After the Rulo farm was raided, police confiscated more than $250,000 worth of stolen farm equipment as well as thirty semiautomatic rifles, and thirteen fully automatic submachine guns and rifles, a sawed-off shotgun, more than a dozen conventional pistols and 150,000 rounds of ammunition, enough to fill two delivery vans when the evidence was carted away. It was a typical inventory for one of America's many Survivalist compounds. Prosecutors estimated the group had spent $50,000 in stolen funds on their arsenal for Armageddon.

When Ryan's band wasn't out stealing or milling about the compound in a state of agitation over end times, the "Archangel" often stirred up his followers with his sexual code. As noted earlier, the burly Ryan would flaunt the fact that he had taken nearly all the commune's eligible women as his concubines, including Ruth Ryan, Debra Thiele, Cheryl Gibson, and Maxine and Lisa Haverkamp. He then forced the other men into sodomy. The young bachelors were told to copulate with the goat. Ryan disciplined Rick Stice by forcing him to engage in oral sex with his five-year-old son, Luke, trial testimony charged.

"It was pretty harsh stuff," Stice told the author in late 1986.

James Thimm balked at the perversity in the spring of 1985 after being forced to copulate with the goat. In response, Ryan ordered some of his followers to sodomize Thimm with the greased handles of shovels, then to shoot off the tips of the defector's fingers with their pistols. Other commune members broke Thimm's right arm and both legs with heavy boards. Finally, wearing yellow dishwashing gloves, they peeled the flesh from his legs with a straight-edge razor and a pair of pliers, showing Thimm swatches of his own severed skin as the wailing unfortunate groveled in the manure-laden straw of the farm's hog pen. Thimm died screaming in physical anguish and begging "Yahweh" for forgiveness, subsequent trial testimony stated. After he was dead, Thimm was shot in the head with a .45 caliber pistol, wrapped in a sleeping bag and buried in a shallow grave dug with one of the disk plows the group had stolen.

Five-year-old Luke Stice's short and miserable life ended in April 1985 when Ryan tried to discipline the child by wrapping a dog leash about his neck and holding the boy, clad only in his small cotton underpants, aloft while telling Cheryl Gibson and his other queens who watched from the farmhouse windows, "This is the mongrel, the seed of Satan." Cheryl Gibson testified that before hanging the child, Ryan had written the numbers 666 on his tiny back in red paint and tortured him for days with icy showers, beatings and threats. Luke Stice was buried in a shallow grave in sight of the same front porch where his mother had died two years earlier.

Stice confirmed in the interview that he had seen the marks on Luke's tiny body when he helped the commune bury the body of his son. "I don't know what I could have done," he said.

Clearly, the tragedy of Rulo transcends even the bizarre politics of the Survival Right. There was as much psychopathology as ideology driving Michael Ryan and his blighted followers to their fatal combination of Identity and sodomy. Nevertheless, significant aspects of the American movement toward the Survival Right emerged in the wake of Ryan's arrest and trials.

For example, once Nebraska's civic leaders learned of the deadly Posse/Identity chemistry through reading, hearing and watching news reports of the Rulo story, a number of other Survivalist groups came under public scrutiny in that state. Clubs of paramilitary commandos in Omaha's suburbs were interviewed on local TV stations. A group of Survivalists centered on the central Nebraska community of Kearney opened their doors to Omaha TV newsman Kevin Penrod and invited him onto their commune to film their boasts of firepower and warnings of the international conspiracy by Jewish bankers.

Another group of Survivalists were traced to the world-famous Amana Colonies of Iowa, where they tried to blend in with Mennonite "plain people" who still live in the age of the horse and buggy out of their religious beliefs. In Partridge, Kansas, just across the state line from Rulo, Nebraska, a young neo-Nazi named Tim Bishop openly raised a private army of disillusioned farmers, taking advantage of news media interest in the Survivalist movement prompted by the Ryan story to urge his rural members to join him in an offshoot of Richard Butler's Idaho Church of Jesus Christ Christian/Aryan Nations. (Butler told the Hutchinson, Kansas, *News*, during a 1986 interview that Bishop was accurately representing the

Aryan Nations testament even though his uniforms were not in keeping with the color codes adopted by the Idaho neo-Nazis. Noting that Bishop's swastika-draped uniforms were in khaki, Butler told the Kansas newspaper, "We have a light blue shirt and dark blue pants.")

In an interview with *The Village Voice*, Sam Van Pelt spoke of his personal fears that many of the sheriff's offices in Nebraska included deputies, if not sheriffs themselves, who embraced the Posse mind-set. Van Pelt noted that when he did his investigation of Arthur Kirk's death, he detected widespread sympathy for Kirk among other farmers, who frequently pointed out that, just as Posse preachers so frequently warn, Kirk was killed by government agents acting on behalf of bankers.

Underscoring just how widely the Survival Right message has been promulgated, the man who prosecuted Michael Ryan, Richardson County district attorney Douglas Merz, acknowledged that he too had attended Posse revival meetings in his spare time, even as Ryan and his followers were sitting in the next pew. In an interview with the author in his Falls City, Nebraska, office, Merz helpfully ticked off on the fingers of two hands the names of local businessmen and farmers whom he considered "either in the Posse or sympathetic to it."

Despite the suspicions of *The Village Voice* and others about his own orientation, Merz prosecuted Ryan with a vigor that indicated that he, personally, had little sympathy for the Survival Right. Nonetheless, the movement is thriving on the fringes of the American heartland, even if it still must travel far before joining the mainstream.

Preaching that farmers are being victimized by a heartless cabal of international Jewish bankers, Survival Right proselytizers have surfaced in a number of communes. Details of a group of compound dwellers far larger, more sophisticated and somewhat more sane than Ryan's strange band emerged in 1985, when a task force of two hundred heavily armed FBI agents led a raid against a likewise heavily armed compound in Arkansas, just south of the Missouri border, occupied by nearly two hundred men, women and children and called the Covenant, the Sword and the Arm of the Lord.

In their own shorthand they called themselves CSA, noting that the initials also stand for Confederate States of America. Their compound itself was called Zarepath-Horeb, after the biblical places where Moses and the Israelites received the ark of the covenant (Mount Horeb) and the Phoenician city (Zarepath) which became a place of refuge for weary soldiers, like the prophet Elijah, who had raised their swords against false prophets and needed sanctuary. At its peak, Zarepath-Horeb, located on 224 acres of prime Ozark mountain lands along Bull Shoals Lake outside the town of Three Brothers, Arkansas, was a tightly knit polygamous community boasting its own water supply, electrical system, dormitories and a number of factories, including one for making hand grenades and another for manufacturing silencers and other paraphernalia for firearms. It was in this shop that the MAC 10 submachine gun used to slaughter Alan Berg was altered from its legal semiautomatic state to that of an illegal fully automatic machine gun. Using the best tap and die equipment, drill presses and other sophisticated machines, CSA gunsmiths took the off-the-shelf Ingram MAC 10 and installed a switch that at the flip of a thumb enabled the weapon to fire either one shot at a time (semiautomatic) or bursts. A CSA-built silencer reduced the sounds made by the Ingram's .45 caliber bullets to the level of noise produced by slamming a heavy book onto a desk.

For much of the decade during which it flourished, CSA inhabitants financed their activities partly by making the national circuit of gun shows, where they sold shooting accessories made in their own factory and contracted with attendees for custom gunsmithing. Often the CSA booth at National Rifle Association–sanctioned gun shows would include large supplies of Survival Right literature as well as gun accessories. In common with Richard Butler's compound in Idaho, CSA augmented the communal coffers by doing a brisk business in neo-Nazi-style hate literature, including the infamous *Protocols of the Learned Elders of Zion*, *The Talmud Un-*

masked, Who's Who in the Zionist Conspiracy, The Negro and the World Crisis and *A Straight Look at the Third Reich.*

Another moneymaker was a series of CSA seminars that its commando experts, such as Randall Rader, conducted throughout the Midwest and South, at which they demonstrated the use of legal weapons and sold "streetsweeper" riot guns made in the compound gun shop. It was through these traveling seminars that Rader met the members of the Order who later were to bring him to Idaho, where he acted as their trainer and equipment manager as they prepared for their various crimes. Rader later was to become one of the federal prosecutors' prime witnesses in building the case against those who eventually stood trial or pleaded guilty in the Seattle case. In exchange, Rader, the man who built the gun that killed Berg, taught the killers how to use it and then sent the assassins off to do the killing, never spent a day in jail for his role in the crime spree.

While he was in Arkansas, Rader helped the CSA commune dwellers conduct their own version of a military boot camp, where participants drilled in what they called "Christian martial arts" as well as urban warfare, rifle and pistol marksmanship, military tactics and wilderness survival. Between the late 1970s and 1985, when the commune was virtually eliminated by the massive raid of FBI agents and other police, CSA zealots conducted training classes for outsiders who paid fees of $500 and more to go through CSA's "End Time Overcomer Survival Training School." Many attendees combined going through the school with a vacation in the numerous nearby Ozark resorts for which the area is famous. The "End Time Overcomer" training course culminated at an area of the compound called Silhouette City, patterned after the famous urban gunfight training facility the FBI operates at its own fortified training camp at Quantico, Virginia.

Like Quantico, CSA's Silhouette City consisted of a number of mock buildings on several streets where cardboard cutouts would suddenly spring up as trainees walked with their guns at the ready. But whereas the FBI's cutouts tended to be of mothers pushing baby carriages interspersed with hulking brutes carrying tommy guns, often the cutouts that popped up in Silhouette City were of Menachem Begin, Golda Meir and other prominent Jews.

CSA was founded in 1976 by Jim Ellison, a fundamentalist preacher from San Antonio, Texas, who moved to the Ozarks after himself undergoing a conversion from ordinary Protestantism to Identity. Apparently drawn to northern Arkansas because that was where Identity patriarch Wesley Swift had begun his crusade, Ellison found many receptive neighbors in nearby towns like Schell City, Missouri, where Dan Gayman runs his own compound called the Church of Israel, and in Harrison, Arkansas, home to Thom Robb, the Identity preacher who claims to be the national chaplain of the Ku Klux Klan. In fact, the Ozark country's combination of beautiful although rugged terrain and a virtually all-white population dedicated to the idea of "live and let live" has, as will be seen, lured a fairly large number of communal movements with a wide variety of orientations to the area where Arkansas and Missouri join. For example, one area commune, which called itself Sassafras, was populated entirely by lesbians who established a "pan-female" cloister in which books were edited to remove male nouns and pronouns and all farm animals were females who were inseminated artificially when more animals were needed. Another commune, located just outside the tourist town of Branson, Missouri, was established by out-of-work country-and-western musicians who hoped to combine talents and produce hit records.

Unlike guitar pickers and lesbians, however, the CSA Survival Rightists were lured at least partly by the location near state lines. In common with Michael Ryan's Rulo farm near the borders of Kansas, Missouri and Nebraska, the CSA's proximity to the Arkansas–Missouri border allowed members to commit crimes in one jurisdiction and then find sanctuary in another. Likewise, when the Order was in its infancy, members took advantage of the fact that Butler's Idaho compound was within a few minutes' drive of either Washington or Montana to commit crimes against ZOG.

Ryan and Ellison shared far more than just a taste for border locations, the Book of Revelation and boorish racism. Like Ryan, the burly, white-bearded Ellison took four wives from among the women who moved to his compound and subjected the men, who often were confined to a separate dormitory, to harsh discipline. Although no evidence collected suggests that CSA ever approached the depths of sadism Ryan visited upon his followers, there were allegations and suspicions that people had been killed behind the fences of Zarepath-Horeb. One FBI affidavit said an unnamed CSA member had told police that the group obtained at least some of its membership by kidnapping hitchhikers. This FBI source charged that at least one of these reluctant Identity converts, a nineteen-year-old woman, had been murdered and her body left alongside an Oklahoma highway. This affidavit and others filed in Arkansas to obtain the search warrant under which the CSA's compound was raided charged that members fanned out from Zarepath-Horeb to commit numerous crimes. There was a bitter irony in this, for the disclosure of the allegations about recruiting members by kidnapping led to speculation among CSA's Ozark neighbors that the Identity movement was dedicated to stealing children for its religious ser-vices—a charge that until then had been made by Identity preachers against Jews. The "blood libel," as Jews call this allegation that has been raised by anti-Semites at least since the Middle Ages, backfired in the Ozarks.

While no kidnapping charges were ever filed, CSA members were convicted of numerous other crimes. Richard Wayne Snell, a CSA adherent, was charged in the 1983 murder of a black Arkansas state trooper who was killed with a weapon altered in the communal gun shop, and Ellison, along with another CSA resident, William Thomas, was charged in the search warrant application with the burning of the Beth Shalom synagogue in Bloomington, Indiana, in August 1983. Ultimately Ellison was convicted on a raft of federal firearms charges, including conspiracy to manufacture, possess and distribute machine guns and silencers, including the one used to murder the trooper. The synagogue attack, the murder and other crimes were cited in the 1987 sedition indictment, which named Snell along with Miles, Butler, Beam and company. Ellison proved a key witness against his former comrades.

At several of Richard Butler's Aryan Congresses, Ellison boasted of CSA's ties to the Posse and of its ability to furnish the needed firepower and other matériel for a white supremacist revolution. CSA, along with the rest of the Survival Right, viewed the death of Posse figure Gordon Kahl as martyrdom and the beginning of the long-anticipated race war. In one widely quoted address to Butler's 1983 Aryan Congress, Ellison said, "I'm sorry I wasn't with Gordon Kahl when they found him. I just wish I'd been there . . . I'm here to tell you that the sword is out of the sheath, and it's ready to strike. For every one of our people they killed, we ought to kill a hundred of theirs."

Perhaps the most chilling discovery in all the investigations that followed the FBI raid on CSA's compound was that the group had been busily manufacturing cyanide compounds for use in poisoning the water supply of an unnamed city, a form of attack that, indeed, would have allowed CSA to kill a hundred and more for every Posse/Identity zealot who had died. The raiders found thirty gallons of raw cyanide in one CSA lab, which is a massive quantity of a poison so deadly that a single drop is more than enough to kill a full-sized adult. It will never be known whether CSA would ever have used the cyanide for mass murder. Certainly, finding the poison in CSA hands dredges up memories of James Jones, who persuaded more than eight hundred members of his religious commune to drink cyanide-laced Kool-Aid.

The final chapter for CSA opened on April 15, 1985, federal income tax deadline day, when Jimmie Linegar, a thirty-one-year-old Missouri state trooper, was assigned to patrol the short stretch of highway between the tourist town of Branson, Missouri, and the Arkansas state line and make a series of random "routine traffic checks" in a state police effort to crack down on traffic ticket scofflaws, tardy vehicle registrations and drunken driving. At 1:45 p.m., Linegar pulled over a brown van driven by David Tate, twenty-two, of Athol, Idaho. Unbeknownst to either Tate or Linegar, just three hours earlier a federal grand jury in Seattle had indicted Tate along with twenty-two others on the racketeering charges that eventually were heard in the long Order trial.

Linegar, the father of two small children, had a reputation among his fellow highway patrol officers of being ultra-cautious. He always wore a bulletproof vest when making traffic stops and took special pains to follow police procedure to the letter, making radio checks of the license plate numbers of each and every vehicle he stopped. Checking the false name on the driver's license that Tate handed him with files in law enforcement computers via his car radio, Linegar was told that the alias was often used by a neo-Nazi named David Tate who was wanted on a federal firearms charge. Quickly, the young trooper radioed his friend Allen Hines, who was making similar traffic checks nearby. Within minutes Hines's squad car rolled onto the scene and the two troopers approached Tate's van.

From boyhood Tate had trained for this very moment. His parents, who were well-to-do dairy farmers, had encouraged him to study judo, karate and other martial arts as a boy and had taken him to services at Butler's church on most Sundays. After high school, Tate had signed on as one of Butler's Aryan "soldiers," rising quickly through the ranks until he was chief of security and in charge of training members in hand-to-hand combat. As seen earlier, Tate and the street-wise ex-convict Gary Yarbrough operated the printing press that was used in the Order's first, abortive counterfeiting scheme. He later participated in the sundry commando raids against armored cars.

Hines was later to recall that as Linegar approached the Chevrolet van, Tate opened the door and smoothly rolled to the ground, clutching a submachine gun to his hip. As the startled trooper reached for his weapon, Tate let loose with a withering burst of submachine-gun fire that sent several slugs slamming into Linegar's bulletproof vest and several others into his unprotected side. As Linegar fell dead onto the tarmac, Tate deftly moved around the vehicle and fired a burst of three rounds that struck Hines in the shoulder, arm and hip. Hines rolled under the van and began shooting at Tate's legs. Tate fled into the dense underbrush and a massive manhunt was launched.

For the next six days Tate lived by his wits in the thickly wooded Ozark countryside, stealing food and clothes as needed and eluding a combined force of FBI SWAT teams, Missouri state police and deputies from at least three counties in Missouri and Arkansas. Armed Cobra gunship helicopters from the Missouri National Guard flew repeated patterns day and night while bloodhounds broke through the brush and FBI agents tried to pick up Tate using sensors aboard a Bureau spy plane capable of detecting living creatures in total darkness by their body heat. Ultimately, Tate, filthy, exhausted and fearful, was captured without a shot being fired in a city park just north of Branson.

By then it was clear that Tate had been en route to the CSA compound, where he hoped to find shelter among like-minded Identity Christians. And it appeared likely that others from the Order who had been indicted in Seattle may have found refuge at Zarepath-Horeb. Hours after police had flashed Tate's picture on area television newscasts, an Arkansas campground owner had called the troopers to say that he had rented space to both Tate and another man, who turned out to be Frank Silva, the California Klan leader who served as keeper of Order message centers during the armored car capers. Silva was arrested in Bentonville, Arkansas, near the point where the borders of Arkansas, Missouri and Oklahoma come together. Searches of Tate's brown 1975 Chevrolet van and a similar vehicle in which Silva was arrested found substantial arsenals, each sufficient to arm one of the minimal racist cell groups that the Order set out to form after disbanding following Matthews's death in the Whidbey Island shoot-out with the same FBI SWAT team that conducted the Tate manhunt and the raid against CSA.

Armed with the Seattle indictment that named Tate, Silva and Rader as well as another frequent visitor to the CSA compound, tax protest leader Ardie McBrearty of Gentry, Arkansas, the FBI SWAT squad took its case into an Arkansas court seeking a search warrant to allow agents to enter Zarepath-Horeb.

Largely as a result of the efforts of B'nai B'rith's Anti-Defamation League to publicize the anti-Semitic orientation of CSA, news media representatives assigned to cover the dramatic Tate manhunt, including the author, also suspected the connection and repeatedly visited the CSA compound to pose questions to the group's spokesman, hulking Kerry Noble, Ellison's confidant.

The meetings with Noble can hardly be described as interviews. A solid chain link gate closed off the dirt road leading up to the CSA compound, and all visitors were greeted by a group of roughly a half dozen obviously frightened and surly young men carrying Mini-14s, MAC 10s and other automatic and semiautomatic weapons. Other armed CSA soldiers were clearly visible in a fifty-foot-tall guard tower overlooking the front gate, from which they pointed machine guns at reporters. Noble, wearing a bowie knife strapped to one leg and cradling a converted AR-15 automatic rifle in his arm, repeatedly came to the gate to spar verbally with the nervous news media. Noble said on one such occasion, "We will not be taken alive. This we vow in the name of Yahweh and of Yoshua, his son and our Lord."

Noble emphatically agreed with an ADL study distributed to news media representatives in which he was quoted as having described CSA saying, "We are Christian survivalists who believe in preparing for the ultimate holocaust."

Likewise, he said, the ADL had quoted CSA accurately when a representative described the group's credo saying, "We believe the Scandinavian-Germanic-Teutonic-British-American people to be the Lost Sheep of the House of Israel which Jesus was sent for." Jews, he repeated for the humming video cameras, "are the seed of Satan, not the seed of God."

While these strange press conferences were underway it was impossible not to notice the large number of buzzards that circled lazily overhead, almost as if they had some foreknowledge that blood soon would spill. And, like the buzzards, FBI commandos congregated on the fringes of the compound. Trim men in spit-shined paratroop boots sat around assault helicopters just out of sight from the CSA guard tower and painted one another's faces in camouflage makeup. An FBI spy plane monitored events from the air.

When the inevitable raid occurred, the press corps was kept more than two miles from the compound gates and was forced to rely on FBI spokesmen for all information. The SWAT teams first stormed the gate and occupied several outbuildings before demanding a general surrender from the CSA inhabitants, who had fled to a complex of four ragtag buildings in the center of the sprawling compound. Happily, after nearly forty-eight hours of negotiations, the CSA stalwarts surrendered en masse, winning as their only concession a promise that Ellison and Noble would not be placed in cells with black prisoners.

As promised when the FBI sought the search warrants, those who filed out of the CSA gate into federal custody included two of the indicted Order members, Randall Evans and Thomas Bentley.

The presence of the Order members inside the CSA compound was further evidence that the most violent components of the American Survival Right remain a closely knit underground. These haters are poised throughout the country to offer shelter, succor and other support to any initiates who work up enough bile and courage to execute the sort of violent attacks against the establishment that Identity preachers equate with virtue. And nowhere is this support network for haters more solidly entrenched than in the rolling hills of the Midwestern tourist mecca known as the Ozarks.

For example, Dan Gayman, one of the original American religious leaders led into the Identity theology by Wesley Swift, Bertrand Comparet, William Potter Gale and company, carefully built the Schell City compound for his Identity Church of Israel by having members purchase property in the church's name until they had control of a 1,000-acre tract on Missouri's Osage River about twenty-four miles from the Kansas–Missouri line.

An investigation of Gayman's compound by the Springfield, Missouri, *News & Leader* found through county property deeds that roughly a dozen Gayman-affiliated families had acquired adjoining farms, then combined forces to establish their own Identity grade school and high school as well as other community institutions.

Operating out of his own fiefdom, Gayman, a former Missouri high school principal, has raised large sums of money selling audio tapes in which he delivers the Identity credo and urges listeners to shed blood in pursuit of the "Emancipation of the White Seed." His monographs, including *For Fear of the Jews*, are best-sellers among the Identity membership of America. In that work, Gayman urged his audience to "penetrate, expose, unveil, and bring to light the truth about Jews, political Zionism, the racial origin of the Jew and the Satanic origin of the religious philosophy called Judaism." A Gayman book, *The Two Seeds of Genesis*, is widely credited with promulgating the key Identity tenet that Satan gave birth to the Jews even as God brought onto the globe the white chosen race known today as Aryans. At Butler's 1979 Aryan Congress, Gayman was the keynote speaker, delivering a talk entitled "The Aryan Warrior's Stand."

Another member of the fraternity of hatred with an Ozark operation is John R. Harrell, whose Christian-Patriots Defense League uses a 220-acre compound on the edge of the Mark Twain National Forest near Licking, Missouri, for Survivalist training sessions. While only an estimated twelve Harrell followers are full-time residents at the Missouri compound, federal investigators have observed as many as a thousand people passing through military training sessions and other events held there each summer. In 1984 Harrell's C-PDL acquired a similar compound in West Virginia near the town of Smithville, which the group called its "Survival Base."

Harrell, affectionately called "Johnny Bob" by his supporters, is a pivotal figure in the Survival Right because of his role in bringing large numbers of people who were involved in such 1960s right-wing movements as the Minutemen and the John Birch Society into the modern-day fold of Identity, anti-Semitism and Survivalism. Today only Butler's Aryan Congresses attract attention among the Survival Right to match the annual Freedom Festivals that Harrell hosts at his fifty-five-acre estate outside Louisville, Illinois.

Harrell began his crusade in 1959 after receiving what he says was a vision from God while a patient for lymph cancer at the Mayo Clinic in Rochester, Minnesota. As a brilliant young businessman in southern Illinois, Harrell had amassed a fortune of several million dollars by the late 1950s selling mausoleums and agricultural real estate. Subsequent literature produced during Harrell's political campaigns and fund-raising efforts tell how the Holy Spirit extracted the cancerous tissue from his body after doctors had declared him a doomed man. The experience changed his life.

Cured of cancer, Harrell dropped out of business, let his hair grow down to his shoulders and ran for the Senate in Illinois in 1960, where he was soundly defeated despite his efforts—and expenditures of personal wealth—to convince voters that a Jewish conspiracy was about to lead to a nuclear war, after which Americans would have to fight for their lives against invading Soviet troops. One Harrell pamphlet, *The Golden Triangle*, tells how God visited George Washington as he was camped at Valley Forge and gave him a vision of a final great war, pitting America against her global enemies, in which the forces of good withdraw into the interior and defend a triangle starting at the Great Lakes and covering the heartland. Harrell told his audiences that it was necessary to raise a private militia and train its members to defend this triangle, which he called the "Mid-American Survival Zone."

Harrell found an easy ally in Robert DePugh, another midwestern self-made millionaire (pharmaceuticals for animals), who had founded the notorious paramilitary Minutemen. DePugh wrote articles in the Minuteman newspaper, *On Target*, urging each citizen to establish a personal "hide" in some remote area in preparation for the coming Soviet invasion. Hides were supposed to be earthen bunkers, ten feet wide and six feet deep, stocked with enough food for thirty days and enough ammunition to allow two latter-day Minuteman soldiers to fight an occupying army for a month. On the subject of which weapons should go into each hide, DePugh wrote in *On Target* on April 1, 1964:

If you are EVER going to buy a gun, BUY IT NOW. The time may come that almost any gun of any caliber will be worth its weight in gold. Still, your life may depend on it, so why not get the best you can possibly afford? We especially recommend the following: Adult males: .30-06 Garands, 7.62 NATO FNs, .30-06 bolt-action Springfields or Enfields, high caliber sporting rifles as desired, 12-gauge double barrel, pump or semi-automatic shotguns. Adult females: Winchester model 100 in .308 caliber, Remington model 742 in .30-06 caliber or 30 caliber military carbines. Older children: sporting rifles in 6 mm, .243, .270, .222 calibers. Younger children: semi-automatic .22 rifles.

Predictably, law enforcement officials took a keen interest in the Minutemen, and several members were arrested after raiders found illegal weapons and silencers in their hides.

In 1961, as DePugh was creating his Minutemen, Harrell had founded the first of several organizations he heads, this one called the Christian Conservative Church, which advocated tax protests, survivalist training and anti-Zionism. Borrowing from the early Identity Jew baiters, Harrell harangued about how the Zionist conspiracy was working furiously behind the scenes to corrupt the morals of America's military forces in preparation for the coming Soviet invasion. One of Harrell's pamphlets with this message found its way into the hands of an eighteen-year-old Marine stationed at Camp Lejeune, North Carolina, and the young man was so taken with the idea of a Jewish-Communist conspiracy to corrupt the morals of America's fighting men that he went AWOL and traveled to Harrell's estate in Clay County, Illinois, where he said he wanted to tell the world of "debauchery, immorality and atheism" in the Marine Corps.

A keen judge of the news media, Harrell went to reporters and vowed that he would protect the defector with his own life. "He'll stay right here with me and they'll take him over my dead body," said Harrell, adding, "We can't spare one cent to fire a bullet at Khrushchev or Castro, but we'll spend billions to break the hearts of young men."

Then, almost twenty-five years before the raid on the CSA compound, Harrell ordered four fifty-foot-high guard towers erected on his property and strung his riflemen along the estate perimeter to meet any invading law officers. Harrell had converted the Louisville estate into an armed compound with fifteen "soldiers" and at least an equal number of "womenfolk."

The raid came shortly after sunup one hot late August day in 1961 when a force of a hundred law officers broke through Harrell's gate with a half-track armored vehicle and took the entire group captive at gunpoint. Harrell later said they hadn't fought because God simply hadn't responded when asked whether they should resist. On the Illinois compound, authorities were to find the traditional Survivalist stores of weapons, food, canned water and at least four underground bunkers along the lines of the hides recommended by DePugh.

Ultimately Harrell served four years in a federal penitentiary for harboring a federal fugitive and for a raft of tax charges filed after he first clashed with the federal officials he was to come to call ZOG. Throughout the long ordeal surrounding his prosecution, DePugh and the Minuteman organization at large remained staunch Harrell allies. On Target, the group's hate sheet with its logo picturing the cross hairs of a telescopic sight, supported Harrell in his fight with the "Red feds," and space was given liberally in the newspaper for Harrell to espouse his views about how God had divinely inspired founding fathers like George Washington, only to have the Semitic sons and daughters of Babylon come along to corrupt American life by amending the Constitution, inaugurating the income tax and enacting government programs designed to encourage mixing of the races and other Communistic mischief.

There soon would come a time when Harrell was to return the Minutemen's favors, a time when he was in a position to help DePugh and other group leaders after they brought the wrath of the federal establishment and public opinion down on their own heads and those of their followers.

For much of the early 1960s, the flamboyant Minutemen had displayed a reckless disregard for popular public taste and conventional wisdom that repeatedly propelled its leaders and membership into the media limelight. In a country just emerging from the peaceful if dull post-World War II Eisenhower decade, the talk of stockpiling freeze-dried food, silencers and other survival gear for use in a war against invading forces was strange enough to win DePugh and company copious media attention. With American high school students writing endless essays about the moral dilemma of deciding whether to share one's fallout shelter and food with one's less prepared neighbors, DePugh's rhetoric and conspiracy theorizing were, at least, relevant to the topic of the day. But, as DePugh himself was to recall later, the Minutemen went too far.

Within months of the November 22, 1963, assassination of President John F. Kennedy by telescopic rifle in Dallas, DePugh stunned much of the country by reprinting as posters a challenge to the federal establishment that had first run on the front page of *On Target* shortly before the assassination. The statement attacked twenty members of Congress for a vote that the Minutemen decided would lead to the abolition of the House Committee on Un-American Activities.

The copy read in part: "Traitors, beware! Even now the cross hairs are on the back of your necks . . ." At the bottom of the text was a headline reading "IN MEMORIAM," followed by the names of the twenty lawmakers targeted by the group.

With films of John Kennedy's violent assassination a very fresh memory in the minds of nearly all Americans, the *On Target* ad about "cross hairs on the back of your necks" was an ultimate expression of bad taste. It also was a reminder that no matter how enlightened the body politic may have seemed, American society still included the same sort of fanatics that had made Hitler's ascent possible in Germany.

DePugh recalled later how he had hungrily sought out publicity after the assassination. He reasoned—rightly enough—that even the most negative publicity at least served to inform millions of Americans that groups like the Minutemen existed, and that these groups were always seeking new members.

The December 1, 1963, issue of *On Target* said of the assassination: "Now that John F. Kennedy is dead, we can expect to hear millions of words about his greatness. Even his most bitter political enemies will praise him. We will not be hypocrites—we will not soon forget that he ignored the best interests of his country from the day he took the oath of office to the day he died. Still, very little is really changed. The 'power behind the throne' remains the same as before."

In the months following the Kennedy assassination, the Minutemen frequently put up their posters with the cross-hair logo reading:

> See the old man at the corner where you buy your paper? He may have a silencer-equipped pistol under his coat. That extra fountain pen in the pocket of the insurance salesman that calls on you might be a cyanide-gas gun. What about your milkman? Arsenic works slow but sure. Your auto mechanic may stay up nights studying booby traps.
>
> These patriots are not going to let you take their freedom away from them. They have learned the silent knife, the strangler's cord, the target rifle that hits sparrows at 200 yards. Only their leaders restrain them.
>
> Traitors, beware! Even now the cross hairs are on the back of your necks . . ."

TV cameras and newspaper reporters focused great attention on this group of self-styled patriots. DePugh's voluminous writings about how white people would soon have to take up arms and fight guerrilla wars against their black neighbors captured the imagination of many news organizations where editors were eager to document just how the traditional white majority was reacting to the emergence of formerly disenfranchised blacks as a political force. Left-leaning circles eagerly seized upon the hyperbole espoused by the Minutemen as living proof of the dangerous nature of the political right.

Meanwhile, James Garrison, the volatile prosecutor in New Orleans, captured the headlines with a number of pronouncements that he had uncovered a conspiracy behind the Kennedy assassination, including evidence that the triggerman, Lee Harvey Oswald, was a member of the heavily armed extremists known as Minutemen.

The Minuteman theory was but one of many that the prosecutor was to cite in his long and generally discredited probes of the assassination, but the resulting heat from officialdom was so intense that DePugh and his inner circle were swept into virtual oblivion. From Colorado to Seattle, Kansas to North Carolina, Minutemen were arrested on charges ranging from conspiracy to rob banks to planning to slip gallons of cyanide into the air conditioners at the United Nations. As in the investigations into the Order, prosecutors charged that various Minutemen had robbed banks to finance their political activity and that many group members had been assigned prominent assassination targets, including President Johnson and former Supreme Court Justice and UN Ambassador Arthur Goldberg. It was found that top confidants of DePugh, such as Wally Peyson, had made repeated trips to California, where they studied Identity Christianity at the feet of Wesley Swift, then took the message back to group headquarters in Norborne, Missouri. Minuteman ties to the neo-Nazis were dramatized in an interview by Kansas City journalist and author J. Harry Jones, Jr., with George Lincoln Rockwell in March 1967, just five months before Rockwell's assassination. The neo-Nazi confirmed to Jones that the Minutemen had recruited dozens of his members and had won over three of his best financial supporters. "I'm all for what the Minutemen stand for," Rockwell told Jones. "People should be armed and prepared to defend themselves."

DePugh himself went to federal prison in 1968 for numerous firearms and conspiracy charges. In the Virginia suburbs of Washington, D.C., Rockwell was gunned down by a trusted lieutenant in a laundromat. Clearly, being identified as a neo-Nazi or as a Minuteman was the kiss of death, and many sycophants slipped out of the public view to embrace such less visible credos as that of the Posse Comitatus or that preached by Harrell, who by this time was out of prison and back in his Louisville, Illinois, compound ready to fill the void in Survival Right leadership.

Harrell operated four organizations to keep the Identity/Survivalist movement viable. First was his Christian Conservative Church of America, which states as its purpose "to blend Christianity and Patriotism together to effectively oppose Zionism and Communism." The political group, the Christian-Patriots Defense League, uses the hyphen to emphasize that its members can be either practicing members of Identity or just secular patriots. The compounds in West Virginia and Licking, Missouri, operate as part of C-PDL's Citizens Emergency Defense System, a private militia. Finally, the Paul Revere Club is the group's fund-raising arm.

Roughly twice each year these groups join forces for C-PDL Freedom Festivals at the Louisville facility. The centerpiece of Harrell's fenced establishment is the mansion, a replica of George Washington's house at Mount Vernon built to a scale 10 percent larger than the original. Federal law enforcement documents estimate that many of the Freedom Festivals draw crowds of upwards of a thousand persons, who are allowed to camp or park their recreational vehicles in the wooded areas alongside the Wabash River on the compound grounds.

Like Butler's sessions, Harrell's festivals center on Identity sermonizing, paramilitary seminars and sales of survival gear, literature and other items. One IRS document lists typical seminars at C-PDL sessions as: "Handgun Use for Personal Defense," "Concealment of Valuables and Weaponry," "Archery, Crossbow, Black Powder Guns," "Street Action" and "Knife Fighting."

As seen earlier, the Covenant, the Sword and the Arm of the Lord was particularly active at these festival training sessions, with commando experts like Randall Rader conducting firearms classes, while the commune's leaders, Jim Ellison and Kerry Noble, delivered Identity sermons. One prominent Identity preacher who is a fixture at the Harrell sessions is Colonel Jack Mohr, author of a work quoted earlier, *Know Your Enemies!* A distinguished Korean War combat veteran, Mohr was a member of the John Birch Society's National Speakers' Bureau before parting company with the Birchers after some members complained about his anti-Jewish focus. Mohr then signed on as national military commander of C-PDL.

Nobody knows just how many Survival Right compounds exist in America today. It's not the sort of thing noted on census forms, so news accounts remain virtually the only source of information and such secondhand material often doesn't clearly indicate the ideology of the group in question.

A group with many similarities to Identity congregations called the Church of the Living Word operates a twenty-acre compound near Pineville, Missouri, in the state's extreme southwest corner.

Sympathizers of the Order are said to be living on a 160-acre tract of land in southern Missouri purchased with funds stolen in the West Coast armored car robberies for a paramilitary training camp.

Likewise, there are reports that a communal religious group called Elohim City, in the Ozark foothills near Stillwell, Oklahoma, is another paramilitary Identity/Survivalist operation. When the federal SWAT team swooped down on the CSA compound, FBI officials noted that persons inside Zarepath-Horeb had also lived at Elohim City. After one alienated husband complained in court that his wife had taken his children illegally to live in the Elohim City compound, Sheriff Russell Neff of Adair County, Oklahoma, said that he couldn't find any children on the property but he did note that he saw many men carrying semiautomatic rifles. Dan Irwin, the husband who filed the complaint but never got his children back, told the Kansas City *Star*, "They claim to be a Christian group but there is an underlying hatred of Jews and blacks."

In the spring of 1986 yet another Oklahoma Survival Right compound blazed into the headlines as the result of publicity given to efforts by a small-town Georgia bank and a rural sheriff to evict a black farmer from his land near Cochran, Georgia. *People* magazine had devoted a major takeout to the plight of Oscar Lorick, a hardworking man who had given his life to tilling the harsh red clay soil of Georgia only to have his small farm and meager savings threatened when he couldn't repay the local bank.

Other than the fact that he was a black man, Lorick was in a fix identical to that of so many heartlanders who have adopted the Posse Comitatus/Identity Christian solution to their woes. The case captured the imagination of the latest in the pantheon of Identity leaders, thirty-two-year-old Larry Humphreys of Velma, Oklahoma, scion of the locally prominent—and very rich—Humphreys family, which made its money in banking and oil. The large lake north of Velma where townspeople take their boats for happy summer outings is Lake Humphreys.

Blessed with an inheritance of at least $5 million, Larry Humphreys created his personal Survival Right compound on 300 acres of ranchland on the very edge of Velma. There is a sturdy fence protecting the property, and an 1,800-foot airstrip for Humphreys's airplane and those of visitors. The place is called Heritage Library, and large sections of the cathedral-domed mansion that dominates the grounds are given over to a 25,000-volume library of literature bearing on Identity religion as well as what is said to be valuable source material about the German Nazi era. In front of the mansion Humphreys flies the twelve flags of the "Aryan nations" that Identity adherents view as the twelve tribes of Israel. Most of the books are stored in a wing of the building named for Gordon Kahl.

The Heritage Library also advertises a legal research service to help "patriots" file Posse-style "pro se" lawsuits challenging the income tax, denying obligations to repay farm loans, etc. After the CSA raid, Humphreys acknowledged that his organization had purchased weapons from the commune's gun shop.

In the 1986 congressional elections Humphreys won the Republican nomination and ran a "Republican/populist" campaign against the incumbent Democrat, Representative Dave McCurdy, in which Humphreys called for banks to declare a "land sabbath" in which all farm debts would be forgiven. The story about Oscar Lorick in *People* magazine provided Humphreys with an ideal opportunity to flex some Identity muscle and to bolster his own political fortunes.

The day before Sheriff Ed Coley of Bleckley County, Georgia, was to serve foreclosure papers on Lorick, Humphreys and an estimated fifty followers wearing camouflage clothing and sporting semiautomatic weapons moved onto the property and covered the farmhouse windows with posters denouncing "ZOG." When the sheriff arrived with a badly outnumbered contingent of deputies, Humphreys's group began firing their semiautomatics into Lorick's haystack to dramatize their firepower. One of the shooters declared, "We won't fire until fired upon, but if we are fired upon, heaven help the men on the other side." The sheriff and his deputies left the farm without serving papers, and that evening the lawman held a press conference to announce that a deal had been made between Lorick and the bank to allow the embattled farmer more time to raise money to pay off the loan.

As Jeffrey Yitzak Santis, plains states director for the Anti-Defamation League of B'nai B'rith, put it in an interview, "We don't know just how significant this Humphreys thing is going to be. He certainly brought the far right a big victory in Georgia and that worries us. Until he came along they didn't have many victories."

The emergence of Humphreys as a fresh new force illustrates that the Survival Right will outlive its founding fathers, such as the elderly World War II veteran William Potter Gale and the badly aging Richard Girnt Butler.

Butler's compound, which was the forerunner of the rest, has been described at length earlier. It bears repeating, however, that unless one knew that the deeply rutted gravel road that leads up a tree-covered hill to Butler's gate was the Aryan Nations' driveway, it would look just like the entrance to any of the ramshackle farms that surround Butler's bastion. In fact, local leaders like Sandy Emerson, director of the nearby Coeur d'Alene Chamber of Commerce, recalled that until the neo-Nazis started seeking publicity, most residents of the area "had no idea these dangerous people were in our midst." The point is that nobody really knows how many of the rutted dirt roads of rural America lead up to the gates of Survivalist compounds.

And it bears noting, as well, that Survival Right activists are far more widespread than is indicated by those who choose to live out their hatred behind barbed wire and guard towers. In addition to the compound dwellers, there are the lone wolves, Survivalist men and women who react to the prospects of Armageddon with varying degrees of strangeness, but with a chilling commonality as well. Whenever the lone wolves surface, somebody gets hurt.

*The goyim are a flock of sheep, and we are their wolves.
And you know what happens when the wolves get hold
of the flock?*
　　　—*The Protocols of the Learned Elders of Zion*

6: Lone Wolves

If ever there was a lone wolf stalking the streets of America it was
David Lewis Rice in Seattle on Christmas Eve of 1985 when he
used a carving knife and a steam iron to stab and bludgeon to death
Charles Goldmark, forty-one, his wife, Annie, forty-three, and their
two sons, Derek, twelve, and Colin, ten, while the boys' stockings
hung at the fireplace and a Christmas ham baked in the oven.

Until the carnage at the Goldmark house, the holidays had been
a welcome respite for Seattle from talk of hatred, a breather after
months of daily headlines about the bizarre disclosures that had
unfolded in the city's federal courthouse as prosecutors made their
case against the Order. That case now was in the hands of the jury,
and Judge Walter McGovern had sent those jurors home to spend
Christmas with their families before completing their complex de-
liberations.

But not everyone shared in the holiday spirit. Gaunt at six feet
two and 155 pounds, with a long, unkempt black beard and scraggles
of shoulder-length hair, David Rice was on a mission from Yahweh
as the sun set on December 24. He wore camouflage clothing and
carried a toy gun and two real sets of handcuffs as he slipped quietly

157

through the streets of Seattle's upper-class Madrona neighborhood toward the Goldmark family's $200,000 house on a Lake Washington hillside.

At 7 p.m., Rice knocked at the Goldmarks' wreath-draped door carrying a white package. One of the boys, it's not clear which one, answered and, when told the package was for Charles Goldmark, summoned his father and his brother. Rice then pulled his real-looking toy pistol and ordered all three upstairs, where Annie Goldmark was taking a shower. Goldmark, a senior partner in one of Seattle's most prominent law firms, tried to stave off his murderer by offering him money, but he had only fourteen dollars and change in his pockets. So he gave Rice his plastic bank card and told him the number he needed to withdraw money from the machines of Seattle's Seafirst Bank.

"Honey," Charles Goldmark called to his wife, "put on a robe and come out."

Rice forced the four Goldmarks to lie on the floor and cuffed Charles's and Annie's hands behind their backs. Then he tied the boys' hands behind them.

Next, he removed a bottle of chloroform and a rag from his pocket and moved from family member to family member, knocking each out.

"Oh," said Annie Goldmark just before going under, "he's going to kill us."

Rice's lawyers, who pleaded him not guilty by reason of insanity, later were to argue unsuccessfully that their client was so unbalanced and so suggestible that those words from Annie Goldmark convinced him to kill.

Rice knew he had twenty minutes before any of the family revived—he had tested the anesthetic on himself the day before. He went to the kitchen, retrieved a long-bladed carving knife and a heavy steam iron and returned to the bedroom, where he moved among the supine family stabbing and bludgeoning. Then, his clothes drenched in blood, Rice fled. Annie died immediately of a stab wound to the heart. Charles and his boys were found within an hour of the assault by friends who had been invited to the house for a traditional Christmas Eve ham dinner. All three were taken to Harborview Hospital, where, over the next thirty-seven days, one after another died of massive head injuries, even though doctors succeeded in treating the sadistic stab wounds inflicted by their assailant.

As the Goldmarks lay bleeding and dying that Christmas Eve night, Rice drove his dilapidated Volkswagen to a Seafirst Bank automatic teller and was photographed trying to withdraw funds from Goldmark's account using the stolen card and the wrong account number. In his terror Charles Goldmark had given Rice his personal bank card, but had told him the code for his law firm's business account. Within a day those photos would lead to Rice's arrest.

Later Rice would tell a Seattle magazine writer that he acted as he did because he had just read an article by Colonel Jack Mohr reporting that 30,000 Communist Chinese troops were poised over the Canadian border and 40,000 North Korean troops hovered just across the Mexican border, "waiting for the final word from the Federal Reserve to take over." Kenneth Muscatel, court-appointed clinical psychologist, later would conclude that Rice was obsessed about Communists, the Federal Reserve, international bankers and his perception that there are foreign troops just over the border of Canada and Mexico ready to shoot American citizens. "He indicates that his actions with the Goldmarks was the first step in a final war and thus, he saw himself as a soldier," wrote Muscatel in his report to the court. "Sometimes, he said, soldiers have to kill."

For months before the Goldmark tragedy, Rice, a twenty-seven-year-old unemployed salesman, had attended meetings of the ultra-right "Duck Club" chapter on Pike Street in Seattle, where members munched on cookies and discussed the Order trial, which was underway just up the hill at the federal courthouse.

The Duck Club was a nationwide Survival Right movement that blossomed in the waning days of the Carter administration and the early Reagan years as the result of the tireless efforts and expenditure of considerable personal wealth by Robert White, a Cocoa Beach, Florida, millionaire. White started his project by producing a strange publication called the *Duck Book,* crammed with the same old warnings of an international Jewish conspiracy by bankers, tips about surviving the approaching Armageddon and more warnings about how the Trilateral Commission and the Council on Foreign Relations were engineering the downfall of America. The publication was filled with small cartoon drawings of a duck. Sometimes the duck would be in a plane strafing the Russian Bear, other times it would be out to recapture the Panama Canal or flying a B-1 bomber over the Middle East oil fields.

White later insisted that he used the comical duck simply because he liked the birds, but others reminisced about the famous motto of America's prototypical exponent of the international Communist conspiracy, the late Senator Joe McCarthy, who liked to remind his audiences, "If it looks like a duck and walks like a duck and flies like a duck and quacks like a duck, then it's probably a duck."

One cartoon in White's *Duck Book* carries the caption: "Stop Rockefeller's peanut farmer puppet and his Marxist superbrain advisers before they turn our country into a complete socialist welfare state for their one world government crap."

Another asked: "When are you 'ducks' going to wake up and realize nothing has changed in Washington, except the puppets? Haig and Weinberger are giving you that same crap that Brzezinski and Brown gave you. They have Reagan boxed in even more than they had Carter. Don't you realize there's more of Rocky's Trilateralist pimps surrounding Reagan than Carter?"

The Duck movement received widespread national news media attention in 1981 when White went public with his plans to use the old Ponzi chain-letter scheme to build membership in his far-right Duck Clubs. He sent 50,000 sample copies of the *Duck Book* to names culled from other far-right group mailing lists. White offered each of them a lifetime subscription to the monthly in exchange for ten dollars and the name of a friend who was willing to make the same deal for supplying ten dollars and a third name and so on. White claimed to have distributed 500,000 copies of the publication in that fashion and, at his peak, boasted of having 1,000 Duck Club chapters around the country.

Inspired by what he heard at the Seattle Duck Club chapter, Rice decided to eliminate the "head Jew," the "top Communist," in the Pacific Northwest on the eve of the birthday of Jesus Christ, he later told reporters. Rice never explained, however, why he thought that the Protestant Goldmarks with their home decked out in full Christmas finery and a ham cooking in the oven were Jewish.

Later court sessions were to document how Rice attacked Goldmark because of a long-standing animosity by the Survival Right against Goldmark's late father. Psychologists, prosecutors and others at the Rice murder trial explained at length how the Goldmark family had been targeted for the simple reason that Charles was the son of one of the most legendary liberals in the history of the Pacific Northwest, the late John Goldmark.

In the early 1960s John Goldmark had tangled with the Pacific Northwest's right-wing establishment in a nationally celebrated libel trial. That lawsuit sought damages from a local newspaper that had charged that Goldmark was a Communist because he had married a former Communist and because his son, Charles, attended a college where a major Communist figure once had been a speaker. ("If it walks like a duck and quacks like a duck . . .") The case of Goldmark versus the Tonasket *Tribune* et al. played a major role in blocking the far right from its once popular strategy of guilt by association, under which a person was condemned as a traitor simply for associating with people who had, in turn, associated with individuals deemed to be Communists or otherwise enemies of the United States.

A child of Eastern wealth, John Goldmark attended Quaker schools and exclusive Haverford College before going on to Harvard Law School, where he edited the *Law Review* and graduated with honors in 1941. While a student he met and married Sally Ringe, the daughter of a German immigrant, who had been forced to drop out of medical school when her father went bankrupt during the Great

Depression. As Sally Goldmark later explained in testimony before the House Committee on Un-American Activities (HUAC), she reacted to her bitter reversal by joining the Communist Party. She said that shortly after meeting John, she had rejected the ideology and canceled her Communist membership.

Later the couple would proudly point out that HUAC had sent Sally a letter thanking her for her cooperation in helping Congress understand the evolution of the Communist Party in America. They also noted that John was given a top secret Navy clearance after explaining the same issue to his commanding officers during World War II.

The Goldmark family legend continues with John writing Sally from the Pacific suggesting that they abandon the plans they had made to join the Washington, D.C., world of politics and law and instead move to the Cascade region of Washington State, where they could become ranchers among neighbors "less twisted up in tradition, class and inhibitions." In 1946 Sally and John bundled up two-year-old Chuck and moved from Alexandria, Virginia, onto a 5,000-acre ranch and wheat farm near Tonasket in north-central Washington about twenty-five miles south of the Canadian border, a region called Okanogan, the name given to the nearby mountains in the Cascade Range by Indians.

A decade later, in 1956, John ran as a Democrat for the state legislature from the predominantly Republican Okanogan country and won. Over the next six years Goldmark rose in the legislature to the powerful post of chairman of the House Ways and Means Committee.

In the election campaign of 1962, however, the Tonasket *Tribune* printed stories about Sally's past membership in the Communist Party. The paper added that John himself was a member of the American Civil Liberties Union, identified as a Communist front by both the *Tribune*'s editor and the John Birch Society. Further, added the newspaper, Goldmark's son, Charles, had attended Reed College in Oregon, where Communist Party U.S.A. secretary Gus Hall had been invited to speak. ("If it walks like a duck and quacks like a duck . . .") In Spokane, the editors of a hate sheet called *The Vigilante* reprinted the *Tribune*'s charges and embellished on them.

In November, John Goldmark was trounced at the polls, losing his House seat by a margin of 3 to 1. Bitter at his loss and outraged at the unfairness of the cause of it, Goldmark filed his libel suit, which was heard in a rustic county courthouse and received nationwide news media coverage. With the abuses of the McCarthy era fresh in mind, the trial was perceived as a court test of the guilt-by-association tactics still being used to great effect by the Wisconsin senator's spiritual heirs.

Goldmark won a $40,000 judgment, but it was later overturned. He then declared the trial a moral victory and resigned permanently from politics. Thrown from a horse in the late 1960s, Goldmark spent years of anguish undergoing hip surgery and therapy before dying of cancer in 1979. Sally died of emphysema in 1984.

Meanwhile, Charles followed in his father's footsteps, graduating from Yale Law School and serving an Army tour at the Pentagon, where he reportedly was assigned as a liaison with the Central Intelligence Agency, reports that the elder Goldmark later greeted simply with a smile. Sally took great delight in the thought of her son working with "those old right-wingers."

Charles Goldmark went on to become a paradigm of the new breed of affluent liberal-minded conservationists who flourish in the good life of the Pacific Northwest. On a trip to Europe for a student conference he had met his future wife, Annie, a French citizen assigned to act as Goldmark's interpreter. She made a point of raising their two boys, Colin and Derek, as fluent speakers of both French and English.

An avid mountain climber, Charles Goldmark was the subject of news features about his climbing exploits in the South American Andes, where he and a law partner, world-class climber James Wickwire, once conquered 22,834-foot Mount Aconcagua. In 1984 Goldmark attended the Democratic National Convention as a Gary Hart delegate.

Heir to John Goldmark's ranch and fortune, and a senior partner in the downtown Seattle firm of Wickwire, Lewis, Goldmark and Schorr, as well as athletic and adventurous, Charles appeared to be on the brink of following his father into some sort of political role.

It all proved too much to take for the ideological heirs of John Goldmark's opponents from the Birchite era such as Homer Brand, president of the Seattle Duck Club chapter. The court-appointed psychologist, Dr. Muscatel, reported that Rice told him he learned about Goldmark from Brand, who had described Goldmark as the "regional director of the Communist Party." Brand responded by telling reporters that he "vaguely" remembered telling Rice about Goldmark.

Muscatel explained that Rice had been initiated into the Duck Club by a naturopathic physician named Anne Davis, who spoke of the Survival Right's distrust of the traditional American medical establishment and treated Rice for chain smoking with a regime that included drinking nicotine solutions instead of smoking. At the time of the murders Rice was living in Davis's apartment.

A tersely worded affidavit filed by Seattle police seeking a search warrant for Davis's apartment said Rice had told officers he killed the family "out of his belief that Goldmark was a Communist and Jewish." Further, said the warrant, Rice was carrying "papers and writings on Communism and Judaism and pertaining to the Gold-mark family."

Rice himself said he had listened and read since late summer as paid media commentators chewed over the issues raised at the Order trial. In one jailhouse interview he told of working for a Jewish wholesaler in Arizona. "It was then that I discovered what Jews can do to you," said Rice, wearing red prison coveralls that were cavernous when draped over his emaciated frame. "Jews think Gentiles are less than animals. He had me lifting 300- to 400-pound stoves all day for $3.50 an hour. Once he said he'd give me a stove if I could guess the weight. I guessed 385 pounds. He weighed it and said it was 385½ pounds, and he wouldn't give it to me, and he laughed at me for being so stupid."

Rice said he learned about a Jewish conspiracy when invited to attend Duck Club meetings. "I'd listen when they talked. 'Shut your mouth and open your eyes,' I always say." On the basis of what he heard, he decided he would be "proud to die for my country."

When he was contacted by the Seattle news media after Rice surfaced that violent Christmas Eve, Robert White said that he had stopped printing the magazines on a monthly basis in 1982 and that only a handful of his 1,000 Duck Clubs remained, largely in California, and, of course, one in Seattle.

The day after the tragedy in Madrona, Rice dropped by Duck Club president Brand's house. "Hey, Homer," said Rice with a grin, "it's me. The cops are after me. They could be arriving any minute. I've just dumped the top Communist. There were four involved."

At the trial Brand explained that he hadn't heard of the Goldmark murders and assumed Rice was once more indulging in his Survivalist daydreams. Brand recalled how Rice often would dress up in camouflage clothing and urge the Duck Club to engage in paramilitary tactics, tactics which Brand denied ever adopting.

Like so many other mainstream Americans who learn of the emergence of the Survival Right when violence suddenly erupts in their midst, people in Seattle groped for an answer. Why did it happen?

Certainly, David Lewis Rice was a badly troubled man, an ill-educated loner with enough evidence of bizarre behavior that even prosecutors acknowledged that his personality was "schizoid and paranoid." But psychologists also deemed him capable of distinguishing right from wrong, and of functioning in the workaday world. In 1986 the judge and jury agreed that Rice was legally sane, found him guilty and sentenced him to death for the four murders.

Born into a construction worker's family in Durango, Colorado, in 1958, Rice had followed his father from job to job throughout the Southwest as a child. As a four-year-old he had run through a sliding glass door, scarring his face and leaving him blinded in the right eye. His other eye was badly burned in a welding accident in his late teens, and doctors explained that it was his eye problems that gave him the eerie haunted look so dramatic in photos and television appearances.

Trying to explain his background, relatives said that he had attempted suicide at the age of ten and then suffered through his early teens as a figure of ridicule among his classmates because of his appearance. By the age of twelve, he was disfigured, blind in one eye, and at nearly six feet tall he was also the skinniest kid in his school. His sister-in-law told the jury that Rice had been a loner and that despite his size he "let smaller people hit on him, without doing anything about it."

He managed to finish two years of high school before dropping out. In a short marriage he fathered a son, then joined the Navy, but was released during boot camp with an honorable discharge for unstated reasons. After a few years of jobs in sales and as a menial laborer, as he described his job in Arizona lifting stoves, in 1982 Rice arrived in Seattle, where he moved in and out of shelters and held several part-time jobs before moving in with naturopath Davis and joining the Duck Club.

He was, in short, just another of the millions of American losers who wander the streets and countryside in unhappy confusion—people who, as the old commercial for patent medicine used to say, are "not sick enough to stay in bed, but not really well."

Eric Scigliano, a Seattle writer, came up with an explanation for Rice's horrible actions that can be applied to many of the denizens of the Survival Right dealt with earlier—the Michael Ryans, Bruce Carroll Pierces, David Tates and others who have let their hatred and politics carry them over the line separating ideology and murder. Scigliano called it "the Smerdyakov defense."

Smerdyakov was the dull-witted and unbalanced half brother of Dmitri, Ivan and Alexei Karamazov in Dostoevsky's classic novel of patricide and guilt, *The Brothers Karamazov*. While his half brothers endure humiliations and loss of their property at the hands of their loutish father, Feodor Pavlovich Karamazov, Smerdyakov listens to them speak of hatred and of their wish that the overbearing old man were dead. Ivan particularly talks at length about killing their father. But Ivan, an educated and religious man, albeit given to nihilism, never acts on his words.

Born as the result of Feodor Karamazov's drunken rape of a village idiot girl who died in childbirth, Smerdyakov repelled his half brothers in childhood by his taste for hanging cats, then holding full-blown funerals for the animals. Sent to Moscow to study cooking while his half brothers received university training befitting aristocrats, Smerdyakov listens from the wings as Ivan vents his hatred of the old man before the others. Finally, Smerdyakov slays his and Ivan's father with a brass pestle. He then frames another brother, Dmitri, for the murder and commits suicide after telling Ivan that Ivan is the real murderer because it was his continual nihilistic prattle that convinced Smerdyakov to act.

The court psychologist, Dr. Muscatel, reported how Rice had told him in some interviews that he had been told by "friends" from "outer space" to kill the Goldmarks. But Muscatel found instead that "most of the delusional material turned out to be information that he [Rice] found in actual pamphlets and publications, and information that he discussed with and found support in from some of the important individuals in his life." The incessant hate-filled rhetoric of the Survival Right provided the same impetus for David Lewis Rice as had the ravings of Ivan Karamazov that spurred Smerdyakov.

"The point is," wrote Muscatel, "that Mr. Rice did not cook up this stuff by himself, out of touch with society . . . Rather he belonged to a subgroup of individuals who believed in and supported these ideas. In fact, these people validated these ideas as rational and important. In this regard, I think these people share at least a moral responsibility for what happened."

In *The Brothers Karamazov*, Dostoevsky concludes, "We are all responsible for all," a particularly poignant observation of a netherworld in which people such as the members of the Order decide to act out the hatreds being expressed by those around them. Robert Jay Matthews decided to do something after tiring of Richard Butler's failure to translate into action the neo-Nazi rhetoric spouted at the Hayden Lake compound. Similarly, Michael Ryan moved onto the Stice farm to put into practice the hatred he learned from the rantings of Posse Comitatus leader James Wickstrom, just as members of the Covenant, the Sword and the Arm of the Lord slipped out of their compound to murder and steal in furtherance of the prattle they heard from elders Jim Ellison and Kerry Noble.

All across today's Survival Right landscape, strange people react to the talk of conspiracy, anti-Semitism, Armageddon and associated themes with disastrous results for the people living about them. Consider the spring day in 1986 when David and Doris Young bombed the elementary school in Cokeville, Wyoming, as their plan to raise money to start an Aryan "new race" backfired. What voices had they heard that prompted them to attempt the strange crime in which both died after Doris detonated a crude but effective gasoline bomb in a classroom where she huddled with 167 people, most of them schoolchildren?

Cokeville is a tiny Mormon community of 515 people at the extreme southwestern edge of Wyoming, just across the point where the Utah, Idaho and Wyoming borders intersect. Once again the Survival Right was to play out one of its tragedies at a border site.

On May 16, 1986, the Youngs drove up to the front of the red brick Cokeville elementary school in a van loaded with a staggering arsenal of more than fifty-five rifles, pistols and other weapons, several of which the local sheriff would later trace to members of the Posse Comitatus. Stuffed in the ammo cases and scattered about the floor of the van were numerous diaries written by both David, forty-two, and Doris, forty-seven, outlining their plans to commit a crime they called "the Biggie" in order to finance an effort to establish a "new race."

Shortly after the school lunch period the Youngs burst through the school doors brandishing firearms and wheeling a bomb rigged out of two one-gallon jugs of gasoline strapped to an ordinary wire grocery cart and armed with an electrical trigger connected to a wooden clothespin wired to the cart handle.

Guns are so commonplace in the isolated area around Cokeville that the few people who saw the couple wheeling their arsenal into the school simply assumed it was some sort of program related to hunting safety, explained one of the witnesses, Delbert Rentfro, a member of the town council. "We have these kinds of programs on civil defense and gun safety all the time," Rentfro said. He added that one of the teachers saw Doris walking down the hall with an armload of rifles and pistols and asked her if she could bring her class to the show. "Doris said, 'Yes,' " recalled Rentfro.

Then David Young shouted, "You're going to be the new race," and they herded the terrified children along with their teachers into a single ground-floor classroom with alphabet posters over the blackboard and American and Wyoming flags in the corner. David marked out a ten-foot-wide square with masking tape on the floor in the center of the room and Doris wheeled the bomb into the square. They told their hostages that she would set the bomb off if anybody crossed the line. Then David left to broadcast his demands from the nearby school office.

The demands consisted of $300 million in ransom and a talk with President Reagan.

Max Excell, principal of the grade school, recalled acting as intermediary between Young and the law enforcement officers who quickly cordoned off the school after the takeover. "He talked about the new race and taxes and he said over and over that they were revolutionaries who were going to start their own world where the race could begin," said Excell in an interview the day after the tragic siege ended.

As David Young talked to Excell and to police officials who telephoned the school, Doris stood in the center of the classroom with one hand holding the clothespin to keep the two bomb trigger wires from touching and sang to the children cowering on their side of the masking-tape square.

She sang "Happy Birthday" to one little boy, then launched into a version of "The Teddy Bears' Picnic." She also assured the group that her husband "wouldn't hurt us, because children are too precious," one hostage, twelve-year-old Heidi Roberts, told reporters.

The next day, seven-year-old Mike Thompson, one of the children held captive, stood alongside his small bike on the school grounds and told the author, "She seemed like a nice lady at first."

For nearly three hours the people packed into the ordinary-sized classroom endured a nightmare of sobbing children, several of whom threw up out of terror. Young allowed one teacher to bring in a rack of books from the library and to wheel a TV set into the room in hopes that the afternoon cartoon shows would distract the frightened children.

But at roughly 3 p.m., Jean Mitchell, the first-grade teacher, in whose classroom the group huddled, walked to the masking-tape boundary and said, "I have a headache."

"I do too," said Doris. Then she added, "Okay, let's have some quiet time," and turned away from Mitchell.

When she turned, Doris Young's grip on the clothespin slipped and the bomb detonated with terrible force. Doused with burning gasoline, terrified and traumatized, the 167 captives, 150 children and 17 teenagers and adults, jumped through the windows onto the lawn outside.

David Young, who had stepped into the boys' lavatory to relieve himself, looked into the inferno and saw his wife writhing on the blackened floor horribly injured by the blast. An expert marksman, he fired two .44 caliber pistol shots into Doris's brain, ending her suffering. Then David Young held the weapon to his own temple and ended the nightmare in Cokeville.

Of the 167 held captive, 78 were treated at hospitals in Wyoming, Utah and Idaho for burns. Of them 21 were admitted for treatment of severe burns. One teacher had been slightly wounded by a gunshot in the shoulder early in the siege. Many of the children will bear the ugly scars—both mental and physical—for life, but nobody except David and Doris Young died.

Nine years earlier, in 1977, David Young had been the Cokeville town marshal, the single law enforcement officer in the tiny hamlet. Cokeville's mayor, John Dayton, recalled in an interview that Young had been nicknamed "Wyatt Earp" by the locals because he persisted in strutting up and down Cokeville's single street wearing a gun-slinger's six-shooter in a quick-draw holster tied to his thigh with a thong of buckskin.

Wyoming investigators were to learn that David Young was highly intelligent—an IQ of 180 with almost straight A's in college. Moving from town to town taking jobs as a peace officer, he had also been the law in tiny Loup City, Nebraska, and the man with the star in Mountain Home, Idaho, as well as marshal in Cokeville.

Power to the county. Posse Comitatus. David Young agreed that the local lawman should be considered the highest form of government. And he agreed that God's chosen people, the white race, was doomed to extinction by a conspiracy of race mixers. A onetime Young family friend in Idaho, Ellen Kearney, told the Casper, Wyoming, *Star-Tribune* that she once had a long discussion with Young about politics in which he urged her to vote for the candidates who would do the least to enforce the laws of the corrupt establishmentarian government. Beyond such hints, whatever went on in Young's brain probably will never be known with certainty. Police found that he rarely spoke of his political views. Nonetheless, enough can be gleaned from the forty disjointed and rambling journals and diaries he left behind to see that once again a Smerdyakov had surfaced on the Survival Right. Interspersed among such imponderables as "zero equals infinity" and "2 + 2 may not equal 4" are references to nuclear war, Hitler and the need to "come apart and start a new race."

Police such as Ed Carroll of the Lincoln County, Wyoming, sheriff's office later told about how acquaintances of Young recalled his intense concern with surviving an imminent nuclear war. They said Young had made repeated solitary trips to the deserts in Wyoming and Idaho to contemplate the coming of the end and to explore ways to survive in the wilderness, Carroll said in an interview.

Later Carroll told the Associated Press, "Young told someone that after they got the money they were going to take half the kids to an island where they were going to live in a new world—happily ever after."

Even less is known about Doris Young. News media interviews with people who knew the couple painted her as a typical house-wifely type of Western woman willing to subordinate her own in-terests to those of her man. Cokeville mayor Dayton recalled that she had been a "real pretty" waitress in the local cafe with a truck driver for a husband in 1977 when Young came to town "and swept her off her feet, as they say." Young took his coffee breaks at the Red Dog Cafe lunch counter. Six months later, when he was fired "for harassing our good citizens and letting the bad apples get away," the two "rode off into the sunset on a motorcycle," leaving their respective spouses behind, the mayor recalled.

Some friends remembered that Doris had dreamed of becoming a country-and-western singer. She apparently was an easy person to like, particularly because she was "good with kids," as family friend Ellen Kearney told the Casper *Star-Tribune*. When Kearney knew the Youngs, Doris worked as a substitute teacher in the elementary school in Soda Springs, Idaho. Even David Young's ex-wife spoke fondly of Doris in an interview with the *Arizona Republic* shortly after the tragedy, recalling that Doris "had the most beautiful voice in the world" and that she had sung briefly in several honky-tonks in Tucson after leaving Cokeville.

David Young's plan to finance and create the new race was to hold 150 children for ransom, demanding $2 million for each child from the Mormons' well-heeled Church of Jesus Christ of Latter-day Saints. The Youngs believed that the church would come up with the $300 million because of its strong family orientation. Then, the diaries indicated, once the ransom was paid, Young would take half the hostages aboard a commandeered 747 airplane and fly them off to an unspecified island to start that "new race." The diaries alternately speak of the "new race," "Brave New World"—usually abbreviated as BNW—and "the Biggie." Young wrote in his small crabbed hand on January 2, 1986: "Biggie is always on my mind as I work . . . There will be a new race." The day she died, Doris

Young wrote in her own diary: "I wonder what we will be called in the new world."

The siren call to start a new race before the coming of Armageddon is a familiar one. Up in Montana, in the awesome Spanish Peaks Wilderness Area just north of Yellowstone National Park, self-styled "mountain men" Don Nichols and his son, Dan, heard the same call. But, in the spirit of the frontier, the Nicholses set out to create what they called a new all-white "tribe," rather than a race.

On July 15, 1984, Kari Swenson, a light-complexioned, attractive, long-haired young woman as Nordic-looking as her name sounds, went for a run on a mountain trail behind the famous Big Sky ski resort north of Yellowstone National Park as part of her training as a member of the elite U.S. women's biathlon ski team. At twenty-three, Swenson was a recent honor graduate in microbiology at Montana State University in Bozeman and was virtually certain to be among the first women to compete in the Olympic Games as a biathlete, in a sport combining cross-country skiing and shooting. She had led the American women to victory in world competition at Chamonix, France, earlier that year when they had won the first bronze medal ever for an American team, and now the sport had been added to the Olympic schedule for women. As well as being a personal triumph for Swenson, the addition was a victory for women in general because the arduous sport, which requires one to ski cross-country to the point of exhaustion and then shoot a rifle while controlling one's breathing, had long been an Olympic event only for men. Then Kari Swenson ran up against the Survival Right on a Montana mountainside, and her dreams ended.

Waiting on the trail were Don Nichols, fifty-three, and his nineteen-year-old son, Dan. For months the father and son had lived in the Montana mountains, subsisting on small game, roots and berries, with a skill hardly dreamed of by even the most ardent Survivalists.

In the tradition of Jim Bridger, Jeremiah "Liver-eating" Johnson and other legendary mountain men of frontier times, the Nicholses had established their own survival network in the high country. They had stored weapons, ammunition and such supplies as flour, beans and dried fruit at locations scattered throughout their forest empire. Their gardens of turnips, carrots, radishes, beets and other edibles were planted in dozens of secluded mountain meadows and in protected ravines. They made clothing out of the hides of animals they had trapped or shot and claimed they lived in harmony with the pace and dictates of their natural surroundings. In summer they gardened and gathered food. In the short autumn they hunted and preserved their game for the long winter. And when the howling winds ripped across the Spanish Peaks, they survived nicely, holed up in caves protected by clear plastic tarpaulins and heated by fires of "squaw wood" snapped from low pine branches. They had everything a man needed to keep on going except a woman.

Now, with the stink of weeks of wood fires in their clothing, hair and beards, Don and Dan Nichols accosted Swenson as she jogged past icy-blue Ulerys Lake in her citified Day-Glo orange running shorts and Adidas shoes. At first Don told her he just wanted some "conversation," but then he punched her in the temple and the two tied her wrist to Dan's wrist.

Don explained, "We want you to come up in the mountains with us for a couple of days. We just want you to come up and try living with us." Then they dragged the young athlete into the rugged pine forests and began working their way north, up the side of Lone Mountain, a virtual clone of Europe's Matterhorn.

On a tall slender lodgepole pine tree growing alongside the trail where the kidnapping took place they had scraped away the bark and written in a bold cursive script: "Dan and Don Nichols Live in These Mts. July 14, 1984." With Swenson dragging along, they plunged through the timber for several hours, stopping just before dusk. They chained the young woman to a large pine tree and gave her a copy of *Mad* magazine to read while they expertly set up a camp. Don gathered wood and built a fire and cooked some biscuits while young Dan shot a doe for dinner. The deer, although wounded, fled into the brush. Reluctant to risk the sound of another shot, they confined dinner to Nichols's greasy biscuits, Swenson later recalled during several court appearances. She expressed distaste that the men had felt justified in slaughtering a two-hundred-pound animal just to provide three people with a single meal. Don Nichols responded by telling her of his contempt for "bureaucrats" who wrote laws against poaching just to keep themselves in work. "We take what we want in these mountains," he said. "We don't worry about the machine of society. Society will soon be gone."

The next morning they arose with the robber jays and moved their camp a short distance to take advantage of the cover provided by a stand of looming spruce trees. Then Dan shot and cleaned a squirrel, which they cooked and ate for breakfast. They forced Swenson to remove her shorts, explaining, when she protested fearfully, that the intention was practical, not sexual. Being naked from the waist down would make it too painful for her to make a dash for freedom through the thickly gnarled underbrush. The Nicholses told Swenson over their spartan meal that they had been looking for a mountain woman for some time. Don told her that the chain they used to hold her to the tree was a dog chain that he had bought for that specific purpose in Jackson, Wyoming, in 1978.

Later, at his own trial and that of Dan, Nichols described how his goal had been to abandon civilization for good and to move deep into the wilderness, where he and Dan both would use Swenson to breed his new "tribe." Although extremely taciturn and hostile under questioning, Nichols eventually stated that he felt his new tribe would be superior to the rest of society because its members would be steeped in the ability to survive in nature on the same instinctual basis as animals.

Only a few hours after her kidnapping, a search party had begun combing the forest for Swenson. The daughter of a prominent physicist on the faculty of Montana State University in nearby Bozeman and a world-class athlete, Swenson was quickly missed. She was a summer employee of Bob Schaap, owner of the Lone Mountain Guest Ranch, a dude operation and Nordic ski resort established at Big Sky by the late television news giant Chet Huntley during the early 1960s. When Swenson failed to show up for a waitressing shift at 5 p.m., Schaap, who had recommended that she take the Ulerys Lake trail because he had enjoyed seeing a grizzly bear there the day before, moved quickly. Shortly after five, Schaap and several of his friends and employees, including Jim Schwable and Alan Goldstein, fanned out into the mountainside, where they spent all night scrambling along trails and calling her name.

Schwable and Goldstein came upon the camp and saw Swenson chained to the tree shortly after the Nicholses finished cleaning up the breakfast leavings. All three in the Nichols camp heard the rescuers busting through the brush. Swenson screamed, "Watch out, they'll shoot! They'll kill you!"

Don shouted to his son, "Shut her up, Danny."

Dan pointed his .22 caliber automatic pistol at her chest and pulled back the slide that cocks the weapon in warning. But something went wrong and the pistol fired, slamming Swenson back against the tree with what veterans in Vietnam called a "sucking chest wound."

At that point Schwable strode into the camp and approached Swenson as she lay bleeding and gasping for air under the tree.

Suddenly Goldstein stepped into the clearing brandishing a heavy-duty pistol. Trying a fatal bluff, he shouted, "Drop your guns. You're surrounded by two hundred men. You can't get away."

With that, Don Nichols spun and fired a single shot from his deer rifle. The bullet struck Goldstein square in the face, shattering his jaw and killing him instantly.

At Dan's trial, in a voice devoid of any emotion, the elder Nichols pointed to his own breastbone and said of Goldstein, "I thought I would hit him in the chest and spine." He added, "I guess I missed some."

After Goldstein died, Dan and Don quickly packed their gear and ran off into the forest, leaving Schwable behind with the badly wounded Swenson. The biathlete survived her wound but was forced to postpone her Olympic plans because of physical complications brought on by the injury.

The ensuing "Montana mountain man" story, predictably, became a news media sensation, reaching its climax six months later on December 13, when a storybook Western sheriff named Johnny France, who had grown up with Don Nichols and styled himself a mountain man as well, captured the two on a snow-choked mountainside in a fast-draw showdown worthy of a Louis L'Amour novel. A Hollywood movie was made casting France in the hero's role, and France teamed up with author Malcolm McConnell to write a book about the capture called *Incident at Big Sky*.

But Kari Swenson, along with her parents, John and Jan Swenson, Schaap and many others directly affected by the story, complained that the sensationalist aspects of the incident obscured the fact that what really had occurred on Lone Mountain was the crime of murder against a very likable man named Al Goldstein.

Like Alan Berg bailing out of Chicago, Al Goldstein had hoped to move away from the Midwest rat race by coming into the Rocky Mountain high country. In 1982, at the age of thirty-four, Goldstein had sold his interest in the prosperous men's clothing store of Roberts, David and Alan in Flint, Michigan, and moved to Big Sky. A strapping large man whom Schaap called a "gentle giant," Goldstein signed on at Lone Mountain as a laborer clearing horse trails in the summer and grooming the resort's dozens of miles of cross-country Nordic ski trails in the winter. Although the sale of his business had made him comfortable financially, the "gentle giant" worked with his hands and muscles because that was what he had wanted when he left Michigan. After his murder, Goldstein's family spent large amounts of money hiring psychics, trackers and others in an effort to find his killer.

Donald Boone Nichols had spent most of his adult life learning how to survive in the wilderness. As with David Young, it is difficult to understand exactly what was going on in his head, for he was a loner who rarely said anything at all to those around him and even more rarely spoke of such things as politics or religion. Battered by dozens of hard Montana winters and hardscrabble poor for his entire life, Don Nichols was a perfect example of the personality type that Leslie Fiedler once dubbed "the Montana Face" while writing about his experience as a city-bred New Jersey Jew moving to the Big Sky country.

> I was met unexpectedly by the Montana Face. What I had been expecting I do not clearly know; zest, I suppose, naïveté, a ruddy and straightforward kind of vigor—perhaps even an honest brutality. What I found seemed, at first glance, reticent, sullen, weary—full of self-sufficient stupidity; a little later it appeared simply inarticulate, with all the dumb pathos that cannot declare itself; a face developed not for sociability of feeling but for facing the weather. It had friendly things to say, to be sure, and it meant them, but it had no adequate physical expression for friendliness, and the muscles around the mouth and eyes were obviously unprepared to cope with the demand of any more complicated emotion. *

Nichols was born in Kansas and, when the Dust Bowl was at its Depression-era worst, was brought to Montana by his father, Pat, who found work around Virginia City in the gold and silver mines. His father loved to drink, play the guitar and, above all, hunt and fish. Pat introduced his son to the outdoor life, taking him on numerous trips up the sides of Lone Mountain before being killed in a drunken car crash in the late 1930s. After Pat Nichols's death, Don's mother remarried, presenting her son with a stern, Bible-thumping farmer for a stepfather, a humorless disciplinarian with a ready razor strap. This man, Steve Engleman, had no use for hunting and fishing, which he saw as a waste of leisure time that should be spent in church.

The razor strop and Bible kept Don Nichols in line as he grew into early manhood. He went through the same high school in Harrison, Montana, as did John France and graduated at the top

---

* From "Montana: or The End of Jean Jacques Rousseau," in *Collected Essays* by Leslie Fiedler (Stein & Day, 1971).

of his class. He then joined the peacetime Navy in the late 1940s, only to be dismissed on what was called a "Section Eight," mental instability. Later he would brag that he had feigned mental problems to escape the Navy's clutches after he found the rule-bound military life unbearable.

In the early 1950s he wound up in West Virginia, where he married a daughter of Appalachian poverty named Verdina and took a job at one of Union Carbide's big chemical plants. When they had enough money saved, Don and Verdina took their infant son, Dan, and their daughter, Barbara, to Montana, where he bought a piece of land near the mountains and attempted to establish a farm.

Verdina, however, had grown up on just the sort of rustic farm that Nichols desired. She had no stomach for returning to a life of outhouses, hauling well water and chopping the heads off chickens for Sunday dinner. She insisted on a house in town, even though she had to pay for the privilege by working as a nurse and taking other jobs while Nichols scratched at farming for a while, then took to the backcountry for good.

From the time they reached Montana, Don Nichols worked only sporadically, usually as a welder, putting together enough money to tide him over the next few months, then going his own way. He read incessantly, focusing on books of history, geology, biology and the writings of the early trappers and explorers, Verdina later recalled. Quickly he seized on the same conspiracy theory that today drives followers of political extremist Lyndon LaRouche—that all the world's troubles were caused by the British. Every war ever fought by America, he told Dan and others, had been caused by the British. British agents of influence are attempting to bring the country down by selling drugs and poisoning food supplies.

There were dark forces afoot in the land, enemies out to poison people before an ultimate takeover, Nichols concluded. Foods were being poisoned with deadly additives even as overweight and undernourished people were being coddled to the point where they could do nothing on their own when the hard times came.

The most revealing glimpses into the strange mental landscape of Don Nichols came from a Jackson, Wyoming, woman, Adelle Della Porta, who lived in a trailer near a cabin where the mountain man would stay in the Wyoming tourist town just south of Yellowstone Park when working as a welder to put together enough money for his next trip into the mountains with his son. Della Porta told investigators that Nichols would come down with fits of mirth just looking at the big desk where she kept all of her business papers— bills, tax forms, etc. Laughing and pointing, he would say, "What the hell do you need all that for?" Earning money, paying bills, meeting one's taxes, all were silly exercises in bureaucracy, the meaningless "machine of society," he told her, adding that doctors were dangerous enemies and that people should treat their own ills with steam and herbs.

To emphasize his contempt for civilized conventions, Nichols made a point of using the wrong utensils when invited to Della Porta's home for a meal. On Thanksgiving he ate his turkey with a spoon and he liked to eat his eggs with a knife, she recalled.

He asked her to leave Jackson and become his mountain companion but made it clear that he intended to share her with any other mountain men that joined him. In his new tribe women would be community property, or, as he put it, "fifty-fifty" with the other men. When Della Porta refused in a good-natured fashion, he mocked her and told her how much she would regret things when the coming invasion was at hand and the only safe people were those so far back in the country that no oppressor could find them. He told his friend that she would be a slave, but "they'll never take me alive."

Between 1971, when Verdina divorced him, and the tragic events of 1984, Nichols took Dan into the mountains to live with him every summer just as his father, Pat, had taken him during the 1930s. Several years Nichols failed to bring Dan back until well after the fall school session had begun. When Verdina, who had quickly remarried, complained, the sheriff would go looking for the missing boy. Nichols then would explain that he didn't rely on the calendars of civilization and that he had planned to bring his son down after the mountain strawberries were ripe, which was how he reckoned the coming of fall. France recalled one autumn when, as a sheriff's deputy, he went to help retrieve Dan from the mountains and found the boy wearing a pair of Navy surplus binoculars. When asked what he used them for up in the mountains, Dan said they were his "people watchers."

Obviously, there was an awesome craftiness and sophistication to Don Nichols's practice of the Survivalist's life. If he was short on ideology, he was long on practicality. He taught Dan, for example, that humans must learn to approach nature as do animals and as did the aboriginal Indians whom his new tribe would emulate. To bring the lesson home, in August 1983, Don took Dan with him into the mountains to spend the winter, a retreat that ended nearly a year later in the kidnapping of Swenson and the murder of Goldstein.

For months on end they endured howling winds, temperatures routinely at 50 below zero and snow dozens of feet deep. Dan explained later that his father had taught him that the wild animals in the high country simply are not aware of misery in the cold weather. Only humans are unhappy to be out in the bitter cold. In fact, taught Don Nichols, both cold and heat don't exist for purely natural creatures. So the duo ignored the cold.

Similarly, Don taught Dan to hunt like an animal. The two would have contests in which each would sit motionless in a mountain clearing for hours, ignoring flies, muscle cramps and other irritations until such animals as grouse accepted them as forest fixtures and approached within grabbing distance. "Saves a shot," Don told Dan.

It later would be learned that, on several occasions during the long manhunts by large SWAT teams of state, local and federal police that followed the kidnapping, Don and Dan had sat motionless in a clump of bushes or other minimal cover while pursuers in their camouflage clothing and other gear walked within touching distance of them.

At the same time that they received massive attention in the world's media, the mountain men struck a harmonious chord among many of the year-round residents of the Big Sky country who admired their rugged individualism. On one occasion in late October, for example, a professional hunting guide named Tom Heintz stumbled upon the Nicholses while he was leading a group of Easterners on an elk hunt. Heintz told the "Nichols boys," as Montanans came to call the father-son duo, that Kari Swenson had survived her wound, and he promised not to tell the law about meeting them for "a spell." True to his word, Heintz didn't call the sheriff for three days. "It's not my fight," he later told the Billings *Gazette*.

Virginia City, the seat of Madison County where France served as sheriff and where Don and Dan eventually stood trial, is fourteen miles off the main road connecting Yellowstone National Park with Interstate 90, and despite such efforts as installing frontier-style boardwalks and false fronts on the local stores, the town never has realized its wish to become a major tourist draw. The main local claim to historical fame is Virginia City's role as the birthplace of the Montana Vigilance Committee, which rose up in 1864 to establish its own law as a self-ordained posse. There are twenty-three graves on Boot Hill in the town's cemetery that the vigilantes filled, according to Virginia City's historian in residence, Dick Pace, in his book *Golden Gulch*. Each time a victim was singled out the posse would write the number 777 on his door, a practice probably adapted from some sort of Masonic ritual, Pace speculates.

Locals in Madison County take historical pride in the fact that their posse has the dubious distinction of having hanged a man "for just a misdemeanor," Pace reports. That man, Joseph Slade, got drunk and went into the local saloon, where he made a spectacle out of himself shouting for the bar girls to "take it off." Then he staggered out to his horse and backed the animal through several store windows on the main street before going home to sleep it off. As Slade snored, the posse scrawled 777 on his cabin door, then cured his hangover with a "rope treatment," as legend has it.

To this day Montana law officers such as the state patrol and county sheriffs wear a patch that includes the number 777.

"A lot of the vigilante spirit still lives in these hills, and that's why so many folks are captivated by what Johnny did," Pace said in an interview, adding that a growing number of local ranchers and other county regulars were "at least listening and attending a few meetings" held by Posse Comitatus advocates. Perhaps the best symbol of the region's openness to the Survival Right is the fact that on the sidewalk outside Bettie's Cafe, John France's principal hangout in Virginia City's neighboring town of Ennis, is a box where one can buy each week's edition of *Spotlight*. But there is no box for *USA Today*.

David Young and Don Nichols were not the only lone wolves of the Survival Right out to start new tribes. In fact, as strange as these two men were, a case surfaced—where else?—in California that may have been an even more bizarre outbreak of the Survival sickness.

The story of California Survivalists Charles Chat Ng and Leonard Lake must begin at the end because legal technicalities prevent a clear picture of exactly how their odyssey began. Nevertheless, even the limited court records that are available indicate that something very bad indeed occurred in the underground fallout shelter and sexual torture chamber the two operated in California's Calaveras County to test potential female recruits for the army they planned to raise to fight the battle of Armageddon.

This particular incident came to light on June 2, 1985, at a police substation in the seedy industrial Bay Area city of South San Francisco when officer Paul Ziemer began questioning an overweight and balding ex-Marine with a black beard and a taste for camouflage clothing who had been arrested at a local lumberyard in a minor flap over the alleged theft of a seventy-five-dollar carpenter's vise from a hardware store.

The man had identified himself as "Mr. Stapley," but the picture on Stapley's driver's license didn't resemble the arrestee. Besides, officers had found an "assassin's weapon," a .22 caliber automatic pistol with a silencer, in the trunk of his car. So Ziemer knew that whoever it was he was questioning was trouble; he just didn't know what kind of trouble.

After a round of fruitless questions, the man asked Ziemer for a drink of water. Ziemer took "Mr. Stapley" across the hall and watched from behind as he used a drinking fountain. Back in the interrogation room, the suspect asked for a pencil and paper. He wrote a few hurried words and then announced that his name was Leonard Lake. In a strangely deep voice, he explained that he was a former Marine and that he was wanted on felony weapons charges in nearby Mendocino County. With each sentence, Ziemer later recalled, Lake's breathing became heavier until he started gasping and slumped to the floor in a fatal coma. With his back to the policeman at the drinking fountain, Lake had reached into a secret compartment in his belt buckle, extracted a James Bond-style cyanide pill and swallowed it.

The note was to his family: "I love you. Please forgive me."

Police originally had been summoned to the hardware store by a report that an Asian man, who turned out to be Charles Ng, had stolen the vise and tossed it into the trunk of a brown Honda automobile before fleeing. Lake, who had been shopping at the lumberyard, acknowledged that the car was his and explained that he and Hong Kong-born Ng, twenty-four, a dishonorably discharged Marine with a black belt in karate, were friends and housemates. Lake offered to pay for the vise, but once the illegally silenced .22 automatic was found alongside the vise in the trunk, he was arrested.

The first glimmer of mayhem came when police checked the "vehicle identification number" on the Honda registered to Lake and found that it matched that of a car stolen from Paul Cosner, thirty-nine, an affluent San Francisco auto dealer, who had been missing and feared dead for more than a year.

The name on the driver's license turned out to belong to another prominent missing California figure, Robin "Scott" Stapley, the founder of the San Diego chapter of the urban vigilante group called the Guardian Angels.

License plate records for the Honda showed that Lake lived in the town of Wilseyville, California, a hamlet consisting of a gas station, a convenience store and a couple of antique shops in the "gold country" of Calaveras County, a cattle-dotted scenic area of rolling dry grass hills which caters to tourists from the Bay Area and Sacramento who are drawn on weekends by the memory of the Gold Rush of 1849 and by nostalgia over Mark Twain's famous Calaveras County "jumping frog" story.

Lake's Calaveras County hideaway, which he and Ng had converted into their own Survivalist compound, turned out to be a four-acre "ranchette" concealed by hills and trees from all neighbors. There, up a short dirt road from an iron gate, California authorities found the familiar trappings of the Survival Right—a house stocked with freeze-dried food, guns and ammunition, racist and Survivalist literature, and, dug into a nearby hill, an underground bunker fitted as a fallout shelter.

But on this compound the fallout shelter doubled as a torture chamber where the two men browbeat, tortured and raped an unknown number of women, telling many of them they needed to learn how to be the sort of submissive and helpful females that would be needed in the new world after the coming of a nuclear Armageddon. There were two rooms in the bunker, separated by a one-way window through which one man watched and took video and still pictures while the other tormented a victim on the other side of the glass.

In the house police found a set of sophisticated videotaping equipment, which they quickly traced to a San Francisco free-lance TV camera operator named Harvey Dubs, who, along with his wife, Deborah, and their eighteen-month-old son, Sean, had been missing for nearly one year. A few weeks earlier the Dubses had been featured on an NBC-TV program, *Missing—Have You Seen This Person?* A cabinet in the house contained a number of videotapes apparently made with Dubs's equipment to record subsequent murders and discipline sessions. There also were a half dozen notebooks containing Lake's diaries and several photo albums of pictures taken on the property by Ng that gave investigators a stomach-turning account of the horror that had erupted there. The day the story broke, San Francisco police chief Cornelius Murphy grimly described the content of this material as "plans for survival in bunkers, nuclear explosions, that kind of thing." The chief said that Lake appeared in videotapes standing in front of his bunker like a TV news reporter, explaining that he would need "sex slaves" to continue the human race. He also described the types of guns to use and outlined a strategy for fighting a guerrilla war.

Lake's diaries were full of talk of the final battle and of his plans to survive it. One section, entitled "Operation Miranda," which particularly galled the investigators indicated strongly that Lake had been captivated by the short story "The Most Dangerous Game" by R. E. Connell, about a jaded millionaire who takes to hunting humans as game animals, and that Lake and Ng had done just that with several of the men on the videotapes. A motto scrawled repeatedly in the diaries read: "If you love something, let it go. If it doesn't come back, hunt it down and kill it."

Even as detectives were sifting through the Lake-Ng tapes and other material, other officers were combing the grounds. A Calaveras County sheriff's deputy poked a stick into a cluster of ants on one piece of ground and quickly turned over a charred human bone. Within hours four separate "burn sites" were found on the property, each containing a horrible mishmash of things like baby teeth, human fingernails, bits of skull, leg, arm, finger and toe bones and other human detritus. More than two dozen plastic bags were filled with this material and taken to San Francisco for further study. To this day nobody really knows how many people are represented by the gory collection, although some estimates have been as high as twenty-five. Prosecutors finally put together cases charging that nine murders had occurred, making it clear at the same time that many other murders had obviously been committed but that the victims' remains were simply beyond recognition.

Fanning out across northern California, Lake and Ng had lured a variety of men, women and children—particularly young women— to the ranchette, where they had subjected them to torture, sexual abuse and, finally, murder, all the while describing the qualities they were seeking in "warriors" and "warriors' wives" to meet the coming challenges of Armageddon.

The videotapes appeared to show the torture and murder of several people. One horrible tape was said to record such brutal mutilation that there could be no doubt that the woman died. Most, however, were of bondage sessions in which the two men forced their victims into various sexual acts, slashed their clothes away and otherwise tormented them.

Although knowledgeable sources have given some details of what goes on in the tapes, only limited transcripts have been made public because of a legal impasse that arose when Ng ultimately was arrested in the Canadian province of Alberta, where he was protected from extradition by a Canadian law that bans extraditing anyone to the United States if that person would face the death penalty in U.S. courts. Several weeks after he fled California, Ng had been apprehended while attempting to steal food in a Calgary department store. With Lake dead and Ng sentenced to a long term in a Canadian prison for assaulting a store guard in the fracas during which he was arrested, almost none of the evidence gleaned from the Calaveras County killing ground has ever been presented in a public court.

But perhaps the material that has been released to date—800 pages of partial tape transcripts made public in late 1985 by the California Supreme Court—provides all the details sane people need to know about what Lake and Ng did anyway. These partial transcripts were quoted in various court filings by police seeking search and arrest warrants against friends and relatives of Lake. They include fairly complete descriptions of the torture, rape and murder of Kathleen Allen, eighteen, and Brenda O'Connor, twenty-three, both of whom the men attempted to teach the sort of discipline needed for the coming end times.

Allen had worked as a bagger in a Bay Area Safeway grocery store before being lured to the compound by her boyfriend, Michael Sean Carroll, who appears to have been a follower of Lake and Ng. In the tape Allen sits in a chair while Lake tells her they have killed Carroll because he was her boyfriend.

"If you don't agree this evening, right now, to cooperate with us, we'll probably put a round through your head and take you out and bury you in the same area we buried Mike [Carroll]," Lake taunted. "You'll wash for us. You'll clean for us. Cook for us. Fuck for us. That's your choice in a nutshell. It's not much of a choice unless you've got a death wish." Carroll had served time in the federal prison in Leavenworth, Kansas, along with Ng, who was incarcerated there on charges of stealing $11,000 worth of automatic and semiautomatic weapons from a Marine arsenal in Hawaii. In the search warrant requests that contain the dismal transcripts of Allen's debasement, police suggested that Carroll had become a follower of Lake and Ng, and that he was killed by Ng after he and Ng went into San Francisco on a mission to kill gay men. Ng allegedly persuaded Carroll, twenty-three, to dress as a gay to lure their victims and then shot Carroll to death along with one of the duo's alleged victims, San Francisco disc jockey Donald Giulietti, thirty-six.

The transcripts also show how Lake and Ng apparently eliminated their next-door neighbors, Brenda O'Connor, her husband, Lonnie Bond, and their infant son, as well as Guardian Angel founder Stapley, whom the frightened young couple had persuaded to come to Calaveras County to protect them from their dangerous neighbors, just as the Guardian Angels protect inner-city residents from street crime in cities everywhere from New York to Los Angeles.

O'Connor had told several of her friends in Wilseyville that she was afraid of Lake because he had made sexual advances to her. She had even told some of her friends the exact location on the grounds where she suspected Lake had buried an unnamed girl.

Lake had introduced himself to O'Connor and Bond as Charles Gunnar. The real Charles Gunnar had been Lake's best friend at one time and the best man at his wedding. However, police now found that Gunnar had been missing for two years. He, too, apparently was counted among the compound's victims.

Unlike Kathy Allen, Brenda O'Connor was defiant in the transcripts as the men fondled and otherwise accosted her while keeping her baby, Lonnie Bond, Jr., two, captive in the next room. "You two are crazy," says O'Connor at one point while sitting handcuffed to a straight-backed chair. "Why do you guys do this? You can't keep my baby from me for sex."

"Charles," she asks later, "why are you doing this?"

Ng replies, "Because we hate you."

The videotaped horrors are compounded by the fact that most of the bodies on the property were so thoroughly burned, broken and scattered around the grounds that nobody will ever know for sure who died there. Perhaps the Bond baby was sold to a Fresno couple, as Lake told O'Connor at one point, but police did find baby teeth in the bone piles.

Unlike the other murderous inhabitants of the Survival Right dealt with heretofore, Lake and Ng appear to have foisted much of their violence on those about them as part of an elaborate and grotesque paramilitary fantasy game rather than out of intensely felt religious or racist views. Of course, for those living around them, the results of the Survival madness were the same.

Lake had met Ng in 1981 when the Hong Kong-born ex-Marine responded to an ad in a newsletter that Lake published called *War Games Magazine*. At the time, Lake was living on a communal ranch near the Northern California town of Ukiah—site of the Order's biggest armored car robbery four years later.

That commune, very unusual even by California standards of fringe-group strangeness, was an attempt to re-create Renaissance society, according to an interview with Lake's ex-wife in the San Francisco *Chronicle*. Men practiced a code of chivalry, women wore pointed hats with veils and there were frequent parties called "festivals" at which dulcimer music was played while people ate with their hands and otherwise tried to capture the medieval spirit. The commune also spent much time and veterinary expertise performing surgery on the horns of billy goats, moving them from the sides of the head to the front so that the animals resembled the mythical unicorn.

A veteran of the Vietnam War, in which he had served as a noncombatant radar operator at Danang, Lake also became deeply involved in modern war games. He would host gatherings, as many survival schools do today, at which participants would run about the woods in mock combat carrying guns that shot dye to indicate when a player was killed. In that game, Lake and his comrades apparently pretended that they were living in the world after a thermonuclear exchange. And the more Lake played the game, the more he believed that that final war was soon to come.

Thomas Southern, one of Lake's neighbors in Wilseyville, told the author in an interview that Lake often came to his house for Bible readings. The last visit from Lake, recalled Southern, had been a bizarre affair in which Lake brought a chocolate cake he had personally baked for the group's children, then read a passage from the Book of Revelation in which God's chosen people arise against the forces of Satan. Lake said that he personally favored the Mormon religion because of its emphasis on getting ready to survive coming natural disasters in preparation for the final days, but added that he "preferred to practice his faith his way in the out-of-doors," Southern recalled.

Lake began preparing for that final battle in earnest after encountering Ng, who wanted to join in the war games at Ukiah. Ng, a Chinese, had his own fantasy, in which he was a reincarnated "Ninja warrior," one of the legendary class of medieval assassins in Japan. After dressing up in his black Ninja robes and playing war games with the Lake group for a while, Ng told about how he had been drummed out of the Marines for stealing a large amount of weapons. He then brought those weapons onto the Ukiah ranch, where he and Lake became local nuisances, firing bursts of auto-matic-weapon fire long into the night.

In 1982, a task force of FBI agents and Bureau of Alcohol, Tobacco and Firearms representatives joined local police in a heli-copter raid on the ranch and arrested both men and confiscated their arsenal of stolen automatic and semiautomatic guns. Ng was denied bail and ultimately was sentenced to six years in the federal penitentiary. Lake, however, posted a $6,000 bond and then went into hiding, where he remained until the day he told Officer Ziemer that he was wanted on the weapons charges and slumped into a coma on the station-house floor.

As Ng served his time, Lake apparently continued to play his fantasy games while in hiding. He killed his best friend, Charles Gunnar, took his name and moved into the gold country, waiting for "Charlie" to join him and resume the game in earnest.

On February 25, 1984, he wrote in one of the diaries: "Leonard Lake, a name not seen or used much these days. My second year as a fugitive. Mostly dull day-to-day routine still with death in my pocket and fantasy my major goal. As last year, I don't recommend this as reading material. Dull at its best, still, there are no great secrets within (at least at this writing). So whatever. I'm older, fatter, balder and not much wiser. Interested to see where I go from here."

Once again, the background noise about the coming of Arma-geddon and all the other psychic baggage of the Survival Right had triggered violence and tragedy. A striking commonality among the cases examined here—David Rice Lewis, David and Doris Young, Don and Dan Nichols, and Leonard Lake and Charles Chat Ng—is, of course, the fact that all were unstable people who probably were headed for disaster anyway. But it should be noted that the route all of these people took, not to mention the route taken by the residents of Michael Ryan's commune, by the Order, by the Covenant, the Sword and the Arm of the Lord and by all the other characters who have played out the drama of the Survival Right, has been hauntingly similar. It is not inappropriate to view them as Smerdyakovs all, twisted people who listened to the background noise of racial hatred, anti-Semitism and conspiracy theories, to preachers thundering from hundreds of television pulpits about the coming of Armageddon, then tried to relate that bedlam to their own personal fears of nuclear annihilation. They started out as mere right-wingers, but as the background noise rose in volume and shrillness they crossed a dangerous line separating the rest of America from those afflicted with the Survivalist sickness.

It behooves all, then, to examine to what extent the selfsame background noise that pushed these people over the brink is being heard by millions of other potential Smerdyakovs who encounter the Survivalist credo with increasing regularity, as its proponents become ever more sophisticated as political organizers and manipulators of the mass media.

I was run out of Denver by the Jewsmedia.
—David Lane

7: The Politics of Hatred

The leaders of Identity Christianity, the Posse Comitatus, the Ku Klux Klan and all the other sundry groups that are examined in this book share common problems when trying to get their message of conspiracy before their fellow Americans. They can't exactly write a letter to the editor of the local newspaper and expect to see it printed. For that matter, virtually all other outlets of mainstream communication are impervious to their cant.

Radio and television stations, mindful of the ever-watchful Federal Communications Commission, remain loath to air the Survival Right's tirades, regardless of its adherents' arguments citing their right to be heard under First Amendment guarantees of freedom of speech. The wealth of rhetoric from the Survivalists quoted elsewhere in this book argues most eloquently for editors and station managers who find the Survivalists' rhetoric so rabid as to offend the public taste and therefore to render it unacceptable fare for their family audiences of readers, listeners and viewers. When Identity preacher and Posse leader William Potter Gale persuaded KTTL-FM, a 100,000-watt country music radio station in Dodge City, Kansas, to air a tape of one of his sermons calling for attacks on "every damn Jew rabbi in this land" in 1983, the station was brought before the FCC. KTTL's lawyers were able to save the license only by explaining that the tape had been played as part of a marital dispute between a feuding husband and wife who were part owners of the station.

In their difficulty getting access to the media, those inflicted with the Survivalist sickness are not unlike fringe elements throughout history who, once denied the establishment's access to the people, were forced to take their case to the public by passing out pamphlets and haranguing crowds while standing on soapboxes or on tables in Bavarian beer halls. But the Survival Right's emergence on the American scene coincided with a number of household technological breakthroughs that have made its message far more accessible than were the preachings of those who espoused such causes in the past.

Instead of handing out crude mimeographed fliers and making street-corner speeches, the Survival Right often disseminates its messages by such newly available methods as:

—Sophisticated personal computer "bulletin boards," such as the Aryan Nations Net, that can be called up with a home computer, a modem and a telephone.

—Home video cassettes that allow the faithful as well as potential converts to watch programs on their own TV sets, starring leaders like the Posse's James Wickstrom and the Ku Klux Klan's Louis Beam.

—Audio cassettes of Identity sermons by such figures as Gale, Butler, Thom Robb and others that can be ordered through ads in the back pages of *Spotlight* and other publications.

—Telephone "hot lines" that interested parties can call to hear the latest tape-recorded conspiracy theory played on an initiate's phone-answering machine. Michael Ryan made his communal servants call one such "Jew hot line" virtually every day during his reign of terror.

All across the country Survivalists have seized on these pervasive new technologies to get their message before the voters as they press to realize their seemingly impossible dream of turning the United States into a late-twentieth-century version of Hitler's Germany.

While political realities make such an eventuality so remote as to merit consignment to the same category of worries as being struck by a Boeing 747 while on the golf course, the tragic incidents of mayhem, murder and cruelty perpetrated by the relative handfuls of zealots documented in earlier pages are evidence aplenty that the Survival Right's message is being heard.

And despite a rather dramatic lack of success to date, the far-right and often anti-Semitic Populist Party has served up dozens of Identity and Posse adherents as candidates for state, local and national office. Further, the spotty but exceptionally dramatic election successes of followers of Lyndon LaRouche underscore the Survival Right's potential for making inroads at the polls.

The Anti-Defamation League began closely monitoring public opinion in the farm belt in the early 1980s to learn whether the wrenching dislocations brought on by the crisis in the agricultural economy were allowing neo-Nazis, the Posse and other elements of the Survival Right to make political gains. It was clear from the outset that the more sophisticated Survivalist elements had quickly seized upon talk of a farm crisis to promote their movement's political fortunes.

As early as 1984 the Liberty Lobby and its weekly tabloid, *Spotlight*, began promoting a new Populist Party as the way to "revitalize the family farm" and fulfill six other planks of a national platform that evoked virtually all the tenets of the Survival Right. In a special supplement to *Spotlight* promoting the newly created party, Populist chairman Bill Baker pledged the party to a goal of "taking back control of our money system from the mattoid international crooks who have stolen it . . ." (Liberty Lobby founder Willis Carto defined the word "mattoid" as "a criminal of high intelligence. Mattoids often gravitate into international banking or politics . . .")

For years the Liberty Lobby has played an elaborate word game over the extraordinarily touchy subject of anti-Semitism. The columns of *Spotlight*, for example, are just as free of direct racial or ethnic epithets as are those of *The New York Times*. Instead of blatant Jew baiting, the tabloid uses code words such as "international bankers" or "culture distorters" or "the privately owned Federal Reserve Bank." In 1985 the Lobby unsuccessfully sued *The Wall Street Journal* and investigative columnist Jack Anderson for libel after each had called the group anti-Semitic. Liberty Lobby describes itself instead as "anti-Zionist," a distinction that carries very little weight with Jews anywhere or, for that matter, with philologists.

In a glossary appended to *Profiles in Populism*, a collection of essays on thirteen historical figures deemed as Populist forerunners, Carto defines Zionism as follows: "A secular conspiratorial scheme overtly aimed at ingathering the Jews of the world to Israel but in reality a world political engine of massive power which, allied with the power of the supercapitalists, effectively controls all aspects of Western political, intellectual, religious and cultural life. Zionism overlaps substantially into both capitalism and communism. Without Zionist support, neither capitalism nor communism could survive. Zionism is strongly antagonistic to all nationalisms except Jewish nationalism."

Populist chairman Baker boasted in a special *Spotlight* supplement that the tabloid's circulation of well above 150,000 made it bigger than *National Review, Human Events, Conservative Digest* and *Commentary* combined. In its first year of operation, the party put together a presidential ticket consisting of two-time Olympic gold medal track star Bob Richards and his vice-presidential running mate, Maureen Salaman, president of the National Health Federation and an advocate of the argument that "special interests" have covered up evidence that proper nutritional habits can cure cancer.

The 1984 Richards-Salaman presidential ticket managed only 66,000 votes in the fourteen states where the Populist Party managed to get on the ballot, and shortly afterward, Richards, a household name as the official spokesman for Wheaties, "The Breakfast of Champions," parted company with the party over the issue of anti-Semitism. But the campaign had succeeded in putting the Survival Right manifesto before millions of people, even if they later rejected it resoundingly in the voting booth.

A major poll taken in early 1986 by the Louis Harris organization for the ADL found disturbing evidence that the conspiracy theories about international bankers and shadowy Trilateralists were widely known in the Midwestern heartland states of Iowa and Nebraska. Harris found that 46 percent of college graduates in the two states were aware of the Populist Party and that 29 percent of all citizens knew about it. Harris also found that 24 percent of people in those states were familiar with the Posse Comitatus and that 15 percent followed the activities of the Covenant, the Sword and the Arm of the Lord.

More importantly, however, the Harris survey found an appalling "penetration" of anti-Semitism in the Midwest. For example, 75 percent of those polled in Iowa and Nebraska agreed that both the Reagan administration and "big international bankers" were responsible for farm woes, while a plurality placed "a lot of blame" for the problem on the Trilateral Commission, a favorite target of the fringe right. Perhaps the most dismal poll result was that 13 percent of residents in both states flatly agreed that "a good deal of the blame for what has happened to farmers can be laid at the doorstep of 'certain religious groups, such as Jews for example,' " Harris found.

When questioners asked whether respondents agreed or disagreed with the statement that "farmers have always been exploited by international Jewish bankers who are behind those who overcharge them for farm equipment or jack up the interest on their loans"— 27 percent agreed.

Worse yet, Harris found that a 45 percent plurality of people over sixty-five endorsed the statement that Jewish bankers were behind farm woes, as did a 44 percent plurality of people who never finished high school.

Harris advised B'nai B'rith: "The political explosiveness of the farm issue is immediately apparent from these results . . . [which] lay out as clearly as any evidence in this study the magnitude and nature of the problem of anti-Semitism in the Iowa and Nebraska farm belt . . . One can argue, of course, that the 27 percent [who blamed "Jewish bankers"] are not simply more than about one in four rural residents of these pivotal Midwestern farm states, but that it also means that the residue of 73 percent are not prepared to make such a charge against Jews. However, it must be pointed out that any phenomenon which affects over one in four residents must be viewed as a mass phenomenon, even if it is not massive."

Another unexpected popular attitude emerged when the Harris pollsters asked whether respondents agreed with the statement that "Jews should stop complaining about what happened to them in Nazi Germany." Nebraska and Iowa farmers were about equally split on that question. Overall, they disagreed that Jews complain too much about the Holocaust by a narrow 48–42 percent plurality. But among high school graduates, 48 percent agreed that Jews complain too much about the Nazi death camps and only 42 percent disagreed.

Perhaps the best indicator of what Harris called "penetration" of the Survival Right message came when people were asked whether they agreed or disagreed with the statement that "when it comes to choosing between people and money, Jews will choose money." In virtually every category, a plurality of Nebraskans and Iowans bought the stereotype of the money-grasping Jew. In Nebraska, 48 percent agreed with the caricature while 40 percent rejected it. Jews fared slightly better in Iowa, where the charge was rejected by 44–39 percent. Among people in both states over sixty-five years old, however, 70 percent agreed that Jews choose money over people while only 19 percent did not.

Harris concluded that this question indicated that anti-Semitism is far more prevalent in the farm belt than in the rest of America. In 1985, a nationwide Harris poll found that 63 percent of Americans overall reject the thesis that Jews are more interested in money than people, while only 29 percent accept it.

Noting that the poll deliberately asked emotionally loaded questions about stereotypes, Harris advised the ADL that although between 42 and 43 percent of those questioned in the two farm states indicated fairly strong anti-Semitic views, the actual situation is slightly better than that. "The judgment of the Harris firm is that these levels state a serious potential for anti-Semitism, but not its active level today in these areas. Instead, we would put the proper level at somewhere between 25 percent and 30 percent. Of course, from an operational standpoint, the precise number when it is above one in four may not be critical. One-quarter of any group of people must be viewed as substantial, when it involves prejudice," Harris warned.

With such a base of potential supporters already in place, extremists are likely to keep on pushing for political acceptance in the farm belt, but poor showings by Populist candidates and other denizens of the far right in the 1986 congressional elections indicate that they still have a long way to go.

Sam Van Pelt, the retired Nebraska judge who began monitoring the movement after completing a study for Nebraska governor Robert Kerrey of the gunfight death of Arthur Kirk, speculated that a big reason that people in Nebraska and Iowa rejected Populist and Posse-style candidates in 1986 was extreme disgust at what happened on the Rulo farm, a story that was widely publicized in the two states. Yet this hardly amounts to a permanent reversal: with time, the memory of Rulo will fade, and people once again will start listening to the rap from the far right. And those listening will be the same people who already hold substantial anti-Semitic views even before the first Survivalist orator steps up to a soapbox or a video camera.

With Populists and Posse members in at least temporary disfavor during 1986, the most potent political force from the far right proved to be that displayed by the political network of extremist Lyndon LaRouche, which is visible to most Americans as a group of insistent men and women who set up card tables at most major urban airports and try to harangue harried travelers with their arguments in favor of nuclear power, the Star Wars defense project and other hawkish crusades. During the 1986 elections no fewer than two hundred candidates with ties to LaRouche ran for office at the state, local and national level. And while the LaRouches failed to capture a single congressional seat or governor's chair, they did pile up millions of votes and had a profound and surprising impact on national political life, particularly in California and Illinois.

Lyndon LaRouche was born in 1922 into a prominent New Hampshire Quaker family, and in the 1940s joined the Socialist Workers Party. He remained an active old-line Marxist for nearly two decades before being swept up in the turbulent movement politics of the 1960s. During the Vietnam War, LaRouche rose as a leader in the radical-left Students for a Democratic Society and, by the late 1960s, he had a following of several hundred operating out of a headquarters in New York City. He took the name Lyn Marcus and was the leader of the headline-grabbing takeover of Columbia University by student radicals in 1968. In those years, LaRouche zealots, operating under the banner of the U.S. Labor Party, pressed a world view in which right-wing capitalists like Nelson Rockefeller, Richard Nixon and lesser lights were out to start a nuclear war with the Soviet Union.

LaRouches staked out NATO meetings in Brussels and provided reporters with numerous documents purporting to outline the capitalists' plans to destroy the Soviets by a preemptive nuclear strike. The umbrella group for the LaRouche operation was called the National Caucus of Labor Committees and his followers often would tell journalists and other listeners that they had proof that the terminal nuclear war would be launched in, say, ninety days. After the ninety days passed without the onset of Armageddon, the LaRouche representatives would inform questioners that the only reason the missiles hadn't flown was that they had sounded the warning in time to stop it.

The sea change came in 1973, when LaRouche suddenly ordered his followers to begin studying karate and street fighting. He complained that the Soviet KGB was out to kill him, and began spouting the same anti-Semitic cant that was being heard from Liberty Lobby and the rest of the Survival Right. By 1974 the LaRouches were on what they described as a wartime footing. Many supporters quit their jobs and left husbands, wives and parents to become full-time adherents. The incessant talk of an imminent cataclysm continued, only now the perpetrators were viewed as Jews, international bankers, Trilateralists and other targets of the far right. Once again, when confronted with the fact that the predicted attack from evil outsiders had failed to materialize, the LaRouche group would counter that they had headed off catastrophe by sounding a warning in time.

They trotted out one of the most bizarre scenarios ever proffered by a fringe group:

Jewish bankers are behind the drug trade, and are peddling their wares with the collusion of the royal family of Britain . . . B'nai B'rith is actively involved in kidnapping children for fiendish Jewish temple rituals . . . Henry Kissinger is a "faggot" . . . Carter administration Vice-President Walter Mondale is "an agent of influence" of the KGB . . . Abraham Lincoln was assassinated by a Jewish spy hired by interests in Great Britain, where the government and royal family supported the Confederate cause . . . The only hope for mankind is to colonize Mars before nuclear war eradicates all sentient life on Earth . . .

Liberty Lobby was so taken by these arguments that its various publishing enterprises began selling books, magazines and pamphlets produced by the LaRouches. When old-guard members of the Survival Right expressed natural distrust of the former SDS leader, Liberty Lobby responded by issuing a "White Paper" defending the LaRouche group as a legitimate ally of right-wing interests.

In short order LaRouche set up a number of allied organizations to press his crusade—the Fusion Energy Foundation to press for nuclear power plants and Star Wars; the National Anti-Drug Coalition to press the charges that a conspiracy by the crowned heads of Britain was behind the global drug trade; and the National Democratic Policy Committee, the group under whose banner many LaRouche-backed political candidates raised money and sought election.

The LaRouches also operated an international wire service and published several Survival Right magazines and newspapers, including *New Solidarity, Campaigner, Executive Intelligence Review, Investigative Leads* and *Fusion.*

Outrageous as his viewpoints may seem, LaRouche proved phenomenally successful as a political organizer. Grand juries in Massachusetts and Virginia estimated in 1986 that at his peak he was bringing in $10 million per year in contributions for his various crusades and political candidacies.

In 1986 a series of federal crackdowns led to indictments against LaRouche intimates—including at least two Ku Klux Klan leaders—which charged among other things that the airport Star Wars advocates were conning travelers into providing credit card numbers, which the group then used to withdraw large amounts of money from their victims' bank accounts.

It was disclosed in court documents that the LaRouches had also solicited funds by telephone appeals, telling those they contacted that money was desperately needed to stave off imminent catastrophe, such as a nuclear holocaust or an AIDS epidemic. Afterward, contributors were told that they had prevented disaster by making timely donations to LaRouche. One LaRouche defector described life within the fold in terms reminiscent of the recollections of religious cult escapees, telling John Mintz of *The Washington Post,* "It's a seven-day-a-week, twenty-four-hour-a-day total immersion."

In 1986, LaRouche moved his operation from New York City to the Virginia country town of Leesburg, where he was ensconced in a fourteen-room manor house on a 171-acre compound guarded by followers carrying semiautomatic rifles and other commando gear. *The Washington Post,* which devoted substantial efforts to following the new political force in the nearby Virginia countryside, counted nearly a thousand followers moving in and out of the estate.

In April of 1987 federal prosecutors badly damaged the LaRouche apparatus by winning court orders allowing the government to take over control of the group's assets at seventeen locations around the United States, in order to collect more than $16 million in outstanding court fines that were set during the inquiries into alleged fund-raising abuses.

Like the Liberty Lobby, LaRouche denied that his operation was anti-Semitic, insisting that he was merely anti-Zionist. And just as the Harris poll for B'nai B'rith indicated, by 1987 many workaday Americans were willing to listen to the LaRouche skein of hard-line "anti-Zionist" rhetoric about conspiracies of international bankers and other obsessions of the far right.

In California during 1986, LaRouche forces had persuaded 700,000 people to sign a highly controversial petition that would have assigned persons carrying the AIDS virus to virtually the same status as that to which Hitler had consigned Jews in the early days of his German chancellorship. Those carrying the virus would have been declared "infectious" and their identities reported to police authorities. While the referendum on the question failed, the LaRouche group nevertheless won the support of nearly three-quarters of a million people for its AIDS project, an undertaking brimful of the sort of scapegoating and persecution that long has proven the key to success for totalitarian crusades.

During the LaRouche AIDS drive, the California White Resistance Movement circulated an essay from prison by the Order's David Lane, who wrote: "It is universally acknowledged that the disease comes from Africa and is transmitted primarily by sexual acts. THAT MEANS IT COMES FROM NEGROES, and mostly from Negro males . . . No White person on earth would have AIDS if they did not engage in inter-racial sex . . . The doctors and scientists who are searching for a cure for AIDS are almost exclusively Jewish. This is not surprising in view of two facts: (a) All race-mixing has been promoted by the Jews through their total control of the media, politicians, government and judiciary. (b) Jews are the ultimate mongrel race."

While California LaRouches were making political hay using the AIDS tragedy to promote racism and anti-Semitism, their brothers and sisters in Illinois stunned political observers by spoiling that state's 1986 Democratic primary.

In the spring of 1986, Illinois Democratic politics were in their typical state of disarray. Forces led by old-guard Chicago pol Edward Vrdolyak were sparring with the budding political apparatus of the city's first black mayor, Harold Washington. With sparks flying between Vrdolyak and Washington, the well-known Illinois Democratic machine had almost perfunctorily given its endorsement to former Illinois senator Adlai Stevenson III in the governor's race to oppose longtime incumbent James Thompson. Stevenson, in turn, had handpicked his own slate of candidates for the jobs of lieutenant governor and secretary of state, posts traditionally filled by people who will rubber-stamp the programs, policies and orders of their governor.

Adlai III, son of the legendary two-time Democratic presidential nominee and former Ambassador to the United Nations, Adlai Stevenson II, was infamous in political circles for his turgid rhetoric and lack of charisma. He ran a predictably lackluster 1986 primary campaign that was largely eclipsed by the shenanigans of those jockeying for power elsewhere in the Illinois Democratic Party in the aftermath of Washington's challenge to the awesome—and virtually all-white—political machine left behind by the late Mayor Richard J. Daley.

As a result of this preoccupation, the machine was blind-sided in the governor's race, and the morning after the March 18, 1986, primary election, Stevenson found himself leading an organization Democratic ticket that included LaRouche followers Janice Hart for secretary of state and Mark Fairchild for lieutenant governor. As *The Washington Post*'s Myra MacPherson so aptly put it, "Suddenly Stevenson found himself running on the Democratic ticket with people whose platform includes the colonization of Mars, who threaten their detractors and denounce the 'British crown as in fact the head of the drug lobby.' "

Stevenson had little choice. He declined the Democratic nomination and launched a campaign for governor by starting a new "Solidarity" Party, apparently unaware that the LaRouche group often describes its programs as seeking solidarity and that the major

LaRouche group publication is called *New Solidarity*. Both he and the two LaRouche advocates were handily wiped out by Thompson and his Republican slate in the November general election, but the LaRouches found they had won a new respect as a serious political force.

Subsequent political analysis found that LaRouche's National Democratic Policy Committee had sponsored more than two hundred candidates in twenty-six state primaries during 1986. A clear LaRouche strategy had been to place candidates in several Democratic primaries where the local Republican opponents were so powerful that mainstream Democrats had been reluctant to go out on a limb as hopeless candidates. LaRouche followers Harold Kniffen and Susan Director were unopposed in the Democratic primaries in Texas, as were candidates Clem Cratty in Ohio and Dominick Jeffrey in Illinois. Winning such primaries, of course, gave the impression that the LaRouche candidates were a political force of consequence even though their standard-bearers were overwhelmed in the general elections by popular Republicans.

A poll in California by Mervin Field found that 65 percent of registered voters had heard of LaRouche but that only 10 percent had a strongly favorable view of his political credo, as opposed to 55 percent who had an unfavorable or strongly unfavorable view. Still, one can take scant comfort in the discovery that only one in ten California voters became enthusiastic LaRouche backers after hearing his message.

In California primaries three LaRouche-backed congressional candidates, Art Hoffmann, Alex Maruniak and Maureen Pike, received more than one-third of the vote in their respective districts. While none of the LaRouches went beyond the primaries to win actual national offices, their performances underscored a rising support for the movement. A study of the 1986 primaries by B'nai B'rith found that 119 LaRouche candidates won between 0 and 10 percent of the vote, while 60 scored between 11 and 20 percent, 22 won between 21 and 30 percent, and another 33 LaRouche candidates received more than 30 percent of the vote.

Political experts trying to make sense out of the LaRouche phenomenon in the 1986 elections were quick to note that these particular extremists are hard to classify because they exhibit an annoying propensity for changing direction. (LaRouche himself went from ultraleft to ultraright over a single summer. It should be noted as well, however, that LaRouche, while he was on the extreme left, never enjoyed the sort of successes that he did after the swing to the far right.)

As demonstrated by the energy displayed in recent years by forces as diverse as Richard Butler in his seedy Idaho fenced compound and Lyndon LaRouche in his porticoed $14 million Virginia manor house, it is clear that the Survival Right will continue its underground political organizing in years to come. It remains to be seen whether future years will bring conditions that are more or less favorable to its message. If the farm economy continues to droop, as virtually all experts predict, the movement's prospects for further growth would appear good.

It is worthwhile, then, to learn the ways these interlocking fringe groups keep their message circulating as they go about their own version of the time-honored American tradition of political organizing. It is here, at the level of grass-roots politics, that the Survivalists have shown an ability to seize on new technologies.

By far the most sophisticated underground communication channel established by the right-wing Survivalists has been the computer bulletin board.

Richard Butler likes to recall how he and Texas Klan Titan Louis Beam—both men were engineers by training—seized on the idea of communicating over phone lines with personal computers after authorities in Canada started confiscating hate literature the neo-Nazis were shipping to followers in that country, where laws governing freedom of speech and of the press are far less liberal than specified in the U.S. Constitution.

In the early 1980s, just as the neo-Nazis were being denied access to potential Canadian adherents, the world's computer hobbyists were discovering "telecommunications," a technique whereby Morse code-like electronic signals are sent over telephone lines and then translated into text on monitor screens. To pass messages back and forth, participants need only a computer such as the early Apple, Commodore, Osborne and Kaypro models, as well as a device called a modem (modulator/demodulator). With that equipment and the inexpensive software that allows a computer to perform the transfers, they can easily send alphabetic code over phone lines and read it on their computer screens as text.

Most hobbyists used the intriguing new technology to subscribe to commercial bulletin boards like CompuServe and The Source, which offer such things as up-to-date news bulletins, computerized banking, transfer of software and "chat" sessions during which different individuals go "online" and communicate via keyboards and phone lines.

Butler and Beam established the Ayran Nations Net, a system of bulletin boards located throughout the country through which their followers could both keep in touch and spread their message of hatred. Computer technology allows the bulletin board system (BBS) to keep certain data secret until a code word is invoked, while at the same time public messages can be played for any and all callers. Thus the boards serve both as an avenue of propagandizing among outsiders as well as a fairly secure message center for initiates.

Here are excerpts from one session downloaded from a BBS number in Chicago in early 1987:

YOU ARE CONNECTED TO THE CHICAGO LIBERTY NET, AN AFFILIATE OF THE ARYAN NATIONS LIBERTY NET.

THIS SYSTEM IS DEDICATED TO THE FREE EXCHANGE OF IDEAS.

IF YOU ARE AN ANTI-COMMUNIST YOU HAVE MADE THE RIGHT CONNECTION. IF YOU LOVE THE HERITAGE, CULTURE, AND TRADITIONS OF THE WHITE RACE THEN YOU ARE AT HOME.

IF, ON THE OTHER HAND, YOU ARE CONSUMED WITH ONE OF THE MODERN MALIGNANT SOCIAL DISEASES SUCH AS LIBERALISM, ATHEISM, OR EGALITARIANISM, THEN YOU MOST DEFINITELY DIALED THE WRONG NUMBER.

THIS SYSTEM IS DEDICATED TO THE INTERESTS AND NEEDS OF WHITE PEOPLE. WE WISH TO BRING THE MOST LIED TO PEOPLE ON THE FACE OF EARTH THE TRUTH AS WE SEE IT. FOR ONCE IT IS HOPED TO PROVIDE YOU WITH THE OTHER SIDE OF ISSUES THAT AFFECT YOU ON A DAILY BASIS.

Press <SPACE-BAR> —

THIS SYSTEM IS MADE POSSIBLE BY THE WORK, SACRIFICE, AND MOST OF ALL
– LOVE –
OF THOSE WHO FIGHT FOR FAITH AND FOLK.

NOTICE!

Due to the large number of requests that we have received to open up the previously restricted side of the board, we are now giving the password necessary to access that part of the board. The password for the private side of the board is:

FREE AMERICA FROM THE ZIONIST OCCUPATIONAL GOVERNMENT

This is the password and must be entered in its entirety to access the "ESSAY" side of the board.

WELCOME TO THE CHICAGO LIBERTY NET!

Press <SPACE-BAR> —

Enter Password—free america from the zionist occupational government

1) ON REVOLUTIONARY MAJORITIES by Louis Beam
2) WHY AMERICANS WERE TAKEN HOSTAGE
3) OUR JUDEO–CHRISTIAN HERITAGE
4) THE BIRTH OF A NATION — AN ESSAY by Robert Miles
5) ADDRESS TO THE ARYAN NATIONS CONGRESS by Louis Beam
6) CHINA REPORT — SOME REFLECTIONS AND AFTERTHOUGHTS
7) ARE THE JEWS MURDERING CHRISTIAN CHILDREN ONCE AGAIN?
8) JUSTICE IN AMERICA?
9) ..no title line..
0) MORE TOPICS is a Menu

Choose [1,2,3,4,5,6,7,8,9,0,H,R,E,U,M] — 3

WE MAY NEED TO ROUND THEM UP SOON

Because of the terrible crisis this nation faces over the AIDS epidemic there can be no doubt that in a short time it will become necessary to round up all the queers in America for internment and quarantine. The Liberty Net has ordered and will soon take delivery of a new advanced computer program that will allow online acquisition of data via modem survey of callers.

This new program will allow us to compile the names and addresses of homosexuals into a single data base that can be acted upon when deemed expedient. We advise all callers to start collecting now the names and addresses of queers in their local area for entry into this online data base. You should also include in your list the addresses of all known deviant establishments where sodomites are known to congregate, as well as the names of restaurants where they work.

Press <SPACE-BAR> —

The data base once created will be an online nationwide hot line that allows any person to call up and see if someone he knows or works with is listed as a potential carrier of AIDS.

Information that will be needed on individual queers is as follows:

1. Full name
2. Address
3. Age
4. The names of all family members and close associates
5. Occupation if known

Start gathering this vital information now in anticipation of the Liberty Net going online with the new program. Remember, your health, the health of your children, and America's future may very well depend on this information.

If you have not yet read the article entitled AIDS Plague on this board, please do so now.

Let's wipe out AIDS in our lifetime . . .

Press <SPACE-BAR> —

You're at MAIN MENU

```
I)ntroduction
P)ublic menu
E)ssays
Q)uit
```

                              Choose__Q

        THANK YOU FOR CALLING THE CHICAGO LIBERTY NET
****

                         GOD! – FOLK! – NATION!

****

The above excerpt from a single Survival Right BBS is typical of others spread throughout the country.

The material quoted above is the barest glimpse of the contents of a neo-Nazi BBS. Each board, if read to its fullest, would be a document of well over 100,000 words, enough material to fill a substantial book.

Particularly appalling are a number of "essays" circulated among the Aryan Nations Net by Texas Klan leader Beam which are a bald effort to recruit an assassin to eliminate Morris Dees, an old-guard civil rights Democrat active in the South who has become a particular target for the fathers of the Survivalist computer network. A common message on the boards advises that Dees is a "sodomite" and that "it is believed by many Ku Klux Klan leaders around the nation that the real reason Morris Dees is so anti-Klan is because the Ku Klux Klan has called for the execution of every homosexual in America as per the injunction of the Holy Bible (see Leviticus 20, Verses 12 and 13). According to the word of our God, Morris Dees has earned two (2) death sentences. . . . Thy will be done in earth as it is in heaven."

Beam also offers for sale a videotape he made after taking a film crew to Montgomery—apparently with Order donations—"showing the abortion clinic, Dees's homosexual hangouts, and much more" for any members inclined to carry out the death sentence.

In 1986 Dees turned the situation to his favor somewhat by

sending a mailing to thousands of civil rights supporters asking for donations so that he could hire guards and fortify his home against neo-Nazi attacks.

One popular source of far-right video material was a Red Oaks, Iowa, barber named Paul Johnson, who circulated a catalogue of Survivalist videotapes that he was offering for sale through the mail to persons whose credentials were first thoroughly checked. One flier that Johnson enclosed with most of his catalogues observed:

> Wouldn't it be good to sit in front of your tv and watch speeches and interviews of Thomas Jefferson, Benjamin Franklin, John Adams, George Washington and Patrick Henry?
> I believe I am documenting on video tape some of the many leaders in the "second" fight for independence!
> This Giant is Waking Up!
> Are You a "Son of Liberty" or a "Red" coat?

The catalogue offers eighty-four two-hour videotapes for twenty-five dollars each. Among titles offered are these:

> —The Origins of Christmas (anti-Santa) by Paul Johnson
> —Black Power, Jew Power, White Weakness by Thom Robb. Iowa City, Iowa
> —About Gordon Kahl by Ed Udey
> —Spotlight Magazine by Lois Petersen
> —Relocation in Time of Crisis by B. F. M. von Stahl
> —The Populist Party by Robert Weems
> —When Jack Mohr Came to Colorado by Pastor Pete Peters
> —Friend or Foe? Jack Mohr delivers this talk to a church full of Baptists about whether the Jews are our friends or not. Very interesting.
> —Will Russia Invade the United States? by Jack Mohr—Jacksonville Conference
> —The Death of Farmer Arthur Kirk by State of Nebraska Senator Ernest Chambers
> —Heritage Library Up-Date on Farmers in Trouble by Larry Humphreys
> —The Sin that Will Destroy America by Pete Peters. A talk about interracial marriage.

As noted earlier, muckraking journalist Peter Lake was able to capitalize on the Survival Right's fascination with videotapes to infiltrate the group of Idaho neo-Nazis who turned out to be the Order. The importance of the new technology was further dramatized by the members of Michael Ryan's commune, who repeatedly viewed tapes of James Wickstrom sermons and made frequent calls to Wickstrom's "Fed Up American" hot line.

Also used to great effect are simple audio cassettes containing speeches such as the ones Lester Gibson recalled hearing in the Norton, Kansas, blacksmith's shop. The classified ads in the back of *Spotlight* often include pitches for audio cassettes of Identity sermons. One catalogue obtained through one of these ads from the Heirs of the Blessing in Herrin, Illinois, contained 165 titles. Here is a sampling:

> 9. Gordon Kahl's Last Words! Hear this collection of taped interviews with Kahl made shortly before his murder in Medina. This Martyr was an Identity Christian. (He knew Anglo-Saxons are the true descendants of the Israelites.) C-90 tape $5
>
> 23. Illuminati's Darkest Secrets Exposed! World-noted intelligence analyst reveals names of corporations, sub-organizations, and banksters behind the push for one-world-government. You must hear this up-to-date info. 2 C-90 tapes $6
>
> 27. Commander George Lincoln Rockwell Collection. An exciting, informative montage of speeches by this American hero. Hear Rockwell speak at his alma mater, Brown University. Listen as Jew terrorists and Jew supremacists try to drown him out, then thousands of white truth-seeking students shouting "Shut Up, Jews" as Rockwell drives home the Gospel! This Series also includes a debate tape between Rockwell and black agitator Stokely Carmichael. 5 C-60 tapes $7.50
>
> 41. The Danger of Eating Pork! Worms, Cancer and God's Judgment. C-60 tape $3
>
> 43. Ian Stuart's White Power Rock and Roll Band! A great gift tape for youngsters! No dope or sex stuff, just a crisp beat and patriotic lyrics! England's top underground band. Songs include: Hail the New Dawn, White Power, Race and Nation, Sick Society and more. Different !!!!!!!!!!!!!!!!!!! Cassette Only $5

46. Henry Kissinger—Agent of Doom! He is STILL the master controller that weaves the strands of conspiracy that aim for the downfall of America. C-90 tape $5

58. America's Alien Invasion. Illegal red aliens are swarming to our country on all shores and across both borders! You may be surprised to learn that this invasion of Christian-America is in Bible prophecy! C-60 tape $6

86. Who Are the Conspirators? The names of the people, families, institutions and companies who would enslave your children's children!!! C-60 tape $4

90. The Hate Campaign Against Dr. Mengele. The plot's purpose! C-90 tape $5

92. Triumph of the Will. The soundtrack of the 1934 Nazi Nuremberg Party Rally. Hear with your own ears what a people alive with the power of the Holy Spirit sound like after being born again as a nation with the restoration of all the laws of God (Racial, Economic, Agricultural, etc.) while the rest of the world slides into the pits of depression under Jewish capitalism and the slavery of Jewish communism. Great tape for German friends. C-90 tape $5

145. Revisionists Expose the Hoaxocausters! Our best single tape on the subject! Listen as the experts shine the light of truth down the dark historical holes of the single biggest lie to come out of World War Two! C-90 tape only $4

With most automobiles now equipped with tape players, and with portable models selling at places like K Mart for under twenty dollars complete with stereo headphones, the audiotape operation seems to be flourishing. In less than two years, the Heirs to the Blessing outfit's catalogue went from a dozen titles to more than a gross of different cassettes, from which the above sampling was taken.

Butler apparently took advantage of the tape cassette boom as early as 1979, when he set up his Aryan Cassette Service, which for a monthly donation of fifteen dollars will provide tapes of each of his Sunday sermons. His monthly Aryan Nations Catalog offers a wide selection of books, pamphlets and other materials along with the cassettes.

In addition to promulgating the credo of hatred, the sale of tapes, books and other materials has become a major financial resource for outfits like Butler's or the neo-Nazi group National Vanguard, operated by William Pierce, author of the novel *The Turner Diaries*. Ironically enough, the exploits of the Order transformed *The Turner Diaries* into something of an underground best-seller and therefore a major Survival Right recruiting aid. First published in 1978, the book was dormant until 1985, when Pierce issued a second printing through his National Vanguard Books in Arlington, Virginia.

An ad for Pierce's pornographically violent racist novel brags: "The FBI has labeled *The Turner Diaries* as a 'manual of hatred.' Liberals in the news media likewise have condemned it and over the past few months have joined the campaign to expose it as 'the bible of right-wing extremists.' *The Turner Diaries* is the most controversial book in America. If the government had the power to ban books, *The Turner Diaries* would be at the top of the list. Order your copy today."

In terms of spreading the message of hatred, Pierce has become the Mortimer Adler of the Survival Right. His National Vanguard Books sells scores of titles he has selected, and while many are the product of fringe-group publishers like his own house, the catalogue also offers titles from major publishers in the United States and Europe, particularly selections on Nazi Germany, Nordic sagas, anthropology and Zionism. It includes dozens of slick paperback coffee table books about Vikings as well as *Adolf Hitler: The Unknown Artist*, featuring 900 plates of Hitler's paintings, drawings and designs, which, the catalogue gushes, "testify to the talent and artistic ability of the preeminent individual of this century." It also offers a wide selection on the topic of race, including *Race and Reason* and *Race and Reality* by Carleton Putnam, "written in an easy-to-read style for those new to racial thinking." Under the category "Communism, Zionism, and the Second World War" are Henry Ford's infamous *International Jew* and *Did Six Million Really Die?*, which concludes that the Holocaust was a hoax designed "to gain undeserved sympathy for Israel and world Jewry."

Each catalogue suggests to would-be Smerdyakovs that they embark on a Survivalist's version of the Great Books Program, citing thirty titles as "must reading" in the categories of "History," "Legend and Folkways," "Race: Science & Sociology," "The Enemy" and, naturally, "The Solution."

"Every responsible, racially conscious White person must read *Which Way Western Man, The Might of the West, Mein Kampf* (Mannheim edition) . . ." advises Pierce. "Then, and only then, should he read *The Turner Diaries*, which will be too strong a dish for any reader who has not thoroughly prepared himself for it."

It bears recalling that Matthews, in the letter to his hometown newspaper explaining his own road to the Survival Right quoted earlier, tells how he undertook the precise reading program prescribed by Pierce before topping it off with *The Turner Diaries*.

An even larger rightist book sales operation is run by the Liberty Lobby and called Liberty Library, which sells hundreds of titles, ranging from Willis Carto's *Profiles in Populism*, used to launch the Populist Party, to reprints of past *Spotlight* special editions on such topics as "The Trilateral Connection," "Israel and the Bible," "Will Meddling in the Mideast Trigger Nuclear Holocaust?," "Christian Holocaust," "One Worlders Will Destroy Constitution" and the ever-popular "The Great Holocaust Debate," which includes such articles as "Famous 'Gas Chamber Victims' Living Well" and "Patriot Smeared in Phony 'Nazi' Hunt."

A newly burgeoning vehicle for pushing the ideology is the various public-access cable television channels which were created under federal laws passed when the nation began wiring itself for cable in the early 1980s. That legislation requires cable operators to make several of the dozens of channels they operate available for public service programming, including public-access channels which are available to anybody in the community. While promoted as ideal outlets for playing videotapes of high school class plays, lectures by the county agricultural extension agent on gardening tips, small-town city council meetings and other items not usually covered by

Dan Rather and his big-time colleagues, the public-access channels can also be used in lieu of a soapbox by any political visionary with the persistence and stamina to demand a share of airtime.

Tom Metzger, the Southern California television repairman who ran as a Klansman in the 1980 congressional races and received 13 percent of the vote in his San Diego County district, began using public-access channels in that state during 1984 to produce master tapes which are now being aired in many states by Survivalist followers. Demanding his share of public access, Metzger forced Group W Cable Co. to allow him to use its Channel 38 in Southern California and the station's recording facilities at California State College in Fullerton to tape and broadcast a program he called "Race and Reason" after the Putnam book of the same title recommended in Pierce's reading program.

Using the recording studios at the university's Instructional Media Center, which had been designated the main production site for Group W's public-access program in the Los Angeles area, Metzger taped interviews in which he and other Survival Right luminaries discussed their credo. Then Metzger, who prosecutors say received money from the Order's infamous crime wave, distributed copies of tapes of those programs to allies around the United States, who, in turn, took the tapes to their local cable operators and demanded that they be played on the public-access channel.

Metzger eventually found local sponsors who managed to get "Race and Reason" played on cable stations throughout California and Pennsylvania, as well as in areas of New York, Georgia, Texas and Tennessee. Much of the successful drive was coordinated through WAR, the tabloid published by Metzger's White Aryan Resistance and billed as "the newspaper of the international white racist."

In WAR's columns Metzger urged his followers: "Why haven't you contacted your cable company yet to get an Aryan show on TV? Write Race & Reason care of WAR to find out how to go about it. Do it today, instead of just complaining about Jew TV. Jews didn't take over TV by sitting around complaining and you won't liberate the TV from them by anything other than guts and action."

In fact, Metzger became something of a mastermind in the Survival Right's efforts to exploit relatively commonplace but newly emerging technologies as part of its political organizing. He advised his readers to go out and buy telephone-answering machines for use as telephone hot lines. Proselytizers simply dictate their spiel onto the outgoing message tape and then advertise their phone number everywhere from laundromat bulletin boards to classified ads in major newspapers.

Metzger's personal 1986 Holiday Season telephone hot-line message opened with tinny music playing the Christmas carol "Deck the Halls with Boughs of Holly." Then a deliberately nasal voice chimes in: "Hello. What, you may ask, am I, George Cohen, doing standing here in a Santa Claus suit? Why should I, a Jew, love Christmas? Well, if you owned stock in all the big Jew-owned department stores—Macy's, Saks, Neiman-Marcus—you'd love Christmas too. And Christmas is a time people buy furs, diamonds, all the high-markup items. It's a time we Jews really rake in the shekels. Question: why did God make Gentiles? Somebody's got to buy retail. So now's the time to put out that Christmas Day coin . . ." Sophomoric as the message may have been, the medium illustrates how the new breed of Survivalists cleverly exploits new technology to keep its message current.

Another innovative Survival Right strategy has been an ambitious drive to use American prisons as a major recruiting ground. Largely as a result of firsthand knowledge of prisons by leaders such as Robert Miles and the Order's Gary Yarbrough, who themselves served sentences, the Survival Right has been involved in a major—and very successful—prison crusade since the late 1970s, when Miles was released after serving six years for conspiracy in the bombing of the Pontiac, Michigan, school bus fleet and a plan to tar and feather a local high school principal who advocated integrated classrooms.

It is generally agreed by former inmates and prison authorities alike that there is no penitentiary in the United States rougher than the federal institution at Marion, Illinois, where Miles, gray of hair, thick of waist, in his late fifties and early sixties, served his time. Miles is quick to acknowledge that it was his time in "the cages of ZOG" that inspired him to maintain a highly active prison ministry after his own release in 1979. He likes to point out that currently there are 6,240,000 Americans who have served time in prison. "How does that grab you as a political lobbying group?" he wrote in his bimonthly newsletter, *From the Mountain*, in October 1986.

A prison is an ideal hothouse in which to grow a latter-day American Nazi. Racial tensions are a daily fact of life. In most institutions blacks band together to dominate the pecking order, while whites and Hispanics seek safety in numbers of their own. A 1985 study by the Justice Department's Federal Bureau of Prisons entitled "Prison Gangs, Their Extent, Nature and Impact on Prisons" found a total of 114 gangs in state and federal prisons in the United States. That study noted that gang membership "is based first on race, and is usually connected with racial superiority beliefs."

In fact, prison life in today's America is a world where survival itself often depends upon aligning oneself with members of one's own race. Blacks cluster together in groups like the New African People's Organization, the Black Guerrilla Family, El-Rukin and the Revolutionary Communist Party. Whites join groups with names like Aryan Warriors, Aryan Nations, and the Ku Klux Klan, the Justice Department study found. Perhaps the most dominant group among the whites is the Aryan Brotherhood, a prison gang that may have more chapters and more members than the college fraternity Sigma Chi. Authorities estimate that there are 5,300 hard-core gang members in Illinois prisons alone.

There are strong indications that the Aryan Brotherhood extorts money from white prisoners it pressures to join its ranks. One Arizona State Prison inmate, James Bowen, who once served as the Aryan Brotherhood's minister of finance, said that at one point his group had more money than it could handle and that he sent several thousand dollars in donations to Butler's aides for distribution to Brotherhood members in other jails. The money was raised both from funds that individual inmates donated from their personal trust accounts and from the sale of drugs behind prison walls, Bowen testified in an Arizona state court.

Commonly, white prisoners readily agree with neo-Nazi recruiters who tell them that they are actually prisoners of war, incarcerated by a Jewish-dominated system that favors blacks and other minorities. Even those who don't buy the racist ideas find the Aryan Brotherhood a welcome refuge from the very real dangers of prison life. The Justice Department report found substantial Aryan Brotherhood chapters in federal prisons and state institutions in Arizona, Arkansas, California, Kentucky, Missouri, Nevada, Ohio and Oklahoma.

In New Mexico, state penitentiary warden George Sullivan told the Albuquerque Rotary Club in June 1985 that gang tensions were so high in the state prison at Santa Fe that of the 525 inmates in his penitentiary more than 200 were being kept in protective custody because of threats—usually racially motivated—from prison gangs.

A typical example of racial prison tensions between whites and blacks erupted in late 1986 in Yarbrough's alma mater, the Arizona State Prison in Florence.

On October 23, 1986, Aryan Brotherhood member Paul Engle, twenty-eight, was in the institution's law library, doing research on yet another petition he planned to file demanding access to white supremacist literature, when he got into a shouting match with a black inmate, Mark Allen Osborne. An avid Aryan Brotherhood member, Engle would have been released from prison long before except for an additional sentence imposed for possession of weapons after he joined forces with the Aryans. Osborne, a member of the Black Guerrilla Family, slashed Engle's throat with a homemade knife. The next morning, Dennis Haymon, another black inmate, was blinded by knives wielded by two Aryan Brotherhood members, and a full-scale riot erupted, leading to the hospitalization of nineteen inmates and the death of a black prisoner, Roy J. Ellis.

At a 1985 meeting of his Mountain Kirk, the Identity church that Miles heads on his farm near Cohoctah, Michigan, Miles reported to an audience of neo-Nazis, Klan members and Identity adherents that he was currently corresponding with 1,800 Aryan Brotherhood prisoners using computerized mailing lists. He described his goal as "to alert our people within the institution when one of ours is being imprisoned by the system so the new inmate will receive the proper friendly reception." He added, "White survival activists are encouraged to support movement prisoners either directly or through the Mountain Church in whatever way they choose, as these prisoners will one day be out of prison and will be part of the movement's 'irregular forces.' "

The Survival Right labors mightily to take care of its folk heroes who now reside behind the prison bars of "ZOG." Miles's newsletter, *Beyond the Bars . . . the Stars!*, is mailed to thousands of inmates each month, even though many of them are denied access to the publication by wardens fearful of the sort of violence exemplified by the events in Arizona.

Metzger's White Aryan Resistance tabloid publishes a standing list of inmates, complete with prison addresses, along with a plea to readers to send them letters of encouragement.

Other right-wing groups, such as the publishers of *Justice Times*, a Survivalist tabloid published in Clinton, Arkansas, work to help the families of inmates in the fold while they serve penalties for crimes such as failure to file income tax returns. *Justice Times* maintains a "Remembrance Club" by publishing names and addresses of the families of tax protesters who are in prison so that sympathizers can make donations and pass along notes of encouragement that can be forwarded by the families to the inmates.

Yet another branch of the Survivalist prison outreach is the Aryan Resistance Movement (ARM), a group made up of past and current inmates who make a distinction between those who join the Aryan prisoner groups for pure survival and those who are involved in the movement largely for ideological reasons. ARM's publication, *Whitefire*, urges inmates to work within the prison system and "not to break ZOG's rules and regulations, if possible," in an effort to hasten their release from prison so they can become active in the movement.

Another major role of ARM, according to Miles's *From the Mountain*, is to help racists determine if the inmates they are communicating with are truly members of the movement and not federal informants. "In the event that you are communicating with a POW, and you feel that something is not right/White, send us that POW's name, number and address, and any information about him (i.e., people he has mentioned, groups he or she is supposedly connected to, etc.) and we will investigate such for you," an ARM member identified only as "Thunder" offered in Miles's September–October 1986 newsletter. "ARM has an outstanding network of communications in prisons across the nation." Thunder's letter continues: "There are times when ZOG puts one of our POWs in a place like the [Washington] DC jail, where the population is 99 percent black, and then passes the word that he is a White racist, hoping that the congoids will kill him. The federals love to do that where they seek leverage in other matters from such prisoners. However, that usually backfires against ZOG. Even the congoids see through it. Our kinsmen inside ZOG's cages do not live in constant battle with the mud races, as so many of you seem to believe."

Although he lacked the hands-on experience with prisons that Miles acquired at Marion, Richard Butler has long maintained a prison outreach project of his own. Butler's pitch centered more on religion, and Janet Hounsell, the secretary at Butler's Aryan Nations compound, said she personally was writing letters to hundreds of inmates and sending each one the group's monthly publication, *Calling Our Nations*. In frequent court testimony, Butler demanded that inmates who said they belonged to his Church of Jesus Christ Christian should be allowed to receive its materials despite objections from prison administrators that the publications in question advocated open violence ag :nst minority prisoners.

After his arrest in the Order case, Gary Yarbrough told reporters that he joined the movement after studying Aryan Nations literature.

He said that he had been sitting in an isolation cell at Arizona State Prison praying for a sign from God when a guard came in with a letter from Hounsell asking him to join the organization. When he was released in 1979, Yarbrough moved onto Butler's compound, where he used the training he received in the penitentiary's printshop to set up Butler's printing press, the same machine he was to use half a decade later to produce counterfeit currency for the Order's "Assault on the Gold of ZOG."

A study of anti-Semitic activism in American prisons conducted in 1986 by B'nai B'rith found that inmates routinely receive mailings from a number of hate groups who clearly find prisons a potentially fertile seedbed for new members.

One publication commonly mailed behind bars is *Michigan Briefing*, the newsletter of the Detroit-based SS Action Group, which announced in its July 1984 issue: "We of the SS are 'at war' with the Jew-controlled system. Our White brothers and sisters who are prisoners in this war and are currently incarcerated in our nation's prisons will receive the *Michigan Briefing* at no charge, courtesy of our prison program . . ."

The Talon, published by the Euro-American Alliance in Milwaukee, is distributed free to inmates who request it and often has been used to raise funds from prisoners for such causes as the Greensboro Eight Defense Fund, which was used to help the Klansmen who shot five left-wing activists to death on a Greensboro, North Carolina, street on November 3, 1979.

The National Socialist Liberation Front, a neo-Nazi group in Louisiana, distributes a newsletter called *Sinn Fein* ("ourselves alone"), described as "the only national publication written by and for imprisoned Aryan Partisans."

The 1985 Justice Department study of prison gangs found major Ku Klux Klan groups in prisons in Arkansas, Georgia and Texas and noted that a number of Klan publications, such as *White Man's Bible*, were being mailed to inmates in several states.

In October 1986 Miles wrote: "528,945 residents reside in the prisons of America. Multiply that by ten and you have approximately the number of people with prison records alive. Add to that a million or so more who were put on probation, and you have an idea as to the convictions of felonies, state or federal. Since convicted felons may never again legally own or have possession of firearms and their spouses should not, either, there is already gun control in this country. Interesting."

The always quotable Miles sent this homily to his prison ministry and other followers:

> We were asked about bank robbers recently. Your editor replied that he knew quite a few. The reporter raised his eyebrows and asked for names. The reply was "Hmm, the banks who robbed Mexico; the banks who robbed Brazil; the banks who are robbing America's farmers; the banks who are robbing the American small businessmen." The reporter objected that he didn't mean that type of bank robber. We replied that they are the real robbers. The kind who waltz into a bank with a gun, we call "impatient withdrawers," while the really dangerous robbers are the ones who own and operate the banks.

The Survival Right's prison outreach got a big boost in Seattle when the ten "impatient withdrawers" known as the Order were sent to prison for terms ranging from sixty to one hundred years. Even as they were being led away Order members vowed to concentrate on recruiting in the penal institutions for which they were bound.

Yarbrough, perhaps anticipating the nature of his new surroundings, said in a jailhouse interview the day after his conviction, "I do not hate blacks, or Mexicans, or Jews, but I don't want to live with them." He said he was certain that he would win the Aryan Nations many converts through his own on-the-scene prison ministry. "When people first see me, they think of all these things they've seen on TV, calling me a white supremacist, neo-Nazi—which I am not—but let me talk to them a half hour. They'll change their minds."

Even as the Order trial was underway, Frank Silva, the relatively minor group member who helped Jean Craig maintain message centers for the commandos after several of the armored car robberies, was actively proselytizing from his jail cell.

The Seattle *Post-Intelligencer* quoted officials at the Pierce County Jail, where the Order defendants were kept during the five-month trial, who said that Silva sent a steady stream of letters and other materials to inmates in various prisons during the hours he wasn't sitting in the courtroom.

Bruce Carroll Pierce, the gunman in the Berg assassination, told Kevin Flynn of the *Rocky Mountain News* during an interview at Leavenworth Prison that he and his cellmate, Order member Randolph Duey, have been active in recruiting other prisoners to the racist movement since being jailed. Of the Order, he said, "We're still a group, albeit incarcerated. But the ideas and principles of the group and what we wanted are still intact, even though we're in prison right now. Just exactly what that can mean, whether that means someone else will rise up and do some of the same things, I don't have the slightest idea. But the ideas that we had, what we wanted to accomplish, I think that will continue to live within the movement for as long as this earth is intact, which I don't feel is going to be very long."

Perhaps the most active incarcerated Order member has been David Lane. First jailed at the federal penitentiary in Fort Wayne, Indiana, Lane was transferred to Miles's alma mater, the maximum security institution at Marion, after prison officials concluded that his constant haranguing of fellow inmates was disruptive.

Once in the penitentiary at Marion, Lane became an active correspondent with a neo-Nazi group in northern Idaho who called themselves Bruder Schweigen II. That group was broken up after several members were charged with the September 1986 bombings of three buildings in Coeur d'Alene, including the federal building and the house of the Reverend Bill Wassmuth, a Roman Catholic priest who emerged as the leading Idaho establishment critic of Butler and his followers in the neighboring hamlet of Hayden Lake.

The Survival Right, then, is active in its political organizing all across the American landscape. It operates out of prison cells in

Indiana just as it does from LaRouche card tables in America's airports. The message is beamed electronically to home computers and carried as well by hundreds of tabloids and magazines. Zealots tie up their home phones to operate racist and anti-Semitic "hot lines," and there appears to be a brisk market in videotapes and audio cassettes bearing the same message now being beamed across America via cable television. Meanwhile, polls taken by Louis Harris, Marvin Field and others indicate an alarming acceptance of that message both in the American heartland and in California, where so many national trends first surface.

To be sure, the movement in question is very much on the fringes of current American political life. But it is, for all that, a fairly substantial fringe and, above all, a very dangerous one. Far too many people already have suffered and died at the hands of the Survival Right for its minions to be taken lightly. It is important to attempt to fathom just what is it that makes otherwise normal-appearing men and women accept the credo best described as the Survival Sickness.

You can certainly destroy enough of humanity so that only the greatest act of faith can persuade you that what's left will be human.

—J. Robert Oppenheimer, chief bomb designer for the Manhattan Project

8: Survival of the Fittest

When America's incurably upbeat newspaper *USA Today* took one of its innumerable polls on the eve of Ronald Reagan's 1985 Geneva Nuclear Arms Control summit meeting with Mikhail Gorbachev, 81 percent of those questioned said they believed a nuclear war would kill everybody in both countries within a few years of opening day.

That left 19 percent, or roughly one of every five Americans questioned, taking the view shared by the Survival Right, that "the end time" can be overcome. The article by John Omicinski and Paul Clancey. "If an all-out U.S.–U.S.S.R. nuclear exchange comes there is widespread agreement that it would be a doomsday war, leaving an unlivable globe in its ashes. Most of those surveyed felt that neither the Soviets nor the U.S.A. is so stupid as to launch such a war."

Robert S. McNamara, Defense Secretary during the Kennedy and Johnson administrations, articulated this same hopeful view in a 1982 interview with author Robert Scheer of the *Los Angeles Times*:

The Russians are people that I would not trust to act in other than their own narrow national interest, so I am not naive. But they are not mad. They are not mad. They have suffered casualties, and their government feels responsible to their people to avoid those situations in the future. They are more sensitive to the impact of casualties on their people than we appear to be in some of our statements and analyses of fighting and winning nuclear wars which would extend over a period of months.

So they are not mad. They are aggressive; they are ideological; they need to be restrained and contained by the existence of our defense forces, but they are not mad, and I see no evidence that they would accept the risks associated with a first strike against the United States.

Almost as if he was reassuring himself, McNamara stated four times in less than two hundred words on the subject that the Soviets are not mad enough to launch their nuclear missiles.

But while McNamara and virtually all other relatively normal Americans fret over hopes that the other side will not be so mad as to open the floodgates to Armageddon, the Survival Right remains convinced that evil forces are at work behind the scenes and that the machinations of these vile conspirators will bring the long-dreaded global nuclear war. To those infected with the Survival Sickness, fate is out of the hands of mere Russians, whether they are mad or not.

The Survival Right knows that the end is coming courtesy of satanic forces that have conspired throughout history to undermine America. Often this conspiracy is viewed in religious terms as a crusade by Satan and his seed to wreak havoc upon God's true chosen people, the Celts, Lombards, Aryans and other members of Yahweh's true chosen white race. Other times, Survivalists cling to this paranoid perspective without any religious overlay. Either way, they and their counterparts in mainstream America are reacting to the same environment, the existential background noise of terror that plays in the minds of virtually every human operating above the subsistence level on the globe today.

Just listing the facts is numbing:

The United States has 1,043 intercontinental ballistic missiles; the Soviet Union possesses 1,398 ICBMs.

United States, 568 nuclear missile submarines; Soviet Union, 950 missile subs.

United States, 297 manned strategic bombers; Soviet Union, 356 nuclear bombers.

Counting the racks of bombs aboard the planes, the multiple nuclear warheads on the missiles and other inventories in the U.S. arsenal, American commanders have an estimated 10,000 nuclear weapons at their disposal and the number is growing as new generations of cruise missiles enter the field.

Soviet inventories are generally estimated at 7,000 warheads, all with explosive forces ranging between 70 kilotons and 10 megatons. Every one of these warheads is several orders of magnitude more powerful than the devastating 25-kiloton bombs, "Big Boy" and "Fat Man," that President Truman ordered dropped on Nagasaki and Hiroshima to usher in the era of nuclear terror that is now well into its fifth decade.

The sixteen missile tubes on just one American Poseidon submarine carry more explosive power than the hundreds of thousands of tons of bombs that produced the horrible firestorms at Dresden and Tokyo, the massive destruction of London and Berlin, Warsaw and Manila, and all the other devastation that took place during World War II. Every bullet fired, every bomb exploded, every hand grenade tossed, every artillery shell lobbed during World War II, if combined, would not contain the explosive force of a single American or Russian sub.

Furthermore, Americans have grown up with the knowledge that unbelievable terrors await those unlucky enough to survive Day One of World War III. They recall how the late Soviet Premier Nikita Khrushchev once described the world after a thermonuclear exchange as one in which "the living will curse the dead" out of envy. A relatively small one-megaton nuclear blast over even a medium-sized city would, for example, cause grave third-degree burns in at least 10,000 people, but in the entire United States there are facilities to treat only about 2,500 burn victims.

That one-megaton warhead detonated in the center of a city would produce explosive forces between 10 and 30 pounds per square inch of pressure (psi), generating winds of between 290 and 470 miles an hour. Pressures of 12 psi would suffice to topple and pulverize the twin towers of New York's World Trade Center and kill some 98 percent of the people within a three-mile radius.

Such a blast detonated in Chicago's downtown Loop would generate sudden pressure waves of at least 95 miles per hour three-quarters of the way to the remote North Shore suburb of Evanston, killing anyone standing unprotected in the streets.

Planners anticipate that in a full-scale nuclear war such major cities might expect to receive as many as a dozen warheads.

A major nuclear exchange would saturate the U.S. landscape with deadly radioactive fallout. A one-megaton nuclear detonation on the ground in downtown Detroit on a day with a prevailing 15-mile-per-hour wind blowing out of the northwest would send a plume containing fatal radioactive doses of 900 rems all the way across Lake Erie to Cleveland. A 300-rem plume would reach from Motown almost to Pittsburgh, and one of 90 rems—causing at least serious radiation sickness—would reach all the way from Detroit to the Maryland border.

One of the more dramatic illustrations of how World War III would threaten oblivion for humanity came when Defense Department planners were studying the now abandoned plan to move 200 MX missiles back and forth among a complex of 4,600 silos in Nevada and Utah, which would have forced the Soviets to target 4,600 of their warheads to be certain of wiping out the American missiles. Such a Soviet attack would have produced a plume that would have ridden on prevailing winds from the west to drop enough fallout to produce fatalities as far east as Kansas and radiation sickness as far away as Virginia.

Dr. Helen Caldicott, the Australian pediatrician who became a major leader in the U.S. nuclear disarmament movement, dramatically described the consequences of this massive fallout in her book *Missile Envy: The Arms Race and Nuclear War*. According to Caldicott, people ensconced in fallout shelters after a nuclear bombardment would live in unbelievably horrendous squalor. Since many of the people in the shelter would have arrived after the detonations, there would be widespread radiation sickness, including "vomiting with liquid and bloody diarrhea." "Of course," writes Caldicott, "there will be no adequate sanitation, no toilets or sewage system. At best, there may be a small chemical unit. People will have to live with decomposing bodies and revolting sanitary conditions. They cannot go outside without risking exposure to lethal levels of radiation."

In any case, Caldicott concludes that after withstanding these horrors for weeks or months, the shelter denizens will die anyway as a result of climatic changes brought on by the nuclear explosions. Cornell University's immensely popular astronomer-writer Carl Sagan produced a series of controversial studies in the early 1980s that found that after a substantial majority of all Americans were killed outright or by lingering radiation sickness, the rest of the world's population likely would perish within a few months or years as a result of a "nuclear winter" created when blast-borne dust particles blocked out natural sunlight long enough to cause catastrophic weather changes.

The U.S. government's Federal Emergency Management Agency (FEMA), the branch now in charge of civil defense, has drawn up numerous scenarios in which persons fleeing from such horrors in the cities would find refuge and sanctuary among their neighbors in outlying rural areas—a bureaucratic fantasy known as the Crisis Relocation Program (CRP). The CRP for Denver, for example, calculates that the expressways would allow "1,000 vehicles per lane per hour" to flee a nuclear attack against that relatively small city. At that rate, however, FEMA estimated it would take twenty-eight hours to evacuate the Mile-High City. Denverites then would have to find shelter with hosts in mountain communities like Idaho

Springs, Glenwood Springs, Grand Lake and Granby, according to the contingency plan. Predictably, community leaders in those towns were less than avid supporters of the plan to provide shelter and succor for Denverites who would outnumber the entire population of their communities thousands of times over.

Faced with this calculus of terror, most people, especially those living in metropolitan areas, quickly reject speculation about surviving the initial thermonuclear exchange or the horrors that would follow. But, particularly in rural precincts, it still is possible to believe that one can survive even while people concentrated in urban pockets perish wholesale.

Every living man, woman and child, of course, must come to terms with the nuclear monkey so firmly lodged on everybody's back. While a child of urban America most likely will have to reason that the best thing to hope for would be a quick death, it is not totally irrational for somebody living in a village in Wyoming, on a dairy ranch in Idaho or in a small city in Montana to conclude that with the proper weapons, the requisite food, medicine, clothing and other survival gear, one can get past the crisis.

Similarly, it is not irrational for somebody living even deep in the heart of Chicago, St. Louis, Los Angeles or any other major city to speculate whether it might be possible to pack up and flee to safety in the countryside once it becomes clear that the world's leadership is moving toward the brink. More than one canny rural real estate dealer has made a fortune selling survival plots to people from the city. Live Free Inc. of Harvey, Illinois, for example, boasts a thirty-nine-acre survivalist center near Baraboo, Wisconsin, a hundred miles from the Chicago suburbs.

Thus is born the workaday American survivalist. For the purpose at hand this is a survivalist with a small *s*, not a political zealot, not a racist, not an anti-Semite or adherent of Identity, the Posse or any other right-wing credo. This survivalist is just somebody with a natural drive for self-preservation and a hope for getting past the inevitable nuclear exchange. But as has been clearly shown in earlier pages, there is an increasingly fine line that separates ordinary and presumably mentally healthy people who begin dabbling in small-*s* survivalism from those who burst forth on the scene with semi-automatics and machine guns blazing, full-blown members of the Survival Right.

Many social scientists have speculated that simply embracing survivalist goals is a symptom of looming psychic problems. In his 1982 book *The Chosen Few: Surviving the Nuclear Holocaust*, sociologist Edward Myers speculated that ordinary survivalists are simply people who adopt the same sort of world view that kept pioneer mountain men like Jim Bridger going in times of stress—a conception of humanity focused on "me and my world" that made them the sort of rugged individualists who became American icons.

Unfortunately, that self-centered mentality removes these people from the ranks of humankind, Myers argues. Otherwise they might have worked to change the balance of terror instead of simply becoming iconoclastic doomsayers out to save their own hides. Warning of survivalism, Myers quotes Harvard psychiatrist John E. Mack:

> It is sinister because people don't want to deal with painful reality. Survivalism helps them avoid it. People do this all the time [avoid reality]. We all do this, including when we have to think about nuclear war. The point is that in order really to survive, people need to take responsibility for facing this nuclear reality which is so scary, and shouldn't succumb to fatalism—shouldn't assume that war is inevitable. The result of survivalism is that a lot of people who aren't working to prevent nuclear war are deceiving others by helping them think they can avoid the problem.

At this point in exploring the landscape of the Survival Right one comes up against a classic chicken-and-egg problem. Do normal people lapse into ultraright madness as a result of pursuing their dreams of surviving? Or do individuals already affected with such forms of right-wing fervor as the Ku Klux Klan, the John Birch Society, neo-Nazism and Christian Identity just naturally gravitate toward Survivalism as they pursue their credos of hatred?

It bears keeping in mind that a person with a typically right-leaning mind-set would appear much more likely to gravitate toward the Survivalist's world of combat weapons, camouflage clothing and practice at guerrilla warfare than would somebody with a leftward pacifistic bent. If there is a left-wing component of Survivalism, it probably consists of people who cast their plans along the lines of the *Whole Earth Catalog* and *Mother Earth News* and don't let their children play with toy guns out of a sense of social commitment.

As Harvard psychiatrist Mack noted, the very process of laying survivalist plans is an antisocial act. One does not have to think very deeply about the realities of attempting post-nuclear-blast survival to realize that the most important question, after stockpiling food, water, clothing, machine guns and other gear, is protecting these treasures from the hordes of the less foresighted who are likely to start streaming out of the cities either just before or just after the missiles fly. In fact, it seems that preparation for waging war against these hordes of desperate fellow Americans, as well as any invading Soviet troops, is the common thread that draws survivalists of both the small-*s* and the large-*S* variety together.

At this point, one thing can be stated with certainty. When the small-*s* survivalists set out to swap ideas with like-minded people, they don't have very far to look before running up against the Survival Right. Whether answering an ad in the back of a magazine offering tips on finding drinking water in a post-nuclear environment or hanging around the local gun shop, anyone planning for survival soon will encounter the large-*S* crowd.

It also can be said with some certainty that the godfather of latter-day American survivalism of both the big-*S* and the small-*s* variety is Robert DePugh, the Missouri manufacturer of vitamins for pets and livestock who took up Christian Identity and race hatred in the late 1950s and founded the notorious precursor of the Posse Comitatus, the ardently Survivalist group called the Minutemen.

DePugh's activities as founder of the Minutemen have been dealt with earlier (Chapter 5). After leading the group to national notoriety for almost a decade, DePugh was imprisoned for nearly four years on federal firearms charges. While in prison, according to his later writings, he spent much time in solitary confinement thinking about the Survivalist movement. Unlike most denizens of the Survival Right, DePugh had acquired substantial experience living off the land as a hunted fugitive during the seventeen months between when he jumped bail on the firearms charges and the day he was apprehended. Part of that time DePugh survived above 12,000 feet in the Colorado Rockies, and the rest was spent moving about the New Mexico deserts before his 1970 arrest in the aptly named town of Truth or Consequences, New Mexico.

Within three months of his release from prison in 1973, DePugh published *Can You Survive? Guidelines for Resistance to Tyranny for You and Your Family*, a 214-page treatise on how to prepare for the coming catastrophe, whether it is to be race rioting, economic chaos caused when the Federal Reserve Board calls in all U.S. currency, or the long-awaited nuclear attack.

This amazing publication is chock-full of extremely imaginative tips about how to survive in a house in the city, on a farm, while foraging through populated countrysides and, finally, in wilderness areas like the Colorado mountains where DePugh remained a fugitive for nearly a year.

DePugh advises city dwellers to cut gunports into their houses just above the basement line and remove all shrubbery from the grounds to deny approaching intruders cover. Wire mesh should be placed over windows to deflect hand grenades and Molotov cocktails. Fire extinguishers should be kept near each shooting adult. Families should practice listening from the basement as somebody walks on the floor above so they can locate any intruders and fire at them through the floorboards.

An alternative urban survival plan that DePugh calls "deception" consists of hiding family members in crawl spaces, fake heating ducts and other specially prepared refuges while the expected marauders sweep through the house. His favorite tactic is to conceal an entire fallout shelter by putting up a false concrete or cinder-block wall in the basement. DePugh describes how to build a trapdoor and then bolt a piece of furniture to it so that the family can swiftly slip away when trouble erupts.

Substantial space is given to such esoteric techniques as hunting and fighting on moonless nights by using the faintest of sky glows to "background" a targeted person or animal. There also is material, similar to that found in a Boy Scout manual, telling how to start a fire, which direction to face a lean-to, how thick a sleeping bag must be for a given temperature and, of course, the relative merits of various guns for the various members of a Survivalist family.

After an appropriately reverent discussion of the sexy firearms so favored by people like Robert Matthews, David Young, Gordon Kahl and others of the movement, DePugh advises that the best bet is a sturdy .22 caliber semiautomatic pistol, the sort farm boys use to "plink away" at rabbits, squirrels and other varmints.

Such a weapon is extremely lightweight and, when equipped with a rest, is nearly as accurate as a rifle at up to fifty yards, says DePugh, and .22 ammunition is very cheap compared with bullets for more ambitious weapons. Better yet, it is lightweight and small. DePugh notes that 500 rounds of .22 ammo weigh only 3.5 pounds and can easily be carried in one's pockets. By comparison, 500 rounds of .357 Magnum pistol ammunition weighs 35 pounds and would fill a briefcase, while that much .30-06 hunting rifle ammo would fill an automobile trunk.

Acknowledging that .22s lack the killing power of the bigger guns, DePugh suggests that Survivalists buy bullets with hollow points and fill them with lye, thereby greatly enhancing their death-dealing ability.

Perhaps the most striking—and unexpected—advice the canny old survivor has to offer is in the realm of food. He bears ultimate scorn for the freeze-dried foods that have long been sold through Survivalist catalogues such as those offered in the back of *Soldier of Fortune* magazine. To be consumed, these dehydrated meals require three or four times their weight in precious water, and, DePugh emphasizes, the most difficult commodity for a Survivalist to maintain is a steady water supply.

If one is really serious about surviving, DePugh advises, there is a readily available food that precisely fills the bill. This food costs about twenty-five cents for three daily servings and contains virtually all needed vitamins, minerals, proteins, carbohydrates, etc. It is dry dog food, explains the Survivalist who became a wealthy man selling vitamins for pets under the name Fidomins.

Dry dog food is better than the canned variety because it takes up less space, but even more importantly, it tastes much better, DePugh explains. He likens the taste to that of dry breakfast cereal and advises that the serving can be dressed up with a little sugar and some reconstituted dried milk. He notes that a hundred-pound sack of dry dog food contains as many calories as a ton of potatoes. Speaking with professional expertise, DePugh tells his readers to keep in mind that since dogs and cats don't have the same high requirements for vitamin C as do humans, the dry pet food tends to be deficient in just this one ingredient. So, he advises, buy a few jars of vitamin C tablets and take one every few days.

There is, however, one topic that DePugh stresses more than any other—"philosophical survival." A Survivalist must never forget why he or she is fighting to stay alive. The nature of the enemy must never be forgotten, and the Survivalist keeps alive with one goal in mind: victory. After surviving, says DePugh, the victor will inherit whatever world is left and build a society along the lines dreamed of by visionaries like his own very good friend, the late Reverend Kenneth Goff, whose work as a founder of today's Christian Identity movement was described in Chapter 3.

Goff was DePugh's closest ally for many years, a co-founder of the Minutemen and the first to combine the explosive elements of Survivalism and Identity. While DePugh concentrated on such nitty-gritty questions as whether canned or dry dog food makes the most nourishing meal for a Christian soldier, Goff occupied himself with promoting the full gamut of conspiracy beliefs that lie behind the Survival Right.

Absolutely integral to vast segments of the Survivalist movement is a set of conspiracy theories about evil influences working behind the scenes that have fueled anti-Semitic forces since at least the time of the French Revolution. In the world view promoted by Goff, the "Hidden Hand" of this conspiracy—attributed to Satan and his seed on earth, the Jews—has worked clandestinely for centuries to bring about the ruin of the Christian white race.

According to this bizarre and complex view of history, the Jews who were recruited by Satan in Babylon became Khazars, a tribe of Indo-Europeans, who were dispersed in 1016 A.D. after being defeated in an enormous battle by the Slavs. These Khazars, known today as Ashkenazi Jews, then dispersed throughout Europe, where they became a "Hidden Hand" operating against the Christian majorities in each country where they settled.

Proponents of the Hidden Hand conspiracy say that the phenomenon most visibly surfaced on May 1, 1776, in Bavaria, Germany, when one Adam Weishaupt changed his name to Spartacus and established a clandestine group of European leaders called the Order of the Illuminati. The American far right long has cited the Illuminati as the forerunners of modern-day Communists. Robert Welch, the founder of the John Birch Society, for example, made much out of the fact that according to tradition the Order of the Illuminati was formed on May 1, the very day Communists honor their ideology with May Day events.

It is an undisputed historical fact that Weishaupt did indeed form a group he called the Order of the Illuminati to work for enlightened or "illuminated" revolutionary social change, including a rejection of Christianity, an abandonment of superstition and, of all things, the practice of free love. When the secret society was discovered by authorities in Bavaria it was disbanded and outlawed. Then, according to Welch, Goff and many other Survival Right ideologues, the Illuminati infiltrated the various Freemason groups throughout the world and continued to work their mischief against the rest of society. In the mid-1800s, one initiate of this group named Karl Marx laid the groundwork for the Bolshevik Revolution, according to *The Protocols of the Elders of Zion*.

Most historians tend to view the secret order called the Illuminati in somewhat less sinister terms than does the American ultraright. The prevailing view among modern scholars, such as Pulitzer Prize-winning historian David Brion Davis, is that Weishaupt was simply the leader of a relatively small group of men inspired by the philosophical movement now called the Enlightenment, whose genius had been to realize that men were capable of reacting to one another in a decent and sane manner without the trappings of religion. This movement, whose central figures included the French philosophers Voltaire and Diderot, rebelled against revealed religion and scorned superstition, the Catholic Church and Europe's various Protestant sects as well.

Under Weishaupt's tenure the Illuminati expressed their hopes for a rational and humanistic world with the slogan "Liberty, Equality, Fraternity," a phrase, of course, that came to symbolize the bloody French Revolution. Initiates of today's far-right fringes commonly point to the symbol of a pyramid with an eye at the top on the back of the one-dollar bill as proof that the Illuminati, with their three-pronged creed of Liberty, Equality, Fraternity, are secretly in control of the U.S. Treasury.

The Illuminati's stated central goal was "making mankind happy," and they held that any number of corrupt means were justified if the end resulted in the happiness of all humanity. The Illuminati concluded that such lofty goals could only be realized by an enlightened (illuminated) elite ruthlessly working behind the scenes. Opposed to the religious establishment of the day, the Illuminati held that death was a perpetual sleep and that while one carries the spark of life, one should seek to be happy. It was, in short, a group of rebels who, almost like schoolboys, delighted in violating the prevailing standards of the day.

It is generally conceded by mainstream historians that the Revolutionary Jacobins, the force behind the relentless mobs that led so many French citizens to the guillotine, were an offshoot of the Illuminati movement. It was under the leadership of the most notorious of all Jacobins, Maximilien de Robespierre, that the group fomented the abuses of the French Revolution by encouraging mobs of the socially inferior to rise up and dethrone the established government, an uprising that backfired with the execution of Robespierre himself.

Present-day conspiratorialists see that uprising of the great unwashed of eighteenth-century France as simply a dry run for the rebellions in recent decades by American blacks, Hispanics and other minorities, which they view as an effort by worldwide Jewish conspirators to mongrelize the white race.

Fairly substantial details of the Illuminati emerged in 1786 when the group was ordered disbanded by the Bavarian government after a trial. Today the major source of material on the topic is Scottish scholar John Robison's 1797 work, *Proofs of a Conspiracy Against All the Religions and Governments of Europe, Carried on in the Secret Meetings of Free Masons, Illuminati, and Reading Societies.*

Neophytes in the group were called "Minervals." They underwent a period of three years of indoctrination before being initiated into the next level, that of "Illuminatus Minor." The neophyte Illuminatus was taught that a number of major institutions stood in the way of the group's goal of making mankind happy, such as religion, nationalism, patriotism and even racial alignments. As an Illuminatus Minor, the initiate was taught that religion was simply superstition and should be abandoned in favor of "enlightenment," or "illumination," in which reason and not biblical revelation became the dominant force in one's life. The final order was that of "Illuminatus Major," the group that worked actively to implement the revolution. Having rejected religion and the moral teaching of their age, members pledged to work behind the scenes to accomplish their goal of ruling the world.

New to the concepts of atheism, the Illuminati dwelt at length on the implications of rejecting a personal God and Saviour on the rest of life. Hedonism was a prime tenet. Those blessed with the "illumination" of the Enlightenment were given free rein to fulfill their sensual wants. Marriage and the traditional family structure was viewed as merely another way that the superstitious establishment kept ordinary people in line. The Illuminati advocated free love and the abolition of the nuclear family.

In one of his most widely quoted speeches, entitled "More Stately Mansions," Birch founder Welch outlined in 1964 the belief that the Illuminati went underground after the order to disband in 1786 and have been working furiously behind the scenes ever since to wreak havoc on the rest of the world.

Welch told his audience:

> Since by 1800 they were able to pull the veil of secrecy over themselves almost completely and permanently, we do not know to what extent Weishaupt's group became the central core or even one of the main components of a continuing organization with increasing reach and control over all collectivist activities after 1776. But that there have been one or more such organizations, which have now been absorbed into the top echelons of the Communist conspiracy—or vice versa—is supported by too much evidence of too many kinds to permit much doubt.

As is often the case, there is a certain grain of truth in the Survivalists' demented scenario. The Illuminati indeed was a secret society out to effect changes in the world order. It was a group similar, in fact, to today's Masons, and there is a rather grand irony in the fact that most of the Survival Right has concluded that the Illuminati went underground in the opening days of the nineteenth century only to emerge as the Masonic orders, which remain active to this day as last bastions of conservative thinking in virtually every small town in America.

Apart from the fact that the Survival Right considers the Masons to be descendants of the satanic Illuminati, American Freemasonry is an institution far more in keeping with right-wing precepts than are most similar groups. Today's most commonly visible Masonic group is the one called Shriners, a collection of middle-aged men decked out in their Turkish fez hats who are associated by ordinary Americans with their Shrine Circus, their rowdy behavior at conventions and their political conservatism. Catholics often are "black-balled" from the Shrine. So are Jews. Black members often are relegated to "colored" offshoots.

The ultraright rejects Masonry not for what its adherents practice so much as for the stated goals of the institution. The Fraternal Order of the Free and Accepted Masons is the largest such group on earth. Its literature pledges that all men share the fatherhood of God and that no sectarian, ethnic or racial alliances should keep them apart. In practice, however, each Masonic group operates under a system whereby any prospective new member can be denied access by a single negative vote—a black ball—from any established member.

The structure of Masonic groups is highly reminiscent of the three stages of the Illuminati: Minerval, Illuminatus Minor and Illuminatus Major. The basic unit of Freemasonry is the "lodge." Members of a lodge move through three degrees: Entered Apprentice, Fellow Craft and Master Mason. Additional degrees are conferred by two groups of advanced Freemasonry: the York Rite, which awards twelve degrees, and the Scottish Rite, which confers thirty higher degrees. President Harry Truman proudly proclaimed himself a "33rd degree Mason" because he had fulfilled the three basic degrees and then had moved through all thirty steps of the Scottish Rite.

Writing in the Academic American Encyclopedia, Alphonse Cerza says of the movement, "Many great men in history have been Freemasons, including Benjamin Franklin, Mozart, Henry Ford, Rudyard Kipling, Douglas MacArthur, Will Rogers, and George Washington and twelve other presidents of the United States."

According to Goff, while the Jewish conspirators around the world were setting up their infrastructure of subversion through the Freemasonry movement, their brothers and sisters in Russia were laboring as "the Hidden Hand behind the Russian Revolution."

What follows is a summary of Goff's conspiracy theory, a world view with perhaps as many variations as it has adherents. This scenario, or ones very much like it, remains the crucial justification for the hatred and paranoia that drive the Survival Right and make its members the deadly menace they have become:

Driven by the Illuminati-inspired writings of Marx, the Jewish International Assembly of November 1884 in Kattowitz, Poland, near the Russian frontier, drafted the movement known as political Zionism and set out to topple the Czarist government. Attendees left the sessions and infiltrated the "Bolsheviki" movement that was already scheming to rid the class-bound Russian society from the Czars' autocracy.

At a conference in Belgium in the early 1900s a number of the conspirators, including Benito Mussolini, Nikolai Lenin and the sinister Colonel E. Mandell House, chief aide to President Woodrow Wilson, decided that only a global war would make their plans for world domination possible.

For his part, Colonel House returned to the United States and wrote an anonymous blueprint for the coming chaos called *Philip Dru, Administrator: The Story of Tomorrow*. In this book, says Goff, bankers join forces to create an economic depression which allows a man named Rockland to come to power. Rockland, a thinly disguised Franklin Roosevelt, then launches a program called the New Era and "gives fireside chats to keep people in line." The Supreme Court is weakened and Rockland succeeds in fomenting a civil war that puts Philip Dru in absolute power as the American dictator.

While the actual conspiracy never succeeded to the extent dreamed of in the book, House, a close friend as well as adviser to President Wilson, did succeed in getting the Americans to persuade Czar Nicholas II to forfeit his throne and create a civilian government headed by socialists, according to Goff.

But once this government, headed by Alexander Kerensky, was in power, Lenin came out of Switzerland, Stalin emerged from hiding in Russia and Trotsky came from New York to wage their Communist Revolution with the financing of the banking firm of

Kuhn, Loeb & Co., arranged by that institution's Jewish president, Jacob Schiff.

A Jewish Bolshevik, Jankel Sverdlov, president of the Court of Ekaterinburg, ordered the Czar and his family executed, and the conspiracy took power on July 16, 1918. The town of Ekaterinburg later was named Sverdlovsk in honor of the Jewish component of the Revolution.

The Zionists around the world, particularly those in the United States, then launched a major disinformation campaign to paint Stalin, Lenin and the rest as anti-Semites "to destroy, in the minds of well-meaning Christians, any belief that Jewish Zionism was, and still is, the motivating power behind the Communist Criminal Conspiracy." This ploy, says Goff, allowed the Jewish conspiracy both to conceal its own hand in the Communist uprising and to win support among patriotic Americans for the State of Israel.

To this day a favorite tactic of the nefarious Jewish conspiracy has been to discredit its critics by labeling them anti-Semitic, the conspiracy theory continues. Thus, according to the Survival Right, the international Jewish conspiracy fabricated the accounts of Hitler's death camps in order to win sympathy for Jews who otherwise would be castigated by Western society. When critics like the Liberty Lobby dare to question the Holocaust, they are dismissed as evil anti-Semites and, thereafter, ignored.

Actually, according to the Survivalists, the Jewish conspiracy has been conducting its own holocaust against Christians since at least the time of the Bolshevik Revolution. The notorious Soviet programs to install atheism in place of religion were, in fact, nothing more than a Jewish effort to eradicate Christianity from Russian society, in Goff's outlook. Christians were rounded up and placed in concentration camps. Their babies were used for bayonet practice by Red Army goons while leering Jews watched with approval.

The scenario continues with the allegation that while the Revolution was unfolding and during its aftermath, the Jewish conspiracy solidified its hold over the international banking structure through several marriages between members of the Loeb, Warburg and Rothschild families. One of these bankers, Paul Warburg, brother-in-law to Schiff himself, forged an alliance with Senator Nelson Aldrich of Rhode Island, who sponsored the "currency reform" legislation in 1913 that led to the 1914 establishment of the Federal Reserve Bank, an unconstitutional institution that has allowed the Jewish conspiracy to gain virtually total control over the American and world economies, write Goff and others.

John D. Rockefeller, the richest man on earth, amassed his wealth not by oil but by manipulations conducted by the Federal Reserve System. In gratitude, Rockefeller named one of his sons Nelson Aldrich Rockefeller, who went on to become Vice-President of the United States before he died.

It is accepted as an article of faith that for much of the last few decades the conspiracy has operated out of the U.S. State Department, which is said to have shipped nearly a half ton of uranium aboard U.S. planes to Moscow, enabling the Soviets to build their atom bomb. It also supposedly shipped more than 100,000 patents, including many with military applications, to Russia under the guise of the post-World War II Lend-Lease program.

One of the central characters in this conspiracy theory is the "Jewish" agent Alger Hiss, who allegedly began his long mischief in the early 1920s as counsel to a Senate committee headed by Senator Gerald P. Nye that investigated whether World War I had been started by a consortium of international arms companies who needed to market their wares. Hiss would take the secret military documents supplied to Senator Nye to his home, where his co-conspirator, Whittaker Chambers, would copy them and pass them along to a Soviet agent.

As a protégé of Zionist Supreme Court Justice Felix Frankfurter, Hiss received numerous high government appointments before Senator Joseph McCarthy and Representative Richard Nixon unearthed the spy ring that Hiss and Chambers operated out of the State Department. Hiss served as a lawyer with the U.S. delegation to the Yalta Conference, at which he closeted himself with Stalin and

Roosevelt and helped the two men strike a deal whereby Russia would have its infamous veto power once the United Nations was formed.

There, in broad strokes, is the conspiracy theory that drives today's Survival Right with such devastating results. To be sure, various members of the movement have differing views on many of the specifics. But just as Identity Christianity takes traditional Bible research and twists it into the tale of the Khazars and the Lost Tribes of Israel, so do the political theorists of the Survivalist movement reinterpret historical facts and events to justify their paranoia and hatred.

With Alger Hiss long removed from the scene, the Survival Right finds a new sinister gray eminence in the person of David Rockefeller, president of the Chase Manhattan Bank, whose internationalist activities as a leader of the Trilateral Commission and the Council on Foreign Relations are seen as the latest machinations of the Antichrist Jewish banking conspiracy that began with the forerunner of the Trilateralists, the Bilderbergers.

Senator Jacob Javits explained in an article printed in the *Congressional Record* on April 11, 1964, that the idea for forming the Bilderbergers originated in the early 1950s among leaders in NATO countries who decided they needed an informal discussion group to explore such questions as the future of the European alliance, ways to cope with the Communist bloc and how to implement the Marshall Plan, the American aid project to restore the European economy. The meetings were sponsored by Prince Bernhard of the Netherlands and were set up with ground rules that included barring the press and public and keeping discussions confidential. Advocates of the Bilderberg meetings defended the secrecy as a way to get leaders who otherwise were violently in disagreement with one another to sit down and air out their differences. Conspiratorialists, of course, saw more sinister things afoot.

They note, for example, that Prince Bernhard said he was approached by Polish diplomat, writer and political philosopher Joseph Retinger, an advocate of European unity under a central government, with the Bilderberger scheme. Retinger is a dream come true for those in search of a conspiracy. He was, in fact, the Henry Kissinger of his day.

Born in Cracow, Poland, Retinger received a doctorate from the Sorbonne and became one of the leading intellectual and political figures of pre-World War II Europe on the strength of his academic performance and the friendships he built with world leaders. His lifelong goal was to create a unified Europe, and his approach to doing so revolved around the controversial suggestion that the various countries take advantage of their common Catholic traditions and unite under the guidance of the Jesuits. While his pan-Europeanism was rejected by political leaders, Retinger continued to be a close confidant of the subcontinent's ruling elite. His ardent Catholicism also made him most welcome at the Vatican.

During World War II, Retinger served as the representative to the Soviet Union from the London-based Polish government-in-exile. In August 1944, at the age of fifty-eight, Retinger made a clandestine parachute jump into Poland, apparently carrying money to finance Polish partisan forces. This act of bravado served to enhance his access to the world's power centers.

An article inserted into the *Congressional Record* in 1971 by the conservative Representative John Rarick of Louisiana quoted Sir Edward Beddington-Behrens about Retinger's awesome access to power centers: "I remember in the United States [Retinger] picking up the telephone and immediately making an appointment with the President; and in Europe, he had complete entree in every political circle, as a kind of right acquired through the trust, devotion and loyalty he inspired."

Retinger was an amazing embodiment of a long-suspected but shadowy figure in the tenets of European anti-Catholicism, "l'Eminence Grise." The Pope was said to be the White Eminence and the head of the Society of Jesus the Black Eminence, while their hidden secular agents were called the Gray Eminence. Today's conspiratorialists, of course, are electrified by both "Eminence Grise"

Retinger's ties with the Communists and his lifelong affiliation with Vatican diplomats.

Enthusiastic at Retinger's suggestion about setting up a meeting of the European and American elites, in 1952 and 1953 Dutch Prince Bernhard went to Washington, where he got support for forming the discussion group from General Walter Bedell Smith, then director of the CIA, and C. D. Jackson, a top Eisenhower aide who later became publisher of *Life* magazine. Funding was arranged from the Ford and Rockefeller Foundations for the first sessions, and conspiratorialists assume there also was support from the CIA.

The group took its name from the site of the first session, held in 1954 at the Bilderberg Hotel in Oosterbeck, Holland. Among frequent American Bilderberger participants have been David, Nelson and James Rockefeller, U.S. Secretary of State Dean Acheson, diplomat George Ball, CIA director Allen Dulles, Senate Foreign Relations Committee chairman J. William Fulbright, Manhattan Project director J. Robert Oppenheimer, Atlanta *Constitution* editor, Ralph Magill, U.S. ambassador to the Soviet Union George Kennan, Henry Kissinger, CBS president William Paley, longtime arms negotiator Paul Nitze, Secretary of State Dean Rusk, *New York Times* publisher Arthur Hays Sulzberger, Atomic Energy Commission head Louis Strauss, NBC president David Sarnoff, banker Eric Warburg, Johnson administration National Security Adviser McGeorge Bundy, Gerald Ford and Secretary of State Christian Herter.

The list of Europeans is equally impressive, running the gamut from F. D. L. Astor, editor of the London *Observer*, to Giovanni Agnelli, chairman of the Fiat Co., to NATO minister Joseph Luns and Swedish industrialist, Marcus Wallenberg.

A Liberty Lobby booklet called "Spotlight on the Bilderbergers: Irresponsible Power," quotes British writer A. K. Chesterton on the secret group: "Who would the principal have been? Baruch? Frankfurter? The Kuhn, Loeb gang? And why the cloak and dagger stuff? Is the Bilderberg Group an apparatus of Grand Orient Masonry?

Whatever the answer to that question the atmosphere of plotting in the dark which pervades it has a dank and very nasty smell."

The modern world's leadership elite belong to two other groups that arouse the suspicions of proponents of the Hidden Hand. These are the Council on Foreign Relations, directed by David Rockefeller and composed of Americans with heavy credentials, and the Rockefeller-supported Trilateral Commission, a group designed to include Asians in the bilateral Bilderberger formula, which had included only Americans and Europeans.

In short, the Bilderbergers evolved into the Trilateralists and the Council on Foreign Relations, which dates back to the late 1940s and includes most of the Americans involved in the Trilateral group. Naturally, conspiracy seekers find a gold mine in this organization just as they did in the Bilderbergers.

Trilateralists have included Jimmy Carter, Reagan Vice-President and former CIA director George Bush, Carter National Security Adviser Zbigniew Brzezinski, Carter Vice-President Walter Mondale, arms negotiator Paul Warnke, former U.S. United Nations Ambassador Andrew Young, Carter Treasury Secretary W. Michael Blumenthal, Carter Defense Secretary Harold Brown, Reagan Defense Secretary Caspar Weinberger, Federal Reserve Chairman Paul Volcker and many others with similar lofty credentials.

Predictably, the Council on Foreign Relations and Trilateralist connections became a major political issue both in 1976, when Carter defeated Ford, and in 1980, when Reagan defeated Carter with Trilateralist Bush as a running mate. Both elections, of course, served to convince the Survival Right that neither Republicans nor Democrats are free from the conspiracy of the Jewish international bankers they perceive as the force behind these elite groups.

As the preceding examples illustrate, there is far more substance to the Survival Right than is generally attributed to fringe groups. The hatred and violence they preach are backed up by an extremely complex mixture of religious concepts and an equally complex—and highly detailed—view of history and politics.

The greatest concern, of course, about the Survivalists is whether they will ever succeed in getting their message across to the rest of the American public, which also must live under the pall of bristling world nuclear arsenals.

In his immensely moving book *The Fate of the Earth*, Jonathan Schell writes:

> When one tries to face the nuclear predicament, one feels sick, whereas when one pushes it out of mind, as apparently one must do most of the time in order to carry on with life, one feels well again. But this feeling of well-being is based on a denial of the most important reality of our time, and therefore is itself a kind of sickness. A society that systematically shuts its eyes to an urgent peril to its physical survival and fails to take any steps to save itself cannot be called psychologically well. In effect, whether we think about nuclear weapons or avoid thinking about them, their presence among us makes us sick, and there seems to be little of a purely mental or emotional nature that we can do about it.

After examining the Survivalists' terror and their paranoid hatred of Jews, blacks and other minorities, the answer to the question "How can they be that way?" becomes: Because they are sick.

But, as Schell puts it, so are the rest of us. The question is: Will the day come when our nuclear terror makes significantly greater numbers of people as sick as are those on the Survival Right?

When one turns on the cable television and listens to the cacophony of Apocalypse and intolerance being preached around the clock, the question becomes even more urgent.

He who fights with monsters should be careful lest he thereby become a monster. And if thou gaze long into an abyss, the abyss will also gaze into thee.
—*Friedrich Nietzsche*

Conclusion: Apocalypse Now?

His eyes flashing zeal for the Lord through a pair of horn-rimmed spectacles, brother Jimmy Swaggart waves a copy of the Constitution of the United States of America before his rapt audience. "This is the word of God," shouts the tremendously popular television evangelist with a mighty shake of his leonine hair that sends a halo of perspiration backlighted by klieg lights flying about his head.

And while the substance of his extraordinary sermons comes directly out of the credo of the Posse Comitatus brand of Christian Identity, Jimmy Swaggart is no cockamamie racist preacher spouting venom over some backwoods stump in the Arkansas Ozarks. He is one of the most popular evangelists in America today, the moving force behind a multimillion-dollar media empire whose message is beamed via cable television into millions of American households each week. A cousin to two highly successful musicians, rock-and-roll artist Jerry Lee Lewis and country singer Mickey Gilley, Swaggart is a magnificent showman in his own right. He pounds out hymns on a concert grand piano and sings of Jesus in a stirring molasses-thick Louisiana tenor that sets the neck hairs twitching.

250

His followers include many blacks, and he has been known to purchase Israel bonds. Nevertheless, many of the themes voiced by this riveting proselytizer echo the sermons of Thom Robb, Bob Miles and Richard Butler, whose creed of hatred and paranoia has been delineated at such length earlier.

In common with Posse leaders such as James Wickstrom and Gordon Kahl, Swaggart views the Constitution as a divinely inspired document, and he hints darkly in his sermons that "the Beast" has attempted to corrupt that document since it was first delivered to Americans with just ten amendments, known as the Bill of Rights. Along with Identity doomsayers like Miles and Butler, the immensely popular Swaggart has warned his audiences that the "end times" are at hand and that soon one may expect the rain of nuclear missiles or other cleansing fire that will mark the period of "the Tribulations" that is to usher in the final battle of Armageddon and the Second Coming of Christ. He had made repeated references to Jews that are evocative of the same anti-Semitism documented so dramatically by Louis Harris in the backwaters of Iowa and Nebraska. He once admonished a congregation against bargaining with Jesus by warning them to remember that "Jesus is a Jew."

In tandem with so many others in today's Fundamentalist political movement, Swaggart believes that his brand of Christians with their crusade for literal interpretation of the Bible have a pressing moral duty to seize national power and impose their beliefs on the nation at large because time is now very short. He quickly became a major supporter of his fellow television evangelist Pat Robertson when Robertson announced his plans to use his own tremendously popular television empire, the Christian Broadcasting Network's 700 Club, as a platform for a possible presidential bid.

While covering Swaggart's September 1986 crusade in the national capital, Lloyd Grove of *The Washington Post* recorded an amazing conversation between the evangelist and a female reporter from Israel's largest newspaper, *Yediot Ahronot*, that dramatizes how the currently flourishing "televangelical" Christian movement is promoting the agenda of the Survival Right.

Swaggart gave the journalist a brief Cook's tour of the landscape of the future as laid out in the Book of Revelation and elsewhere:

"One day the nation of Israel will accept the Lord Jesus Christ. Several things are going to happen in the future that are cataclysmic, and most of it involves the State of Israel, to be frank with you.

"There will be a man who will rise in the Middle East not too many years from now that will project himself as the Messiah. He will say, 'I am God.' And the Jewish nation will accept him . . . He will make a seven-year pact with Israel. In the middle of that seven-year pact—three and a half years—he will break that non-aggression treaty with Israel and will set himself up as God in Jerusalem and attack Israel, and Israel for the first time in her history will be defeated and will go to a place that you now know as Petra. It's called the Time of Jacob's Trouble. And the Bible also tells us— Zechariah does—that two-thirds of the nation of Israel will be slaughtered during that time . . .

"They're going to cry, the people of Israel, for the Messiah to come. They're going to cry. As the Bible describes it, at that hour, America will not be able to help Israel, no other nation will be able to help this little, tiny, tiny people—and they're going to cry, 'Lord! You are our only hope and if you don't come now there's no more Israel!' And that moment He's coming back . . . He'll split the skies asunder . . . He'll set his feet on Mount Olivet . . . And the entire nation of Israel—those that are left—will accept the Lord. And then the Jewish people are going to become the most evangelizing, the premier nation on the face of the earth."

According to Grove's account, Swaggart then said to the Israeli journalist, "That's quite a story, isn't it?"

She replied, "It sounds scary."

It does, indeed, sound scary. But it also sounds very familiar. In fact, Swaggart had merely reiterated the same prophesies from the Book of Revelation that had fueled the anti-Papist mobs of the early nineteenth century, the Know-Nothings of the pre-Civil War years and the postwar Klan. He voiced the same chilling scenario that has driven the Survival Right everywhere, from Michael Ryan's dismal Nebraska compound to Richard Butler's infamous retreat in the Idaho panhandle.

Catholics with their Douay Version of Scripture call the final book of the New Testament by a more evocative name, the Apocalypse. To Protestants it's the Book of Revelation, the account of a series of horrific visions visited upon St. John the Divine during the waning years of his life when he was exiled as a hermit on the Aegean island of Patmos. Among today's Fundamentalists, these final twenty-two chapters of the New Testament have become the single most important biblical passage. Likewise, Revelation serves as the scriptural justification for the Survival Right, which finds in John's words both a stirring description of the chaos to come and a mandate to take every step possible to escape that chaos, a mandate to survive at all costs.

As Swaggart explained to the Israeli reporter, Revelation dwells largely on the last seven years of human history before the long-awaited Second Coming of Christ. It is a horribly violent scenario replete with strife, famine, pestilence and war, the legendary "Four Horsemen of the Apocalypse." In the first three and a half years of the seven-year Tribulation, the dreaded Antichrist comes to power in Israel and rebuilds the temple destroyed in Jerusalem by the Romans in 70 A.D. In the second three and a half years, this leader, whose name carries the Mark of the Beast (666), defiles the temple by having his own likeness installed on the altar and plunges the world into the final confrontation between Gog and Magog, entities which most "Tribulationists" view as the United States/Israel and the Soviet Union. It is during these three and a half years that those anointed by God to survive the "end time" must hide themselves in the wilderness.

The Book of Revelation, in turn, is foreshadowed elsewhere in prophetic books of the Bible such as Daniel and Isaiah, which Apocalypse scholars have distilled into the prevailing Fundamentalist view of the so-called end time. This is the scenario that Swaggart endorses, and which has been delineated at tremendous length by best-selling writer Hal Lindsey in a series of Bantam paperbacks that have included *The Rapture, The Terminal Generation, There's a New World Coming, The 1980s: Countdown to Armageddon* and *The Late Great Planet Earth*. This last book has sold 18 million copies, and Lindsey became one of the few authors in history to have three books simultaneously on the *New York Times* best-seller list. His blood-soaked vision of the Apocalypse, then, has reached far beyond the Survival Right, although it has had a tremendous impact on these haters as well.

Filled with a perplexing hodgepodge of symbols, John's twenty-two chapters describe the final judgment as the unrolling of a scroll with seven segments, each segment closed off with a seal. The First Seal tells of the coming of the Antichrist and of the first three and a half years before he defiles the temple. The Second Seal tells of a war in Israel which flares briefly and then dies down. The Third Seal unleashes global economic collapse, and the Fourth Seal tells of a war in which one-fourth of mankind dies. The Fifth Seal tells of a massacre in which the forces of the Antichrist set out to kill the forces of goodness. The Sixth Seal ushers in devastating earthquakes, rains of stones and fire that latter-day Tribulationists generally associate with a thermonuclear exchange. Many of the elect escape this nuclear holocaust by finding refuge in the countryside.

After the devastation come the passages of Revelation that raise the quandary of Israel for modern-day Fundamentalists. An angel arrives on the scene with a message from God to stop further torment until 144,000 Jews can be "sealed" as servants of God, 12,000 from each of the twelve tribes of Israel: all others of those tribes must perish. Many Fundamentalists, then, conclude that only 144,000 Jews, what Lindsey likes to call "144,000 Jews for Jesus," will survive the Tribulation. Hellfire, damnation and worse await all other Jews living when the end time begins.

By contrast, far more non-Jews are saved in John's lurid climactic book. He writes in Revelation (7:9–17): "I beheld and, lo, a great multitude, which no man could number, of all nations, and kindreds, and people, and tongues, stood before the throne, and before the Lamb, clothed with white robes and palms in their hands. . . . For the Lamb which is in the midst of the throne shall feed them, and shall lead them into living fountains of waters: and God shall wipe away all tears from their eyes."

With those saved wearing the white robes "washed in the blood of the Lamb," the Apocalypse continues with the Seventh Seal, which opens the way to two other sets of seven horrific catastrophes known to Fundamentalists as the Trumpet Judgments and the Bowl Judgments. The First Trumpet brings the burning of one-third of the earth's surface, the Second Trumpet is frequently interpreted as a nuclear exchange between ships on the high seas, while the Third Trumpet kills one-third of all creatures that live in the water, and the Fourth Trumpet marks a darkening of the globe much like astronomer Carl Sagan's controversial descriptions of a nuclear winter.

The Fifth Trumpet marks an infestation of bizarre locusts, which, instead of feeding on green things, eat at the tormented bodies of those who are not marked as saved on their foreheads. "And in those days shall men seek death, and shall not find it: and shall desire to die, and death shall flee from them," writes John (Revelation 9:6) in a passage evocative of Khrushchev's famous prediction that after a nuclear war the living will curse the dead out of envy. Lindsey speculates that this Fifth Trumpet foretells a biological and chemical war with the arsenals of the United States and the Soviets.

After the Sixth Trumpet blows, an army of 200 million rises in the east and slays one-third of the world's remaining population. To Lindsey, this army is the Red Chinese.

The Seventh Trumpet orders God's vengeful angels to pour seven bowls or "vials of wrath" on the already devastated planet. The first Bowl Judgment causes "noisome and grievous" sores (Lindsey says cancer) to break out on the unsaved. The Second Bowl turns the seas into blood, and the Third Bowl turns the rivers and lakes into blood. The Fourth Bowl brings scorching heat on the tormented, the Fifth Bowl creates darkness that makes the blasphemers chew out their own tongues, while the Sixth Bowl dries out the river Euphrates, bringing plague.

Finally, the Seventh Bowl summons the armies of God and of Satan to the field of Armageddon for the final battle so long awaited by so many. That battle ends with Satan being cast into a pit, heralding a period of a thousand years of peace.

Lindsey's message, as shared by Swaggart and so many other evangelists on TV and off, is essentially a millenarian one. His warning is that all of the biblical evocations of generations, of days and weeks, of epochs and eras, of begats and endings, are literal measurements of time. Further, writes Lindsey, a scholarly study of the matter shows that these biblical measurements indicate that the long-awaited end of the world will coincide roughly with the coming of the millennial year 2000. In essence, this is the same sort of millenarian concept that surfaced in Europe and the Middle East as the year 1000 A.D. approached, a time of confusion and disruption.

It is a valid but still imponderable question whether substantial numbers of people will be driven toward a new period of apocalyptic movements as the end of the second millennium actually arrives over the next decade. Certainly, as things now stand, the approach of the dreaded year 2000 can only serve to benefit the doomsayers.

Particularly important here is the universal obsession that current American Fundamentalist leaders have with the "question" of Israel, and with Jews in general. Whether the speaker is Jerry Falwell, whose Moral Majority campaign of the early 1980s was the first open effort by evangelicals to seize political power, or Ku Klux Klan chaplain Thom Robb, the focus is often the same—Israel, the Jews. The Falwells, Swaggarts and Lindseys insist that they want above all to preserve Israel while the Robbs and Mileses say they want to see it destroyed, but both share a common obsession with the topic prompted by the same Book of Revelation.

Revelation tells them clearly that before the Apocalypse can be played out, 144,000 Jews must be converted to Christ. The Tribulation can begin only in Israel, where the Antichrist is to appear. Likewise, the final battle between Gog and Magog must happen in Israel. In a 1971 statement to the president pro tem of the California

State Senate, Ronald Reagan predicted: "Ezekiel 38 and 39 says that Gog, a northern power, will invade Israel. Gog must be Russia. Most of the prophecies that had to be fulfilled before Armageddon can come have come to pass. Ezekiel said that fire and brimstone will be rained upon the enemies. That must mean that they'll be destroyed by nuclear weapons."

The resulting "pro-Semitism" voiced by so much of the Religious Right is not much more comforting than the anti-Semitism spewing from the mouths of the Survival Right. Noting the growth of attacks against synagogues and other hostilities being visited on American Jews, Rabbi Alexander Schindler, president of the Union of American Hebrew Congregations, told an audience in San Francisco in late 1980 that it was "no coincidence that the rise of right-wing Christian fundamentalism has been accompanied by the most serious outbreak of anti-Semitism in America since the outbreak of World War II."

In their sweeping 1984 portrait of the Fundamentalist movement, *Holy Terror*, Flo Conway and Jim Siegelman note how evangelicals so often trip over their own rhetoric when paying lip service to Israel. Falwell, they recall, once tried to sugarcoat the bitter pill of pro-Semitism by telling an audience in Virginia, "A few of you here today don't like the Jew. And I know why. He can make more money accidentally than you can on purpose."

The two authors likewise observe that although Falwell's ardent support of Israel won him a medal from Israeli Prime Minister Menachem Begin, the preacher also has written in his book *Listen, America* that Jews are "spiritually blind and desperately in need of their Messiah and Saviour." Conway and Siegelman caution that "this new phenomenon of Christian 'pro-Semitism' bears close scrutiny, for it has little to do with human affection. Most Fundamentalist love for the Jews and support for Israel takes its lead from the closing chapters of the New Testament, where the prophecies of Revelation set down the conditions that must be met before Christ's Second Coming and the end of the world."

Holy Terror recalls that Jews have been forced by a lengthy history of pogroms, persecutions and other travails to be ever vigilant for the next threat to their own survival. That awareness has made American Jewry very sensitive to every infringement on religious liberty and human freedom, since history has shown repeatedly that once intolerance is focused against one segment of society, it soon comes to bear against the Jews, no matter who was the original target.

It is painfully obvious to many Jews that the same Fundamentalist leaders who profess their undying loyalty to the State of Israel also vow perpetual enmity toward such minorities as homosexuals and atheists. It is equally disturbing to listen to the racist undertones as Fundamentalist preachers rail against government aid to the poor, to hear them sound anti-feminist themes by waxing poetic about the "sanctity of the Christian family" and call hellfire and brimstone down upon the "liberals" and "secular humanists" who have become the movement's new targets. And what are American Jews to make of the constant vows from the Religious Right to "Christianize" America?

Here it is appropriate once again to raise the question of the Smerdyakov syndrome. What sort of impression is this incessant television thundering about Armageddon and Israel and all the rest having on casual listeners? What are the chances that people who first have been softened up by the awesome persuasive powers of a Jimmy Swaggart or a Pat Robertson will then be receptive to the similar preachings of a Thom Robb or some other Identity fanatic filled with venom about the true nature of the legendary tribes of Israel so crucial to the scenarios of Revelation?

While the blatantly racist and anti-Semitic Identity preachers still struggle for airtime on public-access cable stations, marginally more mainstream evangelists are ubiquitous on the American airwaves. Pat Robertson's 700 Club, with its continual news reports from Israel and discussions about the coming end times, is available on 75 percent of the TV sets in America, according to Christian Broadcasting Network publicity materials. Jimmy Swaggart's weekly audience on the Trinity Broadcasting Network is estimated at more than 8 million in the United States and perhaps ten times that number worldwide. Falwell has claimed a television constituency of more than 25 million. Before their dramatic ouster over sexual revelations in April 1987, Jim and Tammy Bakker reached similar numbers over yet another Christian network, called PTL for Praise the Lord.

A 1985 survey by the Wichita, Kansas, *Eagle-Beacon* found that thirty television evangelists were available each week in that small city alone through its cable television system. When reporter R. Robin McDonald of the *Eagle-Beacon* sent token donations to twenty of them, the result was a deluge of 270 letters asking for more money and promoting the panoply of Fundamentalist ideologies, including repeated requests for funds to travel to Israel, money to help wounded Israeli war veterans and pleas for financing for orphanages in the Holy Land.

A 1985 survey by A. C. Nielsen, the television rating company, commissioned by Robertson's Christian Broadcasting Network, found that the evangelicals were capturing far more public attention than had been thought by scholars up to that time. The study, released at the November 1985 convention of the Society for the Scientific Study of Religion (SSSR), found that more than 61 million people, representing 40 percent of all U.S. households with TV sets, had watched one or more of the top ten syndicated religious programs for at least six minutes in February 1985.

In an address to the SSSR, the group's president, Jeffrey K. Hadden, said the Nielsen study indicates that the Fundamentalists will grow in influence over the coming decade. Hadden said, "Media access is a critical resource in a social movement and . . . the 'televangelists' have greater unrestrained access to media than any other interest group in America." He noted that Robertson alone had a faithful weekly audience of 28 million viewers.

With Robertson's impressive presence as a nationally significant political force, most analysis has focused on such questions as whether the 61 million people who sit and listen to a Jimmy Swaggart or someone like him are likely to move into Republican ranks. What is probably a far more significant question is just how receptive will these same 61 million people be when somebody comes along with the well-honed religious/political package of the Survival Right.

It doesn't take much of a crystal ball to predict a future in which fear of the AIDS epidemic creates a tremendous public animosity toward homosexuals, a future in which worsening relations with the Soviets over building the controversial Star Wars defense system leads to the sort of saber rattling that so terrified people during the 1950s and 1960s and a future in which the approach of the year 2000 may cause many to pause and reflect on the millenarian concepts being offered across the spectrum of the Religious Right.

Since 1979 the U.S. Civil Rights Commission has noted a dramatic increase in instances of serious anti-Semitic violence such as synagogue bombings, cemetery desecrations and physical attacks. In 1979, when record keeping started, the agency found 49 such crimes. In 1984, the commission recorded 705 and in 1985, 638.

What are the prospects that these ugly incidents will increase even more as an indirect result of the efforts of sophisticated political operatives of the American right, such as direct-mail fund-raising wizard Richard Viguerie and Paul Weyrich, whose expertise in setting up Political Action Committees to promote ultraright candidates and causes is something of a legend among political professionals of all stripes? Both men have been active to date in supporting Falwell's Moral Majority, and their efforts are widely credited with putting the country on an ideological course rightward that makes a potential Robertson candidacy far more credible than otherwise would have been conceivable. Will a further mass move to the right make those already at the farthest-right fringes even more dangerous?

As the polls concerning anti-Semitism taken by Louis Harris in early 1986 in Nebraska and Iowa illustrate, there are large segments of rural and small-town America where the growth potential of the Survival Right is considerable.

The Survival Right's own leadership concluded by the mid-1980s that conditions are particularly receptive for their credo in the five adjoining states of Wyoming, Montana, Idaho, Washington and Oregon, a sparsely settled quarter with only tiny numbers of blacks and Jews compared with the rest of the United States. Butler moved his Church of Jesus Christ Christian to Idaho in the early 1970s, for example, after his proclamations about the divinity of Adolf Hitler and the inferiority of blacks made him extremely unpopular in Southern California, where he had collaborated for years with Identity patriarch William Potter Gale.

Many of the oaths taken by the Order members as they prepared for their fund-raising crime wave pledged their efforts to creating a "bastion" for the white race in the Pacific Northwest. Since then, largely through the leadership of school bus bomber Miles, the Survival Right has been urging its members and potential members to join in an exodus to the five states, a movement they call the Northwest Territorial Imperative.

In response to these well-publicized calls for the movement of racists into their backyards, business and social leaders in the Pacific Northwest joined forces to oppose the influx by adopting such tactics as setting up powerful Human Relations Councils in their communities. In Coeur d'Alene, Idaho, for example, the Republican-dominated local Chamber of Commerce joined forces with a well-known left-wing Catholic priest, Father Bill Wassmuth, to form a council and pursue complaints against Butler's Aryan Nations compound.

In late 1986 Wassmuth's home and several other buildings in the area were bombed and prosecutors eventually charged several of Butler's associates in the crime. David Dorr, one of several neo-Nazis charged in Idaho state courts with the bombings, had told undercover FBI informants that the attacks in Coeur d'Alene and a counterfeiting scheme in neighboring Washington had been the work of a new group that called itself Bruder Schweigen Task Force II.

When the national news media descended upon Coeur d'Alene to cover the bombings, Sandy Emerson, director of the local Chamber of Commerce, explained to many a slack-jawed journalist that of the 59,770 persons living in the county only 39 were black.

"Maybe there are a handful of Jewish people here," Emerson told the author, "like maybe a half dozen." Emerson described how once he and a few other local leaders began examining the topic, they found the same sort of "ingrained" prejudice among ordinary Idaho people that Harris's poll documented in Iowa and Nebraska. He noted that the local expression most used to describe getting a bargain was to "Jew down" the seller. Bad genetic traits were ascribed to a "nigger in the woodpile" and giving up on a project was called "Japping out." With no blacks, Jews or Japanese to complain, the slurs have become commonplace, and Butler's rhetoric in such an environment was hardly as disturbing as a drunken prospector saying "hell" or "goddamn" around the womenfolk.

But as the Idaho reformers discovered when the Order burst forth from their midst, casual bigotry all too quickly translates into real hatred. "We found out just how close the gap is between using a careless racial slur in the barroom and bombing a [synagogue]," said Emerson. Unexamined bigotry abounds in rural America, and its existence gives the haters a ready toehold.

Consider the likely impact this small masterpiece downloaded from an Aryan Nations bulletin board in Houston might have on residents of a hard-pressed farm town:

> $2,304,257,900,000.00
> Two trillion three hundred four billion two hundred fifty-seven million nine hundred thousand dollars in foreign aid.
> According to the Library of Congress the net cost (in 1982 dollars) as of January 1, 1983, for foreign aid is the amount shown above.
> Trouble meeting home and/or farm payments and taxes???
> Two trillion three hundred four billion two hundred fifty-seven million nine hundred thousand dollars ($2,304,257,900,000.00) will pay cash for forty-one million eight hundred ninety-five thousand five hundred ninety eight (41,895,598) new diesel tractors at fifty-five thousand dollars ($55,000) each. Are the Orientals in Asia or Jews in Israel somehow more important to the U.S. government than working Americans?

Home or farm being foreclosed on? Trouble meeting 17 percent interest payments?

$2,304,257,900.00 will pay cold cash for 35,450,121 new houses at $65,000 each or 9,217,031 farms at $250,000 each.

At this value, the U.S. government transferred the equivalent of 35,450,121 new homes from the working American to aliens, most of whom live under communist or socialist governments. FMHA (a government agency) foreclosed on 10,000 U.S. farms in the last 15 months, putting an estimated forty thousand (four-member) American families out in the cold. Could that $2,304,257,900,000.00 have been used to help these now destitute American farmers? Simple arithmetic—that is $230,425,790.00 for each and every farm taken by "our" government from its citizens. Home foreclosures are running much higher.

If you love this country, it is time you ask yourself, "Who in the hell is this government being run for?" If you come up with the same answer that this writer did, then you have no choice but to join the "second" American Revolution. Honor demands and duty requires that we rebel against this destruction of our people by the government. For those who think we can vote the tyrants out, they should be reminded that regardless of who has been elected in the last 50 years, confiscation of the wealth of our people has gone ahead. Democrat or Republican, there has been no change. Our founding fathers, lacking success after fifteen years, gave up petitions and letter writing to the government. How about you?

"Rebellion to tyrants is obedience to God."—Thomas Jefferson

As that essay, signed with the name of the Ku Klux Klan's founder, Nathan Bedford Forrest, shows, the mood in America today is growing ever more ugly as economic conditions slip and international tensions increase. The Fundamentalist message likewise paints an ugly picture of a country in moral decay. As pastors shout their condemnation of an abortion rate approaching one in four pregnancies, others see looming disaster as the dreaded AIDS epidemic crosses over from homosexuals to the heterosexual community. A 1986 issue of *Liberty*, the magazine of the Seventh-Day Adventist

Church, lamented in an article about Robertson how "America is turning into a moral outhouse . . . The children of those who watched 'Mayberry R.F.D.,' 'Leave It to Beaver' and 'I Love Lucy' are now entertained with the sex, violence, and drugs of 'Dynasty,' 'Dallas,' and 'Miami Vice.' "

The *Liberty* article, which rejected Robertson's candidacy, nevertheless endorsed his frequent warnings that 4,000 fetuses are aborted each day and the U.S. Customs Service is seizing a massive amount of cocaine annually, which nevertheless accounts for only "a small percentage of what flows in the bloodstream of an estimated 4 million Americans. Crime is rampant, whether committed by E. F. Hutton (2,000 counts of wire and mail fraud) or James Huberty (the 1984 McDonald's restaurant massacre). Meanwhile divorce, AIDS, teenage suicides, alcoholism, and other corporate ills infest America like suppurating sores."

And while the generally pro-defense-spending Fundamentalists aren't complaining, nowhere is the departure from the moral values of even the recent past more dramatic than in the resurgence of militarism in today's popular American culture. That resurgence, of course, is very much in harmony with the styles of those in the Survival Right whose own stores of commando knives, automatic weapons and other hardware often rival the props for such movies as *Rambo: First Blood Part II,* which grossed $75.8 million at the box office in its first twenty-three days. Likewise, blockbusters such as the 1986 hit *Top Gun* extolling the prowess of jet fighters and the 1987 television miniseries *Amerika* about a Soviet takeover of America, all serve to keep in the forefront the themes that drive the Survivalists.

A study of the sudden new phenomenon, "Militarism in America," published in 1986 by the liberal Center for Defense Information, documented a revolution in how post-Vietnam Americans react to guns and things military. The study notes, for example, that after Sylvester Stallone's Rambo movies became popular, twenty-five companies negotiated to obtain distribution rights to Rambo-related merchandise. The U.S. Army replaced its famous Uncle Sam poster with the Rambo figure clutching his machine gun and mowing down hordes of Asian attackers.

Rambo was followed by a deluge of militaristic films, including *Red Dawn*, the one about a Soviet invasion of a small Colorado town that was played over and over by Michael Ryan's Rulo, Nebraska, commune. Others have included the Chuck Norris commando movies, machine-gun operas such as *Missing in Action*, *Iron Eagle* and *Invasion U.S.A.*

The CDI study found that war toy sales soared by more than 600 percent between 1982 and 1986, to over $1 billion annually. Worse, the major toy companies have joined forces with television producers to air cartoons featuring war toys, and the CDI noted that the number of cartoon series publicizing such toys jumped from zero in 1983 to ten in 1985. One popular show, for example, is based on the toy called Laser Tag, in which children strap sensors onto their chests and heads and then shoot at one another with infrared guns ("lasers") that cause the sensors to beep when hit by a light beam. These realistic toys, in turn, were developed from similar models used by military Special Forces members and others in actual training exercises; in early 1987 a teenager in California was shot to death by a sheriff's deputy who mistook the boy's Laser Tag pistol for a real weapon.

"According to the National Coalition on Television Violence, the average American child is now exposed to 250 cartoons with war themes and 800 television advertisements for war toys a year," the CDI reported. "By the age of sixteen, the average child will have watched some 200,000 hours of TV, taking in 200,000 acts of violence and 50,000 attempted murders, 33,000 of which will involve guns."

Of particular interest as far as the impact on the Survival Right is concerned is a study by the Center for Media and Public Affairs in which 500 TV shows were monitored over the past thirty years. The study found "a noticeable shift towards the use of military-style assault weaponry. Popular television series like the

'A-Team' and 'Miami Vice' promote the use of guns as necessary for survival."

And if Americans are introduced to automatics and hand grenades while still crawling about the carpet in front of the TV set, they are growing up to become avid consumers of firearms. The Justice Department estimates that U.S. citizens now own roughly 40 million revolvers and more than 100,000 registered machine guns. Estimates of unregistered machine guns, such as the one used to kill Alan Berg, run as high as 500,000, according to Michael Hancock, general counsel for the National Coalition to Ban Handguns.

Businesses like the Bullet Stop in Atlanta report doing a brisk trade renting machine guns to people who come in off the street eager to fire a burst of lead into a poster of the Ayatollah Khomeini, just as the Order members used to blast away at pictures of Menachem Begin. And the CDI has expressed particular concern that a business called National Survival Inc. runs an ongoing war game, on as many as 600 playing fields around the country, in which participants fight one another using air guns that shoot dye pellets. The game is played over courses with names like Skirmish, Combat Zone and the Ultimate Game, the latter a reference to the short story that police in California think motivated Charles Chat Ng and Leonard Lake to hunt their victims down in the woods of Calaveras County. The CDI study found that as many as 50,000 ordinary citizens were signing up to play that "ultimate" game and others each week with National Survival Inc.

Another indication of the phenomenon cited in the CDI's study is the success of magazines like *Soldier of Fortune, SWAT, International Combat Arms* and *Firepower.* "Over 500,000 people subscribe to magazines put out by the Omega Corporation, the company that publishes *Soldier of Fortune* magazine," the report said. Indeed, Robert K. Brown's *Soldier of Fortune,* published monthly in Boulder, Colorado, and featuring a mixed bag of articles about machine guns, survivalism and other hot modern topics, has become one of America's most successful "men's lifestyle magazines," according to Brown's publicity materials.

Each year Brown hosts a party for his magazine readers at the Sahara Hotel in Las Vegas which features a Combat Weapons Expo where as many as 5,000 visitors swap names and addresses, and buy guns, knives, blowguns, ammunition, freeze-dried food and other survival paraphernalia—all laid out on hundreds of folding tables that fill the hotel's cavernous convention center, a room so large it once was used for Teamsters' Union national conventions. For four days hundreds of men, many of them with potbellies and bald heads, mill about the casino gaming area wearing camouflage clothing, paratroop boots and other military regalia, discussing plans to survive the coming holocaust, how to find work as hired mercenaries and other topics.

Nowhere is the Survival Right's obsession with the Bomb more obvious than at Brown's conventions. Clearly, these people have learned to live with nuclear weapons by making them part of their lore and the focus of much of their humor. One T-shirt showing an irradiated Arab reads: "Nuke Their Ass—Take the Gas." A popular poster shows a B-52 bomber flying away from a mushroom cloud rising above Moscow, with the caption: "And Then It's Miller Time." A button showing a swept-wing nuclear bomber in the same position as the famous peace symbol reads: "Drop It." Another poster depicts a 20-by-29-inch map of the United States with all likely targets for Soviet missiles marked in red so buyers can find "safe zones." Books for sale feature dozens of Survivalist topics, among them: *Survivalist's Medicine Chest, Survival Poaching, Survival Shooting, Survival Retreat, Survival Evasion and Escape, Nuclear War Survival Skills, Fallout Survival* and *Surviving Doomsday.*

As all of the above clearly indicates, the Survival Right was not the only segment of American society turning toward heavy firepower out of nuclear anxiety during the early half of this decade. In reality, the Survivalists were part of a much larger national trend. The fact that these people became immersed in Identity religion, racism and anti-Semitism and became far more extremist than did their fellow citizens could mean simply that they are a vanguard that many more Americans will follow if, and when, things become worse than they already are.

Certainly, increased U.S.–Soviet tensions, the prospect of social panic brought on by the AIDS crisis and the specter of the millennial year 2000 make it crucial that nobody underestimates the Survival Right as a significant potential component of the American political ethos. Indisputably the architects of this movement have left their potential converts with a very complete and complex ideology that has drawn from the most eloquent of history's hate groups to create a comprehensive world view of conspiracy, ranging from the creation of the Talmud in ancient Babylon right up to the latest board meeting at the Rockefeller Foundation. And the religious heritage passed to these Survivalists, complete with all the complicated trackings of the Lost Tribes of Israel and the interpretations of myriad Scriptures, is every bit as complex as what the local Catholic priest or Anglican pastor has to offer.

But as the examples of hatred, violence and suffering described in this book illustrate, the most permanent legacy that the Survivalists offer for the future may simply be more terror and more chaos as an unknown number of potential Smerdyakovs are driven to act by the onerous background noise of Armageddon being sounded everywhere, from the Oval Office of the White House to the flickering channels on late-night television.

Certainly, as of this writing the nightmares that drive the denizens of this book continue. Global nuclear arsenals grow daily even as tremendous international strife compounds the sense of gloom. Economic conditions remain desperate in the farm belt, and urban defenders of hard-won civil liberties find themselves losing ground in the face of the AIDS panic. Frightened and increasingly mean-spirited people perpetuate the blight of racism everywhere, from the boroughs of New York to the backwaters of the Deep South. The millennial year is barely a decade away, and the televangelists' influence already is growing rapidly. These forces all combine to sicken the spirit of people in the mainstream just as they infect the Survivalists whose energies are so intensely focused on overcoming the chaos they believe is imminent.

The ultimate question may not be who has the Survival Sickness, but rather, who is going to survive it.

Acknowledgments

In 1983, as I was wrapping up a tour of duty as the Pentagon correspondent for the Chicago *Tribune*, the newspaper's then-national editor John Crewdson urged me to investigate the story of Gordon Kahl, who had just been killed in a dramatic shoot-out in Arkansas. Crewdson was particularly intent upon learning how widely Kahl and his associates had spread their message of hatred and violence. I lacked Crewdson's interest in the subject and didn't pursue it. A year later, now working in Denver as the newspaper's Western states correspondent, I covered the tragic murder of talk-show host Alan Berg and the subsequent amazing disclosures about the nature of his assassins. Within a few months it became very clear just how correct Crewdson's instincts had been.

Increasingly, the breaking news stories I covered reflected the emergence of the strange behind-the-scenes political force that I have chosen to call the Survival Right—and it soon became apparent that while the phenomenon had surfaced most dramatically in the West, the Survivalist movement was nationwide. This book, then, owes an enormous debt to the Chicago *Tribune* and its editors, who realized the significance of the stories in question and lent substantial resources toward pursuing them. It is important to point out, however, that the positions I have taken are not necessarily those of the *Tribune* or any other of its employees. Further, the facts cited herein and the weight I have chosen to give them are my own responsibility and do not necessarily reflect how the *Tribune* might present the material. I therefore express gratitude to but do not claim the endorsement of *Tribune* editor James Squires, managing editor F. Richard Ciccone, associate managing editor Douglas Kneeland and, of course, Crewdson, who now is based in California for the newspaper.

Many of my reporter colleagues were most helpful as I labored to trace the Survivalists around the country. Among them are Kevin Flynn of the *Rocky Mountain News*, Bill Morlin of the Spokane *Spokesman-Review*,

Don Duncan of the Seattle *Times*, Robert Unger of the Kansas City *Times*, Wayne King of *The New York Times*, Norm Udevitz of the Denver *Post*, Michael Zielenzeiger of the San Jose *Mercury-News*, Bill Walker, formerly of the Denver *Post*, and Eileen Ogintz, former Midwest correspondent for the Chicago *Tribune*.

A particular debt is owed to many people at the Anti-Defamation League of B'nai B'rith, whose early research into the Identity movement, the rise of neo-Nazism, and links between various right-wing groups started me on the way toward the inquiries that culminate here. As with my *Tribune* associates, I must stipulate that what appears here does not necessarily reflect the thoughts of those who helped me at the ADL, such as Michael Lieberman, Michael Kotzin and Jeffrey Yitzak Santis.

My wife, Kay Coates, lived through the writing with me. Her criticism and encouragement during many revisions made possible a book that otherwise never would have existed. My son, Paul, contributed substantially for a twelve-year-old by giving up his father for more than a year, as did my daughter, Marianne. My gratitude to them is immense.

Like many of his other friends, I am indebted to Michael Kilian, a prolific novelist, columnist and writer of non-fiction who introduced me to the joys and miseries of book writing.

Thanks finally to an excellent editor, Hill & Wang's Bill Newlin, whose deft and understanding touches with a pencil are greatly appreciated.

Notes

INTRODUCTION: THE DENVER CONNECTION

The two major Denver daily newspapers, the Denver *Post* and the *Rocky Mountain News*, published scores of articles about the Berg murder and the links the subsequent investigation made to neo-Nazi groups in the Northwest. Representative articles include "5 Named by U.S. in Berg Case" by Kevin Flynn, *Rocky Mountain News*, April 16, 1985; "Vast Dragnet Hunts Neo-Nazi" by Louis Kilzer, Denver *Post*, February 17, 1985; and "The Order: A Humbled Supremacy" by Kevin Flynn, *Rocky Mountain News*, April 22, 1985.

Talked to Death: The Life and Murder of Alan Berg by Stephen Singular (Beech Tree/Morrow, 1987) contains an extensive biography of the man whose slaughter led to disclosures that are the subject of this book.

The Colorado chapter in *The Almanac of American Politics 1986* (National Journal, Inc. 1986) includes a handy summary of how Lamm and Hart rose to power by attacking the entrenched establishment over the Olympics and other issues.

A most insightful treatment of the role of nuclear anxiety in everyday American life is available in *The Fate of the Earth* by Jonathan Schell (Avon Books, 1982), which originally appeared in *The New Yorker*.

An excellent collection of the various conspiracy theories that motivate hate groups is available in *The Fear of Conspiracy: Images of Un-American Subversion from the Revolution to the Present*, edited by David Brion Davis (Cornell University Press, 1971).

Through its Liberty Library in Washington, D.C., the Liberty Lobby offers indexes and back copies of *Spotlight* as well as a large number of books and tabloid reprints outlining the far-right world view.

One of the few books which took note of many of the people and groups that have now emerged as the Survival Right is Phillip Finch's *God, Guts and Guns: A Close Look at the Radical Right* (Seaview/Putnam, 1983).

The events surrounding the farmyard slaying of Minnesota banker Rudy Blyth by debt-ridden farmer Jim Jenkins and his son Steve are the subject of *Final Harvest: An American Tragedy* by Andrew Malcolm (Times Books, 1986).

1: WHERE THEY COME FROM

In a personal communication, religion scholar Gordon Melton, then a visiting professor at the University of California, expressed the view that each time the national political mood shifts either to the right or to the left, a similar shift occurs at the fringes. During periods when the general mood tends to be liberal, such as the Carter years, the extremists on the far left hold sway, whereas when a conservative like Reagan holds office, the far-right fringes tend to be dominant. See "Faith, Hate Crossbreed / Church on the Fringe of the Right Sermonizes on a Creed of Intolerance" by James Coates, Chicago *Tribune*, July 20, 1986.

Alienation and Charisma: A Study of Contemporary American Communes by Benjamin Zablocki (Free Press/Macmillan, 1980) traces the movement by left-wing ideologues into communes during the 1960s and 1970s.

The attacks against various targets ranging from the eighteenth-century Illuminati to the twentieth-century Jewish banking families are documented in the already cited *The Fear of Conspiracy*, edited by David Brion Davis (Cornell University Press, 1971).

The preeminent scholarly work on the American nativist movement, the Know-Nothing phenomenon and other anti-Catholic and anti-Semitic activity in America is *The Protestant Crusade, 1800–1860* by Ray Allen Billington (Macmillan, 1938, and Quadrangle Books, 1964).

An excellent historical treatment of the Ku Klux Klan is available in *The Ku Klux Klan: America's Recurring Nightmare* by Fred J. Cook (Julian Messner, 1980).

More recent and extremely comprehensive is *The Fiery Cross: The Ku Klux Klan in America* by Wyn Craig Wade (Simon and Schuster, 1987).

Another valuable source of information about the Klan, particularly about the current Klan and its members who went on to become active in the Survival Right, is *The Klan* by Patsy Simms (Stein & Day, 1978).

Perhaps the most comprehensive account of the minutiae of day-to-day life within the ranks of the Klan is *My Life in the Klan* by Jerry Thompson (Putnam, 1982).

The links between Klan groups and others in the Survivalist movement is the subject of "The KKK and the Neo-Nazis: A 1984 Status Report" by the Anti-Defamation League of B'nai B'rith, New York.

For a comprehensive listing of the various Identity church operations around the country, see "The 'Identity Churches': A Theology of Hate," *ADL Facts*, Anti-Defamation League of B'nai B'rith/Civil Rights Division, Vol. 28, No. 1 (Spring 1983).

2: THE ORDER

The story of the Order (called Bruder Schweigen by the members themselves) is laid out in great detail in the transcript of the Seattle trial before U.S. District Judge Walter McGovern. A succinct summary of the bizarre crime wave appears on pages 5–140 of the transcript for September 12, 1985, containing the opening statements of federal prosecutors Robert Ward and Eugene Wilson.

Numerous documents about the Order members' philosophy and plans to establish seed groups to start up new cells around the country are among the federal complaints filed in the U.S. District Court for the Middle District of North Carolina, Winston-Salem Division, on April 3, 1985, following the arrest of David Lane.

Similarly, the indictment released on April 24, 1987, in the Fort Smith sedition case against fourteen people with ties to Butler, Miles and Beam shows how neo-Nazi enclaves from Idaho to Arkansas, North Carolina to Colorado worked together to launch various crimes against the federal establishment and to share the proceeds afterward. Federal indictments handed up that same day in Denver offer a comprehensive glimpse at how prosecutors pieced together events surrounding the Berg murder.

" 'Propaganda of the Deed': The Far Right's Desperate Revolution" by the Anti-Defamation League of B'nai B'rith, New York, 1985, traces the various Survivalist compounds around the country and describes how the network attempted to help the members of the Order once they became hunted fugitives.

The Turner Diaries by Andrew Macdonald (pseudonym) (National Vanguard Books, 1985) has become a major source of income for William Pierce's neo-Nazi National Alliance as a result of the publicity the novel received through the Order's actions.

For details about the out-of-print Birchite novel *The Franklin Letters*, see Daniel Bell's essay "The Dispossessed" (1962) in *The Radical Right*, edited by Daniel Bell (Anchor Books, 1964).

The letters from Matthews quoted and mentioned were downloaded from the Aryan Nations Network, a computer bulletin board operated by Survival Right groups and accessible via telephone.

The story of the Yarbrough family is told in "The Yarbroughs: They're an Arizona Legend among Pima County Deputies" by R. H. Ring of the *Arizona Daily Star*, reprinted in the Denver *Post*, January 6, 1985.

Philadelphia *Daily News* reporter Kitty Caparella's interview with Martinez was distributed on the Knight-Ridder News Wire on April 17, 1985.

3: IDENTITY CHRISTIANS

"Neo-Nazis Assert Their 'Identity' at Congress" by Bill Walker was published July 20, 1986, by the Denver *Post* in its Sunday "Perspective" section.

"The 'Identity Churches': A Theology of Hate," *ADL Facts*, Vol. 28, No. 1 (Spring 1983), cited earlier, first disclosed the phenomenon of Christian Identity as a new component of the American far right.

The following Identity tracts cited in this chapter were purchased from Butler's bookstore by the author when admitted to the Hayden Lake compound in 1986 as a journalist:

—*Know Your Enemies!* by Colonel Gordon "Jack" Mohr (Destiny Publishers, Merrimac, Mass., 1982).

—*Still 'Tis Our Ancient Foe* by Kenneth Goff (Salon Publishing Company, Norborne, Mo., undated).

—*End Time Revelation 1979* by William V. Fowler (American Graphic, Mission Hills, Calif., 1976).

—*The Negro: Serpent, Beast and Devil* by Philip Jones (Uriel Publications, North Dakota, 1979).

—*The Holy Book of Adolf Hitler* by James Larratt Battersby (German World Church in Europe, 1952).

—"Dwelling on Two Planes" by Dr. Wesley A. Swift, a sermon delivered in January 1949 in Los Angeles, reprinted by New Christian Crusade Church, Hollywood, Calif.

The historical phenomenon of using Lost Tribe theories to justify anti-Semitism is the subject of *Lost Tribes and Promised Lands: The Origins of American Racism* by Ronald Sanders (Little, Brown, 1978).

4: POSSE COMITATUS

Gordon Kahl's family collaborated with two tax protest movement writers to produce *There Was a Man: The Saga of Gordon Kahl* by Capstan Turner and A. J. Lowery (Sozo Publishing Co., Nashville, Tenn., 1985), which includes a highly sympathetic account of the shoot-outs in North Dakota and Arkansas. See also "Slain Tax Protester's Family Bears the Pain of His Bittersweet Legacy" by Robert Unger, Kansas City *Times*, September 13, 1985, and "Death Kept Its Appointment in a Dakota Town," also by Unger for the Kansas City *Times*, March 5, 1983.

A right-wing treatment of the case is *Why "They" Wanted to Get Gordon Kahl* by Len Martin (Pro-American Press, Detroit Lakes, Minn., 1983).

A major Internal Revenue Service study of the Survival Right was made public in late 1986 after syndicated columnist Jack Anderson obtained the document from unnamed sources. Today copies of that document, "Illegal

Tax Protester Information Book" by intelligence analyst Ruth E. Schweizer and stamped "Official Use Only," is sold by the Liberty Lobby in Washington, D.C., which views the study as a violation of civil liberties against those named. Although it is an extremely comprehensive listing of large amounts of data about dozens of the known major figures in the movement, the study was ridiculed by Identity preacher Bob Miles in his October 1986 *From the Mountain* newsletter, which called it "as accurate as a drunken missileman blindfolded at the controls of a Lower Slobbovian ICBM."

The definitive work on the history of the Minutemen remains *The Minutemen* by Harry Jones (Doubleday, 1968).

William Potter Gale told a group of Chicago *Tribune* reporters in June 1983 that the Posse amounted to a continuation of the Minutemen. See " 'True Believer' Dead, But His Belief Isn't" by Laura Richardson, Bruce Buursma and James Coates, Chicago *Tribune*, June 12, 1983.

"Tax Protesters Fall under Fire from IRS" by Michael Isikoff, *The Washington Post*, August 18, 1985; "U.S. Is Investigating Laundering of Income from Tax Dodgers" by *The Wall Street Journal*, April 10, 1985.

Among articles disclosing the Posse's move into barter banking are:
—"Right-Wingers Circle over Farm Crisis" by Eileen Ogintz, Chicago *Tribune*, May 26, 1985.
—"Tax Protester Waging Lonely War with IRS" by Laura Misch, *Rocky Mountain News*, March 7, 1986, about John Grandbouche's barter operation.
—"IRS Raids Denver Tax Protest Offices" by Jane Hulse, *Rocky Mountain News*, April 6, 1985.
—"Tax Protest's Fort Knox in Indiana" by Jane Hulse, *Rocky Mountain News*, June 11, 1984.
—"Extremists Reap Rewards from Farmers' Plight" by Esther Pessin, United Press International, *Rocky Mountain News*, September 21, 1985.

The document by Randy L. Geiszler showing potential converts how to drop out of the legal system and file "pro se" lawsuits is "Motion to Quash" (Republic vs. Democracy, Oregon City, Ore., 1986).

Don Duncan of the Seattle *Times* wrote a five-part series on the Posse and other far-right groups in the Pacific Northwest that started April 20, 1986, under the heading "They're Marching As to War."

5: THE COMPOUND DWELLERS

The trial of Michael Ryan, his son Dennis and the others associated with the Rulo compound was covered daily by Nebraska news media. See, for example:

—"Witness Tells of Ryan's Religion of Hate" by Mike Mulvey, Lincoln *Star*, March 11, 1986.

—"Many Strange Turns Taken in Life of Jailed Survivalist Michael Ryan" by Jack Croft and Kevin Collison, Omaha *World-Herald*, August 25, 1985.

—"Witness: God, Ryan Talked in 'Arm Tests' " by Nick Schinker, Omaha *World-Herald*, March 11, 1986.

—"Beating, Polygamy among Abuses at Rulo Farm, Woman Testifies" by Nick Schinker, Omaha *World-Herald*, March 12, 1986.

See also "Posse Country Murder and White Supremacy in the Farm Belt" by James Ridgeway, *The Village Voice*, October 22, 1985.

Two articles in Kansas newspapers that illustrate the fascination with Survival Right ideology in the farm belt are "Partridge Man Finds Strength in Aryan Dogma" by Jim Hitch, Hutchinson *News*, July 27, 1986, and "Only White Is Right, Dad Teaches Children" by Sharon Mahric, Wichita *Eagle-Beacon*, September 6, 1986.

The Survival Right communes of the Ozarks were the subject of an article in the Springfield, Missouri, *News & Leader* on April 21, 1985, "Violent Mix of God and Guns Wearing Thin in Tolerant Ozarks."

Two years before the FBI raid against the Covenant, the Sword and the Arm of the Lord in 1985, the ADL had supplied extensive details about the compound in the already cited "The 'Identity Churches': A Theology of Hate," *ADL Facts*, Vol. 28, No. 1 (Spring 1983).

The Kansas City *Times* described the Elohim City compound in "In the Custody of a Cult: Parents Fight to Live with Their Children" by Robert Lever, March 20, 1986.

Two previously cited sources deal at length with John Harrell's Illinois compound and his "Mo-Ark" Survivalist training center on the Missouri–Arkansas border. They are *God, Guts and Guns* by Phillip Finch (Seaview/Putnam, 1983) and *The Minutemen* by Harry Jones (Doubleday, 1968).

For details about Larry Humphreys's compound, see "Candidate for Seat in House Campaigns for Real Money" by Michael Collins Piper, *Spotlight*, October 6, 1986, and "The Sheriff and the Vigilantes" by David E. Lowe, *ADL Bulletin*, March 1986.

6: LONE WOLVES

The lead story in the Seattle *Post-Intelligencer* on Tuesday, December 31, 1985, is "Suspect Held Toy Gun on Goldmark Family" by George Foster and Jack Hopkins. The story given the next prominent play is "The Verdict on 'the Order' Jury Finds 10 Guilty of Terror Campaign" by Steve Miletich, Lisa Schnellinger and Bruce Sherman.

Articles about the Goldmark case in *The Washington Post* in May and June of 1986 explained the killer's motivation in terms of the Smerdyakov syndrome mentioned in the text. See "Drifter Guilty in Deaths of Seattle Family of 4 / Anticommunist Fervor Behind Stabbings" by Bill Prochnau, *The Washington Post*, June 6, 1986, and a two-part series by Prochnau in the May 13 and May 14, 1986, *Post* entitled "The Twisted Tale of a Human Slaughter / Tragedy in Seattle: A Young Itinerant, His 'Friends' in Outer Space—and the Brutal Slaying of the Goldmark Family" and "The Shadows of a Killer after the Goldmark Bloodbath, Questions of Motive and Morality."

Phillip Finch in his previously cited *God, Guts and Guns* (Seaview/Putnam, 1983) deals at length with the *Duck Book*, the Duck Club movement and publisher Robert White's effort to proselytize his vision of anti-Zionism, conspiracy and Survivalism.

The text's version of *The Brothers Karamazov* by Feodor Dostoevsky is from the abridgment by Edmund Fuller (Dell, 1956).

The coverage of the bizarre hostage crisis in Cokeville by Wyoming's largest newspaper, the Casper *Star-Tribune*, includes: "Young Had Own Brand of Madness / Investigators Comb Through His Diaries" by Catherine Warren and Paul Krza, May 25, 1986; "Acquaintances Paint Portrait of Cokeville Bomber" by Paul Krza, May 25, 1986; and "Cokeville Attempts to Cope with Bombing Aftermath" by Paul Krza, May 19, 1986.

See also " 'Gunslinger' Hatched Cokeville Plot / Young Lived, Died a Fantasy" by Joe Garner, *Rocky Mountain News*, May 18, 1986.

The interviews with Young's former wife were published as "Grim 'Genius' / Bomber's Ex-Wife Feared Him," *Arizona Republic*, May 18, 1986.

Other details about the Youngs' mental set emerged in three Associated Press articles printed in the Denver dailies. See "Letter in Cokeville Pair's Trailer Raises Specter of Extremist Group," *Rocky Mountain News*, May 31, 1986; "Hostage-taker Hoped to Start New World Through Mass Death," Denver *Post*, June 2, 1986; and "Cokeville Still Coping with 'the Bomb,' " *Rocky Mountain News*, August 31, 1986.

The most comprehensive account of the Don and Dan Nichols saga is *Incident at Big Sky* by Johnny France and Malcolm McConnell (Norton, 1986). See also "The Ballad of Johnny France" by Richard Ben Cramer, *Esquire*, October 1985.

See also the article by Tad Bartimus of the Associated Press based on interviews with Nichols's ex-wife and others, printed as " 'Mountain Man' Nichols Well-Read, Relatives Say" in the Denver *Post*, July 23, 1984.

The Montana posse tradition is detailed in "Virginia City / Dan and Don Nichols Will Go on Trial in a Town Once Ruled by Vigilantes" by Robert Ekey, Billings *Gazette*, April 21, 1985.

Dick Pace's book about the Montana vigilante tradition is *Golden Gulch* (privately printed by Bovey Restorations, Virginia City, Mont.).

A useful summary of the Lake-Ng case is "A Grisly Dig in California / Bones Sifted for Clues to Disappearances" by Cynthia Gorney, *The Washington Post*, June 13, 1985.

The following articles from California newspapers contain virtually all that is known about the Wilseyville torture compound:
—"2 Lives, 1 Road to Sex, Slavery, Death" by Gretchen Kell and Nancy Weaver, Sacramento *Bee*, November 24, 1985.
—"Death Trail Leads to Humboldt / SF Police to Probe Suspect's Ex-Home" by Thom Akeman, Sacramento *Bee*, June 13, 1985.
—"Treaty Could Stall Return of Fugitive / Canada Holds Man Linked to Deaths" by Jay Matthews, *The Washington Post*, July 9, 1985.
—"Ex-Wife Clams Up, Demands Immunity for Calaveras Help" by Dan Nakaso and Stephen E. Wright, San Jose *Mercury-News*, June 17, 1985.
—"Investigation Moves to South Bay as Evidence Ties 6 to Survivalists" by Linda Goldston, Maline Hazle and Bill Romano, San Jose *Mercury-News*, June 11, 1985.

The interview with Lake's neighbor, Thomas Southern, cited in the text was published in "Cops Followed Trail of Blood to Bare Mass Murders," by James Coates, Chicago *Tribune*, June 13, 1985.

7: THE POLITICS OF HATRED

The Liberty Lobby reprint "Populism: New Ideas for the Future" is dated August 1984 and is available through Liberty Library, Washington, D.C.

Profiles in Populism, edited by Willis A. Carto (Flag Press, Old Greenwich, Conn., 1982).

The Harris poll cited in the text is "A Study of Anti-Semitism in Rural Iowa and Nebraska," February 1986, Louis Harris and Associates, New York.

Major stories about the LaRouche organization from *The Washington Post*, all by John Mintz, include:
—"LaRouche Followers Indicted / 10 Persons, 5 Groups Face Federal Charges: Va. Offices Raided," October 7, 1986.
—"Hard Times in the LaRouche Camp / Suits, Claims Against Extremist's Organization Reach $23 Million," September 14, 1986.

—"An 'Underground' of LaRouche Foes / Loudoun Residents Lauded for Role in Probe of Extremist," October 8, 1986.

—LaRouche and Aides Reacted to Heat from Federal Probe / FBI Tells of Picketing and Harassment," October 10, 1986.

See also "Letting LaRouche Off Easy," *Washington Journalism Review*, November 1986.

Myra MacPherson's treatment of the LaRouche candidates is "Adlai Stevenson's Long, Hot Summer / In Illinois a Troubled Campaign & an Imperiled Legacy," *The Washington Post*, September 5, 1986.

The ADL study of the LaRouche 1986 successes is "The 1986 LaRouche Primary Campaign: An Analysis" by the Fact-Finding Department of the Civil Rights Division of the Anti-Defamation League of B'nai B'rith.

Federal prosecution of the LaRouche group is detailed in "Federal Raids Effectively Shut LaRouche Organization," *Washington Post*, April 22, 1987.

New Mexico prison warden George Sullivan's admission that Aryan Resistance Movement members were riding roughshod over that state's other inmates is described in " 'Predators' Control Pen, Warden Says," by Harold Cousland, Albuquerque *Journal*, August 19, 1986.

Problems with the Aryan Brotherhood in Arizona prisons is the subject of "Prison Gangs Spread Menace into Society" by Albert J. Sitter, *Arizona Republic*, January 25, 1985.

The prison gang situation—both black gangs and white ones—is treated in "Extremism Targets the Prisons / An ADL Special Report," June 1986. Ironically, Robert Miles was so impressed by the document that he made copies and distributed them to followers inside prisons.

The day they were convicted, Order members vowed to use their prison time to recruit new movement members. See " 'Order' Will Survive, Jailed Member Vows" by Lisa Schnellinger, Seattle *Post-Intelligencer*, December 31, 1985.

Kevin Flynn's interview with Pierce appeared as "Racist in Berg Case Compares Self to Job," *Rocky Mountain News*, August 10, 1986.

8: SURVIVAL OF THE FITTEST

The *USA Today* poll appeared on November 12, 1985, in a series entitled "Summit: Hopes High, Expectation Low."

Scheer's interview with McNamara appears in *With Enough Shovels: Reagan, Bush and Nuclear War* by Robert Scheer (Vintage Books, 1983).

For a graphically interesting treatment of the weapons in the U.S. and Soviet nuclear arsenals, see *Nuclear War in the 1980's?*, compiled by Christopher Chant and Ian Hogg (Harper & Row, 1983).

The scenarios describing various nuclear attacks all come from *The Effects of Nuclear Weapons*, Office of Technology Assessment, U.S. Congress, 1979.

Missile Envy: The Arms Race and Nuclear War by Dr. Helen Caldicott (Bantam Books, 1986) is a powerful evocation of the dangerous world situation and the terrors awaiting those unfortunate enough to live through a nuclear exchange.

The Chosen Few: Surviving the Nuclear Holocaust by Edward Myers (and books, South Bend, Ind., 1982).

Can You Survive? by Robert B. DePugh (Desert Publications, Cornville, Ariz., 1973).

What to Do When the Russians Come by Robert Conquest and Jon Manchip White (Stein & Day, 1984).

For a rational treatment of the various writings and theories about a "Hidden Hand" in world affairs, see the already cited compendium *The Fear of Conspiracy*, edited by David Brion Davis (Cornell University Press, 1971).

The material about Goff's version of the "Hidden Hand" comes from his previously cited pamphlet, *Still 'Tis Our Ancient Foe.*

The conspiracy view of the Trilateralists, Bilderbergers and other organizations cited in the text comes largely from "Spotlight on the Bilderbergers: Irresponsible Power" (Liberty Lobby, Washington, D.C., 1975).

The Survival Right's hatred of the Rockefellers is typified by the late Gary Allen's *The Rockefeller File* ('76 Press, Seal Beach, Calif.).

Two *Spotlight* reprints sold by the Liberty Lobby to promote the Hidden Hand paranoia are "The Trilateral Connection: Global Elite Tried to Pick Presidents in Both Parties," March 2, 1981, and "Christian Holocaust," October 18, 1972.

CONCLUSION: APOCALYPSE NOW?

"Jimmy Swaggart: Wonders of the Lord & TV / Reaching Out Through the Small Screen, Bringing in $140 Million a Year for Jesus" by Lloyd Grove, *The Washington Post*, September 29, 1986.

"The Gospel According to Jimmy Lee Swaggart: Whole Lotta Savin' Goin' On" by Steve Chapple, *Mother Jones*, July–August 1986.

The phenomenon of how Fundamentalists invoke the Book of Revelation to deal with nuclear anxiety is the subject of *Blessed Assurance: At Home with the Bomb in Amarillo, Texas* by A. G. Mojtabai (Houghton Mifflin, 1986).

Reagan's widely quoted remarks about the coming of a final war were quoted in *San Diego Magazine*, August 1971.

Holy Terror: The Fundamentalist War on America's Freedoms in Religion, Politics, and Our Private Lives by Flo Conway and Jim Siegelman (Delta, 1984).

R. Robin McDonald's article about the Fundamentalists in Wichita was circulated by the Knight-Ridder News Wire in August 1986.

"The Christian Right: Will It Bring Political Pentecost to America?" by Clifford Goldstein, *Liberty* magazine.

"Militarism in America," *The Defense Monitor*, Vol. XV, No. 3 (1986), Center for Defense Information, Washington, D.C.

Efforts in Idaho to deal with a long-standing tradition of tolerating the intolerant are the subject of Jim Carrier's "Idaho: A State at War with Itself," Denver *Post*, November 9, 1986, and Robert Unger's "Bombings Shatter Town's Tolerance of Hate Group," Kansas City *Times*, October 13, 1986.

Index